D0153956

WILLIAMS

A Streetcar Named Desire

PLAYS IN PRODUCTION

Series editor: Michael Robinson

PUBLISHED VOLUMES

Ibsen: *A Doll's House* by Egil Törnqvist
Miller: *Death of a Salesman* by Brenda Murphy
Molière: *Don Juan* by David Whitton
Wilde: *Salome* by William Tydeman and Steven Price
Brecht: *Mother Courage and Her Children* by Peter Thomson
Williams: *A Streetcar Named Desire* by Philip C. Kolin

Williams: A Streetcar Named Desire

One of the most important plays of the twentieth century, *A Streetcar Named Desire* revolutionized the modern stage. This book offers the first continuous history of the play in production from 1947 to 1998 with an emphasis on the collaborative achievement of Tennessee Williams, Elia Kazan, and Jo Mielziner in the Broadway premiere. From there chapters survey major national premieres by the world's leading directors including those by Seki Sano (Mexico), Luchino Visconti (Italy), Ingmar Bergman (Sweden), Jean Cocteau (France), and Laurence Olivier (England). Philip Kolin also evaluates key English-language revivals and assesses how the script evolved and adapted to cultural changes. Interpretations by black and gay theatre companies also receive analyses, and transformations into other media, such as ballet, film, television, and opera (premiered in 1998), form an important part of the overall study.

WILLIAMS

A Streetcar Named Desire

*

PHILIP C. KOLIN
University of Southern Mississippi

PUBLISHED BY THE PRESS SYNDICATE OF THE UNIVERSITY OF CAMBRIDGE
The Pitt Building, Trumpington Street, Cambridge, United Kingdom

CAMBRIDGE UNIVERSITY PRESS
The Edinburgh Building, Cambridge CB2 2RU, UK
40 West 20th Street, New York, NY 10011-4211, USA
10 Stamford Road, Oakleigh, VIC 3166, Australia
Ruiz de Alarcón 13, 28014 Madrid, Spain
Dock House, The Waterfront, Cape Town 8001, South Africa

http://www.cambridge.org

First published 2000
Reprinted 2001

Printed in the United Kingdom at the University Press, Cambridge

Typeface Adobe Garamond 10.75/14   *System* QuarkXPress™   [SE]

A catalogue record for this book is available from the British Library

Library of Congress Cataloguing in Publication data
Kolin, Philip C.
Williams: A streetcar named desire / Philip C. Kolin.
p.   cm. – (Plays in production)
Includes bibliographical references (p.   ) and index.
ISBN 0 521 62344 8 (hardback) – ISBN 0 521 62610 2 (paperback)
1. Williams, Tennessee, 1911–1983. Streetcar named desire.
2. Williams, Tennessee, 1911–1983 – Dramatic production.
3. Williams, Tennessee, 1911–1983 – Stage history.   4. New Orleans
(La.) – In literature.   I. Title.   II. Series.
PS3545.I5365S824   2000
812'.54–dc21   99–15825   CIP

ISBN 0 521 62344 8 hardback
ISBN 0 521 62610 2 paperback

#41337996

To Margie and Al Parish
with love and prayers
ora et labora

CONTENTS

ILLUSTRATIONS

GENERAL PREFACE

Volumes in the series Plays in Production take major dramatic texts and examine their transposition, firstly on to the stage and, secondly, where appropriate, into other media. Each book includes concise but informed studies of individual dramatic texts, focusing on the original theatrical and historical context of a play in relation to its initial performance and reception followed by subsequent major interpretations on stage, both under the impact of changing social, political and cultural values, and in response to developments in the theatre generally.

Many of the plays also have been transposed into other media – film, opera, television, ballet – which may well be the form in which they are first encountered by a contemporary audience. Thus, a substantial study of the play-text and the issues it raises for theatrical realization is supplemented by an assessment of such adaptations as well as the production history, where the emphasis is on the development of a performance tradition for each work, including staging and acting styles, rather than simply the archaeological reconstruction of past performances.

Plays included in the series are all likely to receive regular performance and individual volumes will be of interest to the informed reader as well as to students of theatre history and literature. Each book also contains an annotated production chronology as well as numerous photographs from key performances.

Michael Robinson
University of East Anglia

PREFACE

A Streetcar Named Desire is one of the most influential plays of the twentieth century. In this volume I have attempted to provide a history of major productions of Williams's play on the world stage since 1947 as well as to offer an assessment of how the play has been translated or adapted for ballet, film, teleplay, and opera. Consistent with the goals of the Plays in Performance Series, I have emphasized the ways in which the script has been validated and transformed through production and how audiences have responded to the changing performance styles through which *Streetcar* has been represented.

This book begins appropriately with, and places greatest emphasis on, the Broadway premiere of 1947 which catapulted Williams to international fame. The premiere saw one of the most powerful and collaborative teams in theatre – director-mentor Elia Kazan, producer Irene Selznick, designer Jo Mielziner, costumer Lucinda Ballard, composer Alex North, and a cast of young actors shaped Williams's script to create a production that directors and actors for decades esteemed as the standard by which *Streetcars* should be enacted. This opening chapter relies heavily on Kazan's *Streetcar Notebook*, William's letters, Jo Mielziner's sketches, and stage manager notes to reflect accurately what audiences saw on stage. Additionally, actors' memoirs and biographies contribute significantly to our understanding of how Williams's characters talked, moved, dressed, and related to props. One of my aims in this chapter was to show *Streetcar*'s indebtedness to the dynamics of collaboration. Moreover, as this beginning and later chapters show, *Streetcar* established the careers of many actors who played in it. The young cast of

Streetcar in 1947 – as well as those actors who starred in the road company productions in 1948–49 – revealed that there was magic in the web of Williams's script.

Chapter 2 focuses on six selective, but in many ways representative, national premieres of *Streetcar* from Mexico City to Tokyo (1948–53). Historically, many of the world's most prominent directors and scenographers reinforced *Streetcar*'s acclaim as a masterpiece of world theatre while they simultaneously reinterpreted the scenography, props, music, and characterization for their particular culture and audience. This chapter explores the performance work of Seki Sano (who directed one of the first premieres outside the US) in Mexico City; Luchino Visconti and Franco Zeffirelli (the designer) in Rome; Ingmar Bergman (who read the script through a cinematic prism) in Sweden; Jean Cocteau, whose sensual adaptation in Paris, 1949 proleptically foregrounded the dark desire that became the focus of later productions; Sir Laurence Olivier, who shortened the script in London; and the Bungakuza Dramatic Company, whose Tokyo premiere helped to westernize Japanese theatre. Seen as an icon of American culture, *Streetcar* quickly acquired an international ethos.

In Chapter 3, the revivals of *Streetcar* (1956–98) on the English-speaking stage illustrate how later decades and tastes renegotiated the performance of the script and how that script consequently evolved through such productions. One major change involved the ways in which Williams's characters were transformed from the social models Kazan envisioned and enshrined in the 1940s: Blanche became far less willowy and more assertive in the 1980s and 1990s and Stanley was more sly, subtle, not nearly as much in control. In revivals, Mielziner's expressionistic scrims were exchanged for much more realistic and provocative sets, including the experience of *Streetcar* in theatres in the round.

Chapter 4 documents alternative *Streetcars* by concentrating on productions by black and gay theatre companies. These non-Eurocentric and cross-gendered productions destabilized the tradi-

tional ideologies upon which the Broadway and many national premieres were based. They radicalized and enlarged Williams's script by
freeing it from expectations based upon conventional valorizations of
ethnicity, race, and gender. Viewed in light of a long, neglected
history of black productions, *Streetcar* in performance encodes racial
and social messages impossible in all-white productions. The black
synesthesia of *Streetcar* reifies the power of transformable characterization and the representation of a different set of cultural anxieties
signified in word and action. Black *Streetcars* also successfully challenged the (false) claims of a seminal Blanche being white in language, gesture, or costume. The last third of the chapter examines
Belle Reprieve, the queer/camp adaptation of *Streetcar* that realigned
the gender roles of woman and man both in the traditional script and
in the famous 1951 Warner Brothers film.

In the last chapter, I turn to *Streetcar* in other media, with emphasis falling upon the process through which the script has been
expanded, cut, literalized, choreographed and contemporized. As
director of the 1951 film, Kazan had to struggle against the imposi-
tion of censorship on the script that he did not face on stage, and he
invented a cinematic code to represent the psychological effects that
stage productions presented more directly. The 1984 *Streetcar* teleplay directed by John Erman intensified the violence and eroticism in
the script, making them far more explicit than Kazan or any stage
production (from 1947 to 1983) ever could. Various ballet versions
of Williams's play also receive meritorious attention as visual representations of jazz and fury inherent in the script. The last section of
this chapter offers one of the first assessments of the transformation
of *Streetcar* into opera – André Previn's score for the San Francisco
Opera – and stresses the ways in which Previn challenged Kazan's valorization of Stanley over Blanche. Previn's opera had to adopt a new
performance language to accommodate a *Streetcar* in song. The
inevitable conclusion of this chapter, and the book as a whole, is that
Streetcar succeeds precisely because performance verifies its non-
static, protean power.

ACKNOWLEDGMENTS

This book has evolved over the years as I pursued the routes *A Streetcar Named Desire* took on the world's stages. Along the way I have happily acquired many debts and been the beneficiary of the kindness of many strangers and friends alike. I want to thank the following individuals for reading earlier drafts of some of these chapters and giving me the wisdom of their criticism: Thomas P. Adler (Purdue University); Allean Hale (University of Illinois); Brian Parker (University of Toronto); Don B. Wilmeth (Brown University); and Jürgen Wolter (Universität Wuppertal). I am also very grateful to Michael Robinson, the Plays in Performance Series editor, and Victoria Cooper at Cambridge University Press for their sage counsel and encouragement throughout this project.

I express a special debt to Cathy Henderson and the staff of the Harry Ransom Humanities Research Center at the University of Texas at Austin, where I spent two sabbaticals working on *Streetcar* materials and where I received their gracious help and knowledgeable assistance about Williams's theatre documents. I am also grateful to the many theatre companies, libraries, and photographers who supplied me with the essential documents that are the foundation of this book.

Sections of Chapters 2 and 4 have appeared in part of my articles in the following publications:

" 'Affectionate and mighty regards from Vivien and me': Sir Laurence Olivier on the London Premiere of *A Streetcar Named Desire*," *Missouri Review* 13.3 (1991): 143–57.

" 'From Coitus to Craziness': The Italian Premiere of *A Streetcar Named Desire*," *Journal of American Drama and Theatre* 10 (Spring 1998): 74–92.

"The Japanese Premiere of *A Streetcar Named Desire*," *Mississippi Quarterly* 48 (Fall 1995): 713–34.

"On a Trolley to the Cinema: Ingmar Bergman and the First Swedish Production of *A Streetcar Named Desire*," *South Carolina Review* 27, nos. 1 and 2 (Fall 1994/Spring 1995): 97–128.

"Williams in Ebony: Black and Multi-Cultural Productions of Williams's *A Streetcar Named Desire*," *Black American Literature Forum* 25 (Spring 1991): 147–81.

I owe a special and continuing debt to the University of Southern Mississippi for supporting my work; in particular I gratefully acknowledge the assistance of President Horace Fleming; Associate Provost James Hollandsworth; Vice President Donald Cotten; Dean of the College of Liberal Arts Glenn T. Harper; and Chair of the English Department Michael N. Salda. My research assistant Terri Ruckel deserves a special place in my heart for all her work in helping me prepare this manuscript.

Finally, I thank my family, Eric Kolin, Theresa Kolin, Evan Kolin and Kristin Kolin, and my extended family for their love and prayers: Margie and Al Parish, Colby Kullman, Frs. Michael Tracey and G. Edward Lundin, Sisters Carmelita Stinn and Annette Seymour, Deacon Ralph Torelli, Cathy and Hilary Englert, Mary Lux, John and Sandy Krumpos, Susan Arrington, Dia Stapleton, Rob and Sally Eddy, and all my St. Thomas Prayer Group partners. My gratitude also goes to Janice Fisk. Finally, I thank God for the grace to complete this book on time.

P. C. K.

CHAPTER ONE

A STREETCAR NAMED DESIRE – THE BROADWAY PREMIERE AND BEYOND

After highly successful tryouts in Boston, New Haven, and Philadelphia, *Streetcar* opened on 3 December 1947 at the Barrymore Theatre and almost immediately entered the world of mimesis and memory. Thomas P. Adler claimed that Williams's play "may arguably be the finest play ever written for the American stage."[1] Running for 855 performances over two years, *Streetcar* was the first play to capture the Pulitzer, Donaldson, and New York Drama Critics' Circle awards. Williams received a thirty-minute ovation on opening night, and was greeted by Howard Barnes "as the Eugene O'Neill of the present period."[2] Louis Kronenberger hailed *Streetcar* as "the most creative new play . . . the one that reveals the most talent, the one that attempts the most truth." Not surprisingly, *Streetcar* quickly became a staple on the world stage, one of the major theatrical experiences and experiments of the twentieth century. In a Public Broadcasting Service interview, Richard Seyd of San Francisco's American Conservatory Theatre estimated that in its first fifty years (1947–97) *Streetcar* received at least 20,000 performances, doubtless an understatement.[3] More accurately, playwright Robert E. Lee (*Inherit the Wind*) affirmed that "There are very few nearly perfect plays. *Streetcar* is one of them. It is indigenous to the speaking theatre."[4] Another playwright, William Hauptman, explained why: "Everything about *Streetcar* is beautifully, uniquely theatrical – right down to the title."[5] Williams's play powerfully influenced the way theatre has been performed in the United States and the world, ushering in new performance styles, launching acting careers, and foregrounding the psychic life of its self-fashioning creator. In an interview on 2 May 1958, Williams told Robert Rice "*Streetcar* said everything I had to say. It has an epic quality that the others [Williams's plays] don't have."[6]

Certainly *Streetcar*'s subject matter partook of epic daring. The play invited and has rewarded risk, testing and teasing a host of mythologies and ideologies – sexual, political, critical. Tenaciously, *Streetcar* is a play of sexual politics. Its language, both blunt and luminous, courted taboo subjects – nymphomania, homosexuality, polysemous desire. *Streetcar* defined desire in 1947 and refines it with each succeeding decade of performance. According to C. W. E. Bigsby, "Sexuality was potently at the core of the lives of all its principal characters, a sexuality with the power to redeem or to destroy."[7] Through *Streetcar* Williams scripted androgyny for generations, celebrating the male form as sexual icon while boldly interrogating female desire, and rejoicing simultaneously in the seduction of both genders. *Streetcar* flaunted censorship, and still does in the theatre and in the academy, defying any boundaries around intimacy or gender valorization. Megan Terry, who wrote the first rock musical, *Viet Rock*, honored *Streetcar* as a "feminist play"[8] while John Clum and David Savran read it in terms of the literature of masculinization.[9]

If *Streetcar* was bold sexually, it was never tame politically. In 1947, Harold Clurman emphasized that *Streetcar*'s "impact at this moment is especially strong, because it is virtually unique as a stage piece that is both personal and social."[10] For Williams the one was inscribed in the other. In many ways, *Streetcar* has been a radical work, challenging status-quo thinking. As Rochelle Owens notes, "What Williams does is to stunningly dissect the psychological habits and fantasies that the American middle class has about itself."[11] Marxist interpretations and performances in Communist-sympathizing societies have released *Streetcar*'s subversive message and mechanisms of revolt. In a production of *Streetcar* by Seattle's General Company in July 1991, Blanche was contextualized for the 1990s. As the playbill proclaimed, Blanche is "anyone who has ever suffered unjustly from a world suddenly gone wrong. She is the bag lady you scurry past on your way to work. She is every AIDS patient abandoned by a misunderstanding society. Blanche is you. Leave here tonight elated, enraged and informed."[12]

Unquestionably, Blanche DuBois and Stanley Kowalski have taken up residence in world theatre and culture. They are Williams's most colorful, memorable yet indeterminate creations. In fact, Blanche, according to Nancy Tischler, may well be Williams's "finest creation."[13] Yet in performance and criticism Blanche has been embroiled in contradictions, ambiguities. On the positive side, she has been enshrined as the guardian of the arts, a hallowed representative of the Old South, a secular saint. Dan Isaac, for example, canonizes her as a "sexual Joan of Arc, who listens to the voices of her body, she is a prophet, and poet, morally superior to her adversaries."[14] Negatively, she has been branded a nymphomaniac, a liar, an infectious source of destructive feminine desire. According to Walter Davis, Blanche plays hardball in a game of sexual politics to gain control.[15] Stanley, too, has been fixed in *Streetcar* dichotomies by directors and critics alike. He vacillates from absolutes to contradictions as the jubilant and "gaudy seed bearer" and keeper and the interpreter of Law to the apelike proponent of a cruel industrial age, the fiery destroyer of the beautiful things of this world. Praising the "*gaudy seed bearer*," Joseph Wood Krutch, for instance, claimed that Stanley's "virility, even orgiastic virility, is the proper answer to decadence." [16]

Challenging Blanche-and-Stanley dichotomies, critics have valorized the contradictions that Williams himself had sewn into the roles. Blanche is both moth (spirit) and tiger (flesh). Like Stanley, she can be aggressive, wily, controlling. Thomas P. Adler stresses that there is "a Blanche side to Stanley," too.[17] Kowalski lays claim to the contraries of his representation – brutishness as well as tenderness; he carries his own set of metaphors and illusions – colored lights and a flag of red pajamas. If Blanche is both Madonna and Venus, Stanley is Pan-Dionysus[18] and protector of the hearth. Inescapably, these two characters embody Williams's androgyny incarnated in the *Streetcar* script. Not surprisingly, the playwright intentionally invited comparisons between himself and Blanche, asserting "I can identify completely with Blanche . . . we are both hysterics,"[19] yet in a letter to his agent Audrey Wood, he subsequently, and more fully, confessed: " I was and still am Blanche . . . [but] I have a Stanley side in me, too."[20] Ironically enough, Georges-Michel Sarotte claimed that "Stanley Kowalski is the Other; he is what Williams is not but would like to be."[21]

Streetcar's magic resides not only in Williams's social/political ideas and in his characters but also in the provocative, new dramaturgy that he had introduced two years earlier through *Glass Menagerie*. Labeled "Williams plastic theatre," "stylized realism," or "psychological realism," *Streetcar's* dramaturgy departed from conventional realism (though not from its Chekhovian heritage and subtleties) with its traditional, unfolding linear plots assuring neat, comfortable closure. Unfamiliar with and unfriendly to such a theatre, early critics misguidedly catalogued Williams's drama as "episodic," "disjointed," "loose." These reviewers failed to see that *Streetcar* innovatively presented a theatre of interiority, converting Blanche's fluctuating mental states into stage action. *Streetcar* staged the disintegration of Blanche's mind and its impact on those around her, including the audience. As Brenda Murphy put it, "The basis . . . for the production was the objectification of . . . subjective reality . . . encoding Blanche's memories, inner life, and emotions [into] stage language."[22] *Streetcar* looked back to Elmer Rice's *Adding Machine* (1923), Pirandellian fantasy, and O'Neillian myth and forward to Brechtian disruptions and Adrienne Kennedy's surrealistic nightmares of the 1960s and 1970s. Williams's dramaturgy reflects the fascination with introspection shaped by the times – the disruption of American society by great social and political upheavals, Freudian theories, and Kinsey's sexual data.

Yet even though Williams was intimately invested in Blanche's hallucinatory stages, his expressionism was mediated through realism. One of *Streetcar's* great paradoxes is that it subverted realistic theatre and at the same time was rooted in the behaviorism of Kazan's Group Theatre techniques. In Williams's theatre, then, realism, expressionism, and naturalism coalesce to (re)present Blanche's illusions, thus accounting for the overwhelming anxiety in the plot. As Ronald Hayman rightly admitted, "None [of Williams's plays] had more tension released into them than *Streetcar*."[23] The ultimate source of that tension can be attributable to what Anne Fleche calls the "restless discourse of desire, that uncontainable movement between inside and outside, soul and body."[24] Like his characters, Williams's dramaturgy of desire remains indeterminate.

STREETCAR — A COLLABORATION IN THE ARTS

Streetcar became the success it did because of the almost unprecedented (in American or for that matter world theatre) blending of diverse talent and extraordinary cooperation among playwright, producer, director, designer, composer, and cast. The contribution of each individual made the Broadway premiere possible and evolutionary. No one artist functioned autonomously. The working methods behind such collaborations were tried and tested in over three months of rehearsals and in tryouts in Boston, New Haven, and Philadelphia. During these months of establishing a performance style *Streetcar* became the most widely admired work ever done on the American stage up to that time.

The producer – Irene Selznick

Making her Broadway debut as a producer with *Streetcar*, 40-year-old Irene Selznick – the daughter of movie mogul Louis B. Mayer of MGM and the wife of David O. Selznick – was one of the powerhouses behind the play. *Streetcar* was only her second attempt at producing; her first play, *Heartsong*, was a flop. She had the honor of being the "first woman to produce a play winning both the coveted Pulitzer Prize and the Drama Critics' Circle Award."[25] A shrewd businesswoman, Selznick knew the value of a hot commodity presented to her by Williams's agent Audrey Wood. Deeply committed to

Streetcar, Selznick invested $25,000 of her own money in the $100,000 production,[26] with Cary Grant and three other investors supplying the remainder.[27] Commenting on the enormous risk Selznick took with the play by comparing her work with that of her husband David, who had produced *Gone with the Wind*, New York theatre juggernaut Billy Rose pointed to the problems she would face on Broadway:

> The whole production of *Streetcar* won't have cost as much as one of his sets in *Gone with the Wind*. There will be no one in the cast who can draw 10 customers a night. Nothing will be riding but talent and know-how. Out front will be the regular assortment of first-night sourpusses and professional runners-down. Irene will be rolling square dice – no Clark Gables or million-dollar advertising campaigns, no buffalo stampedes or bang-up earthquakes. And she'll have to hit her dice up against a brick wall – the New York dramatic critics.[28]

Nonetheless, Selznick and the other investors were amply rewarded. *Streetcar* paid for itself in three months, with nearly two years of unencumbered profits afterwards. Selznick, moreover, sold the movie rights to Warner Brothers for a considerable profit. Responsible for negotiating terms with director Elia Kazan, Selznick may have given in too much, being new to the job of producer, but she thereby ensured the stunning success of the production.

Selznick took an active role in every facet of production. She hired designer Jo Mielziner and costumer Lucinda Ballard, and approved the sketches these two artists provided as well as the revisions Williams did for Kazan. Jean Melgan complimented Selznick for achieving "a feat that seasoned old-timers dream about. Her show is a perfect artistic integration of setting, acting, and script."[29]

The director – Elia Kazan

Like many playwrights of the 1940s and 1950s, Williams wanted Elia Kazan to direct his play. At first Kazan was unwilling, yet after much persuasion Wood and Selznick convinced the 38-year-old director to sign on. Kazan shrewdly negotiated one of the best deals "any New York director ever received,"[30] earning 20 percent of the take for a play that was "a million dollar property" and getting star billing: "Irene Selznick Presents Elia Kazan's Production of *A Streetcar Named Desire*." Kazan was one of the most influential directors (of stage and film) in the 1940s and 1950s with such credits as *Death of a Salesman* and *A Tree Grows in Brooklyn*. During the Boston tryouts, Kazan recognized the enormous earning power of the play. As Wood reports, "Gadge turned to Tennessee one night during a performance and whispered: 'This smells like a hit!' Further events proved that Kazan had delivered the understatement of the decade." [31] Williams regarded Kazan as the guardian angel behind the script: "I don't think any of my plays are complete without a supernatural talent." In *Streetcar* it was Kazan's direction that was supernatural.[32] Kazan truly had extraordinary skills. He was intimately immersed in every phase of *Streetcar* from casting and directing to designing sets, planning light cues, choosing music and colors for costumes. In fact, after Williams approved Marlon Brando to play Stanley, he left the rest of the casting to Kazan, or to Selznick.[33] As the playwright gratefully admitted, Kazan was the "one-man theatre that brought *Streetcar* before the widest audience possible."[34]

Kazan's background prepared him for his diverse contributions. In the 1930s he was a member of the Group Theatre where he directed as well as acted, working closely with Lee Strasberg and Harold Clurman (who directed *Streetcar* after Kazan left the play in 1949). Like the founders of the Group, Kazan had an unshakable sense of theatre as a social agency, a powerful medium to foreground ethical and moral problems. Kazan's sociology of theatre was right for the time – late 1947 – since it evolved from the great domestic and global conflicts (the Depression and World War II) that shaped the hopes and fears of Americans. Yet Kazan successfully modified his strong sense of realism to accommodate the intensely psychological fabric of Williams's play. In 1947 Kazan co-founded, with Cheryl Crawford and Robert Lewis, the Actors Studio, which, like the Group Theatre, taught a Stanislavskian naturalistic style of acting "turning psychological events into behavior."[35] Out of the Actors Studio came such stars as Marlon Brando, Geraldine Page, and James Dean. Kazan was highly and justly regarded as an actor's best mentor.

Brenda Murphy has claimed that "the relentless and climactic pace Kazan maintained . . . was considered the strongest element of his signature on Broadway during the late forties and early fifties."[36] It was Kazan's forcefulness that Williams valued most. When Williams learned that Kazan wanted to revise the *Streetcar* script, the playwright wrote him: "I'm sure a lot of good will come out of consultation between us . . . The cloudy dreamy type, which I admit to being, needs the complementary eye of the more objective and dynamic worker. I believe you are also a dreamer. There are dreamy touches in your direction which are vastly provocative but you have the dynamism my work needs."[37] In consulting with Kazan on *Streetcar*, Williams sent the following letter, excerpted from Kazan's *Life*, on how the director needed to approach the play and the characters. Of all the exchanges between playwright and director, this letter is undoubtedly key to the performance of *Streetcar*:

> It [*Streetcar*] is a tragedy with the classic aim of producing a catharsis of pity and terror and in order to do that, Blanche must finally have the understanding and compassion of the audience. This without creating a black-dyed villain in Stanley. It is a thing (Misunderstanding) not a person (Stanley) that destroys her in the end. In the end you should feel – If only they had known about each other.[38]

The "consultation" between Williams and Kazan begun with *Streetcar* lasted more than twenty years, with Kazan directing four other Williams works – *Camino Real, Baby Doll, Cat on a Hot Tin Roof,* and *Sweet Bird of Youth.*

Reviewers lavishly praised Kazan's achievement in *Streetcar*. John Mason Brown exclaimed that Kazan's direction was "brilliantly creative . . . an achievement of unusual and exciting distinction" while

Edwin H. Schloss of the *Philadelphia Inquirer* asserted: "Elia Kazan's direction has sensitivity, thrust, poetry and an almost savage sincerity" – just the admixture of dreaminess and dynamism Williams sought. Jack O'Brian heralded Kazan as a "wonder lad" whose "job was to establish the mood of Williams' writings, understand his pace, characterization, and put all the components into a single dramatic piece . . . and he more than any other person except the author is to be credited with the play's compassionate commotion."

Kazan's impact on the production was more than dynamic; it was sweepingly profound. He encouraged Williams to make more than 100 changes in the script, including cuts, altering the opening (in an earlier version Blanche meets the blind Mexican woman in Scene 1), and emphasizing more naturalistic details. Kazan changed Blanche's Della Robbia blue dress for a plain white one. The differences between Kazan's *Streetcar* and Williams's are the differences between the acting copy of the play published by Dramatist Play Service and the reading copy published in vol. III of *The Theatre of Tennessee Williams*. Owing to Kazan's influence on the script, Murphy bestows on him the title of Williams's collaborator – "the Williams–Kazan relationship was central to some of the best work that either man did."[39] As Thomas Pauly admits, "Williams created the characters and Kazan brought them to life."[40]

Kazan's concept of *Streetcar* was shaped by the manifestoes of the Group Theatre and most carefully articulated in the *Notebook* that he kept before and during rehearsals (August 1947).[41] A series of working notes, Kazan's *Notebook* (hereafter *N*) was never intended for publication, but is the most valuable window to his ideas about the themes and characters of *Streetcar*. In directing *Streetcar* Kazan foregrounded the idea of social conflict energized through mighty opponents. Stella, for example, becomes the field of battle over which Stanley and Blanche fight. While Kazan labeled *Streetcar* "a poetic tragedy," he also linked it to "classical tragedy," as Williams did, with Blanche as the protagonist. Nevertheless, Kazan read any Aristotelean notion of tragedy through his Stanislavskian, naturalistic perspective.

Privileging the swelling undercurrents of naturalism he detected in *Streetcar*, Kazan portrayed Williams's characters in behavioral terms as social types translated for the stage. For each major character, therefore, Kazan identified his/her "spine," or motivational force, that the actor was to use as a yardstick of his/her performance. His behavioral analyses tacitly dovetailed with Williams's own creative process: "My characters make my play . . . I always start with them."[42]

As Williams did, Kazan read *Streetcar* as a play about Blanche. Accordingly, Blanche is "an emblem of a dying civilization, making its last curlicued and romantic exit" (*N* 365); she is "the last relic of the last century now adrift in our unfriendly day" (*N* 368). Trapped by and in the romantic "Tradition" (Kazan's most definitive word) of the antebellum South, Blanche is true to the "Tradition" she enshrines, seeing protection (her spine) through a man. "All her behavior patterns are those of the dying civilization she represents." But, Kazan argued, she is insecure and looks in vain everywhere for a male protector. Believing she is "special," "superior" – her tragic flaw – Blanche confronts a cruel world that forces her to justify her special existence "in fantasy." Kazan contended that Blanche must be eleven "different people," all of them "self-dramatized and romantic." Yet Blanche's "quest for an accommodation, refuge, is futile, and because she senses this, an incipient madness informs all her actions." Consequently, Kazan instructed Tandy to play Blanche as "heavy at the beginning" – "domineering," displaying her "bad effect on Stella" – but as Stanley "gradually exposes her," the audience needed to see "how warm, tender, loving she can be" and then realize "that they are sitting in at the death of something . . . colorful, varied, passionate, lost, witty, imaginative . . . and then they feel the tragedy" (*N* 367).

While Kazan honored Blanche ("she is better than Stella"; her love of art and beauty is noble), he clearly found Stanley more intriguing. According to Susan Spector, Kazan's "basic sympathies and his most powerful and imaginative descriptions" were reserved for Stanley and even went so far as to justify Stanley's position domestically, socially.[43] In Kazan's reasoning, Stanley fears that Blanche "would wreck his

home – Blanche is dangerous . . . destructive [and] would soon have
him and Stella fighting. He's got things the way he wants them [his
spine] . . . and does not want them upset by a phony, corrupt, sick . . .
woman. *This makes Stanley right*" (*N* 375). A committed hedonist,
Stanley for Kazan was "all sensual." Sex – the rape – was the only way
Stanley could dominate Blanche, reducing her to his level. While
Kazan readily admitted Stanley's liabilities – he is cynical, explosive,
"self-absorbed" – he portrayed him as the "hoodlum aristocrat," the
proletarian hero frequently valorized in the scripts Kazan interpreted
for stage and screen – *On the Waterfront, East of Eden, Tender is the
Night.* Brando's sexual energy and dialectic of male power fulfilled
Kazan's interpretation.

Stella was at the center of the conflict for Kazan. Projecting
"unconscious hostility" toward her older sister Blanche, Stella would
have ended up just like Blanche were it not for Stanley. Stella's spine is
"to hold onto Stanley" (*N* 372), and because of her narcotized sexuality, she pays the price for that allegiance. Critical of Stella's behavior,
Kazan found that she, like Blanche, is "doomed" because she "has
sold herself" through dependence on a man. But, Kazan stressed,
Blanche did succeed in getting Stella to see Stanley in a new light,
whereas she was "blind" to him "until Blanche arrives," thus depriv-
ing Stanley of a complete victory.

Mitch in Kazan's eyes was a "mama's boy," the victim of a matriar-
chy that "robbed him of all daring, initiative, self-reliance." Although
Mitch was "straight out of a Mack Sennett comedy" (*N* 378) for
Kazan, he nonetheless seethes "full of violent desire" for women.
Tragically, Mitch wants the perfect woman, something only the
"Tradition" can give him and, ironically, he is "Blanche's ideal in
comic form, 150 years late." If Mitch was Blanche's last hope, she was
his as well, Kazan firmly believed.

Some critics like Harold Clurman felt Kazan's interpretation was
misleading and inconsistent with Williams's valorized theme of misunderstanding. Clurman claimed that Stanley's "low jeering is sec-
onded by the audience's laughter, which seems to mock the feeble and

hysterical decorativeness of the girl's behavior. The play becomes the triumph of Stanley Kowalski with the collusion of the audience, which is no longer on the side of the angels. This is natural because Miss Tandy is fragile without being touching (except when the author is beyond being overpowered by an actress)."[44] And Williams himself cautioned Kazan not "to take sides or present a moral." Yet performance always tests and modifies authorial intent.

The designer – Jo Mielziner

Essential to fulfilling Williams's and Kazan's plans were the sets designed by Jo Mielziner (1901–76), the most skillful scene designer in New York. Born in Paris, Mielziner, who studied under Robert Edmond Jones, designed his first show in 1924, and by 1947 had a long list of enviable credits, including *Annie Get Your Gun, Hamlet,* and *The Glass Menagerie*. He later designed sets for Williams's *Cat on a Hot Tin Roof, Sweet Bird of Youth,* and *Red Devil Battery Sign*. As he was to do for *Death of a Salesman* two years later, Mielziner worked closely with Kazan on selecting colors, props, and lighting. Robert Garland praised Mielziner's "collaborative background." Brooks Atkinson observed that "since [Williams] is no literal dramatist and writes in none of the conventional forms, he presents the theater with many problems" (4 December 1947). Up to the challenge, Mielziner translated Williams's script into the sights, sounds, and moods of the Broadway premiere. Mielziner's crowning achievement was that he discovered in the *Streetcar* script the unique visual metaphors – the stage language – defining the production. He did this by successfully capturing the stark realism of the Kowalski apartment as well as the illusory world Blanche inhabits without privileging either a realistic or expressionistic theatre, thus being faithful to Kazan's stylized realism. As Irwin Shaw put it, "Mielziner has designed a set that is at once sordid, ugly, dreamlike and glorious."

As he had done with *Menagerie*, Mielziner radically departed from the rigid conventions of a proscenium arch (or boxed) stage.

1. Full stage of Broadway premiere of *Streetcar* (New York, 1947)

Responsible for ushering in an "era of gauze,"[45] Mielziner created a transparent, painted scrim symbolizing the walls of the Kowalski apartment, with appliquéd windows, shutters, and a skylight. Harry Smith pointed out that "The Kowalski apartment . . . reveals even less strict adherence to physical principles. The architectural detail is frankly distorted. No attempt is made to suggest that walls and windows are real. The lines are wavy and indistinct, contributing to the effect of shabbiness and squalor."[46] Light played a major role in capturing this effect. As Mielziner recorded, "When I designed *Streetcar*, I used translucent walls that could be made to appear by the skilled use of light and focus the attention of the audience on only one section of the stage at a given moment. The magic of light opened up a fluid and poetic world of storytelling – selective light that revealed or concealed, advanced a set or made it recede."[47] Light from the front of the stage signaled the interior while light from behind the gauze scrim revealed exterior scenes, or "the desolate street outside" (Wolcott Gibbs) as when Blanche is led off to the madhouse or Stanley eavesdrops on the sisters' conversation in Scene Four. According to Thomas P. Adler, "the most threateningly expressionistic moments in *Streetcar* emanated from the area behind the scrim that forms the back wall of the apartment."[48]

Perceptively, the reviewer for the *New York World Telegram* (16 October 1947) pointed out that the "set is really different scenes demanding further light manipulation" – the interior of the apartment, its exterior, and the environs of the French Quarter, including the Four Deuces. Using "selective lighting," Mielziner improved upon Williams's earlier stage directions that required the scrim for Stanley's apartment to be raised and lowered to indicate exterior and interior locations. A stationary winding staircase that both the Hubbells and Stella used was at the center-point of Mielziner's set, as seen in Figure 1.

Mielziner's lighting provocatively called attention to the subtle distinctions of the *Streetcar* text. As Brenda Murphy stressed, "Lighting was . . . the central element of the new stage language"of stylized realism.[49] Lighting allowed Mielziner to incorporate expressionistic techniques to accommodate Blanche's dreamy trips from reality to illusions and back again. And, as Felicia Londré perceptively pointed out, "The physical interior and exterior of the simultaneous setting also reinforced the mingling of objective reality and the subjective reality . . . seen through the eyes of Blanche."[50] But even more ominously, as Mielziner graphically admitted, "Throughout the play the brooding atmosphere is like an impressionistic X-ray. We are always conscious of the skeletons in this house of terror . . ."[51] Mielziner was the architect of shadows as well as light.

To carry out Mielziner's designs, *Streetcar* included sixty light cues with five electricians in front and behind the stage to implement them on "seven portable switchboards and pre-set switchboards controlling" the hundreds of lights for the production.[52] Most important were the lighting cues to represent the protagonists. As Mielziner confessed, "In almost all the scenes I used a carefully controlled spotlight on the principals, not as an obvious 'follow-spot' but a subtle heightening of the faces of those who dominated the scene."[53] One electrician was assigned just to Blanche, "lovingly following the heroine throughout the evening" (Irwin Shaw). For example, "When Blanche open[ed], the [bath]room door, the smoke curls handsomely into the amber-crisp lighting on the set."[54] Other variations in lighting – the harsh glare of the naked light bulb in Scene 9 or the more kindly glow when Blanche courts the paperboy in Scene 6 – helped audiences to see Blanche's fragile desire for protection and to understand her tragedy. Mielziner also used light to indicate the times of day. "Color framers [were] . . . supplied in both blue and amber for moments in which light on the set supposedly derives from daylight, moonlight, or candle light."[55] Finally, blackouts signaled scene changes for the "two brief, one of them only four minutes, intermissions" (Ibee) after Scenes 4 and 6.

Mielziner also chose highly appropriate props to represent Stanley's squalid world. Wolcott Gibbs admitted: "It's possible that some scenic artist somewhere has contrived a more gruesome interior than the decaying horrors that Jo Mielziner has executed for the Kowalskis' house, but I doubt it." Mielziner's prop list included objects that were frayed, chipped, mismatched, battered, or just plain worn out. For example, a dreadful black telephone, with peeling paint, sat on a rickety pedestal. An armchair, with one arm missing, and a beat-up ice chest and a liquor cabinet on faded carpets signified the only comforts of the Kowalski home. Stanley's poker table was covered with "an old green billiard cloth with a torn edge" and around it were four chairs, each of a different design and color. The "insistent and sometimes jarring iconic realism [of these props] helped to re-emphasize the friction . . . between the world as Blanche saw it and the 'real' world the characters live in."[56] The Chinese paper lanterns – the production's signature symbol – were not cheap; four of them cost $160 to fireproof to meet New York City fire codes.[57] Yet this prop was easy prey for Stanley, whose worldly possessions

were anything but delicate, transparent, or subtle. Stanley's props –
food, beer bottles, T-shirts, cards – physicalized his status as aggressive gamester. Blanche's things – perfume bottles, pillows, or curtains
– proved as ephemeral as their owner and as easily dislodged. Perhaps
Mielziner's greatest triumph was that he gave Blanche magic as well as
realism. Seeing the set as a "wonderful mixture of the qualities of
both" Stanley and Blanche, Tandy characterized it as "decayed elegance and sheer unadulterated guts."[58]

The Streetcar *music*

The music for *Streetcar* was composed by Alex North, who also
scored the film (1951) and ballet versions (1952). North composed
the music for *Death of a Salesman* as well as for several epic films in
the 1960s – *Spartacus, Antony and Cleopatra,* and *The Agony and
Ecstasy.* Working closely with North, Kazan had a hand in the development, arrangement, and placement of the music. Under the direction of Lehman Engel, music came "from two major sources: a
four-piece jazz band" from the Four Deuces and "the phantom rendering of the folk tune Varsouviana heard only by Blanche." The jazz
band, which consisted of a piano, trumpet, drums, and clarinet, was
hidden away in a dressing room at the Barrymore Theatre which
served as a "broadcasting chamber . . . [e]quipped with microphone,
cue lengths, a warning buzzer, and an intercommunication system to
[keep the musicians] in touch with an assistant stage manager" who
signaled when they were to play. Remaining in the broadcasting
room throughout the production, the musicians were "flying
blind."[59] The Varsouviana was played by a novachord, or synthesizer,
backstage. Throughout the performance, audiences heard music
played during some of the blackouts between scenes.

North's music beautifully harmonized with Williams's script and
Kazan's direction. By creating moods and identifying with Stanley's
or Blanche's perceptions of reality, North introduced a varied and
sophisticated score which, according to composer Luigi Zaninelli, led

to the "wonderful phenomenon of the serious American composer using European compositional techniques to create music drawn from American pop culture."[60] The jazz, or blues, played at the conclusion of Scenes 2 ("Jazz music swells and is heard throughout change"), 3 (when Stanley yells for Stella), and 9 (Mitch's midnight visit) evoked the boozy, sleazy world of Stanley's New Orleans – the world of the hot trumpet. The "Wang Wang Blues," pulsating at the end of Scene 10 – the rape – and extending into the blackout, effectively counterpointed Stanley's heinous crime.

Distinctive blues sounds also characterized Blanche. Stressing that the blues "fit the play" and particularly Blanche's life, Kazan noted that the music is "an extension of the loneliness and rejection, the exclusion and isolation of the Negro and their [opposite] longing for love and connection. Blanche, too is 'looking for a home,' abandoned and friendless . . .Thus the Blue Piano catches the soul of Blanche, the miserable . . . side of the girl which is beneath her frenetic duplicity, her trickery . . ." (*N* 371). North similarly maintained in his film work that "lonely people . . . could best be portrayed through small orchestral units."[61] Significantly enough, the "Claremont Blues" was played at the end of Scene 7 when Blanche realized she was losing Mitch. Arguing that the Blue Piano music and the sound of the hot trumpet are not "external to the play," John S. Bak found that Williams's characters were differentiated through music containing Wagnerian echoes:

> the music and the aural accents provide an underlying structure to *Streetcar* which melds all the elements of the play together – literary, dramatic, and thematic – just as Wagner had attempted in the *Ring*. In other words, Williams builds *Streetcar* architectonically, adapting Wagner's use of webbing leitmotifs for his own purpose of reinforcing for the reader or audience the struggle that Blanche experiences with everyone in the play. These leitmotifs create a metalanguage in *Streetcar* . . .[62]

In addition to the music, off-stage noises contributed significantly to the urban ethos Williams strove to create. As Rosamond Gilder graphically noted, surrounding the Kowalski house were "street cries, church bells, the thousand sounds of activity which heighten the sense of palpitating urban life, of brutal intimacies and close-parked, crowded living." Sound merged with staging.

THE CAST

Jessica Tandy as Blanche

Unquestionably the most experienced member of the *Streetcar* company was Jessica Tandy as Blanche. Born in London in 1909, Tandy played opposite Laurence Olivier and John Gielgud in several Shakespearean roles (most notably Ophelia) at the Old Vic, her first appearance being in 1927. When she came to New York in 1940, Tandy was widely regarded as one of the most accomplished actors in England. She spent the next five years making films. In January 1947, Tandy's husband, Hume Cronyn, directed "Portrait of a Madonna" – Williams's one-act play about a spinster, Lucretia Collins, who hallucinates seeing a former beau and is sent to an asylum – at Hollywood's Actors' Lab. For Cronyn, Lucretia "was a first draft for Blanche."[63] It was Cronyn who suggested to Audrey Wood that Tandy be cast as Blanche.[64] Initially, Selznick wanted Hollywood stars Margaret Sullavan or Bette Davis for the role, but when she, Kazan, and Williams saw Tandy perform in "Madonna," there was no question they had found their Blanche.

Tandy looked the way Williams imagined Blanche should – trim, pale, graceful, sophisticated. In a letter to Uta Hagan, Tandy's successor in the role, Williams observed that for him Blanche had a "transparent slightness and frailty."[65] Tandy seemed more appropriate for the role than Williams's earlier choices – Katharine Cornell or Tallulah Bankhead. Cornell was too old (forty-seven) to play the 34-year-old Blanche, and Bankhead, it was feared, was too forceful. In a letter to Williams, Tandy clearly recognized the sensitive side of

Blanche: "I have to make clear Blanche's intricate and complex background – her indomitable spirit – her innate tenderness and honesty – her untruthfulness or manipulating truth – her inevitable tragedy."[66] Because of Tandy's fragile appearance, literary background, and experience playing hysterical women, her Blanche was much more the moth than the tiger.

Many critics followed Elinor Hughes of the *Boston Traveler*, who claimed of Tandy that "the play is largely hers." Blanche was one of the most demanding roles for an actor on the American stage, and "one of the longest in the history of Broadway" (Ibee). Garland observed that it was "a role that would test the talents of a Bernhardt, Anderson, or Cornell," and that Tandy compared favorably with these great actors. Eight times a week, Tandy performed magnificently for over a year and a half. As Atkinson admitted, Tandy's Blanche "is hardly ever off the stage and when she is on stage she is almost constantly talking . . ."(4 December 1947). Tandy received enthusiastic critical applause. George Jean Nathan concluded that she gave "one of the finest performances observed here in seasons," and Atkinson further exclaimed: "Her performance is almost incredibly true. For it does seem almost incredible that she could understand such an elusive part so thoroughly and that she can convey it with so many shades and impulses that are accurate, revealing and true." According to Shaw, "Everything that talent, intelligence, and discipline can do, Miss Tandy does." Writing in 1986, Harry Rasky claimed that Tandy's was "still the Blanche against which every actress must be judged."[67]

Tandy inaugurated a Blanche who was the quintessential "High Bred Lady in Distress" (*N* 371), foregrounding the desperation that Williams saw as central to the character. Her Blanche was neither flamboyant nor aggressive, and certainly not the scrappy survivor as portrayed by later actors. Ironically enough, Tandy's strength lay in pathos, projecting a sensitive and lonely woman terrified by her environment and the tragedy it holds for her. A victim of Stanley's revenge and of her own fantasies, Tandy's Blanche evoked pity, and in so doing won great admiration. Robert Coleman hailed Tandy's rendition as "haunting and volatile." Edwin H. Schloss accurately summarized Tandy's acting talent: "Impersonating Blanche's pitiful gallantries and pathetic struggles, Jessica Tandy . . . gave an arresting and infinitely skillful . . . performance." In his 14 December 1947 review, Brooks Atkinson concluded that Tandy played Blanche with "an insight as vibrant and pitiless as Mr. Williams' writing, for she catches on the wing of terror the bogus refinement, the intellectual alertness, and the madness that can hardly be distinguished from logic and fastidiousness." Most glowing of all, John Chapman affirmed that Tandy "achieve[d] an acting tour de force in the grandly pitiful Blanche that races the pulses."

Yet if the pity that Tandy orchestrated in the role was the secret to her success, it also worked against her. For some reviewers and audiences Tandy's style, developed in concert with Kazan, was overblown, unappealing, not genuine. William Hawkins unabashedly identified Tandy's chief weakness: she "infallibly projects two essential planes of the character . . . unrelenting unhappiness and desperate falseness. She makes her pathos repellent rather than sympathetic," thus unintentionally abetting the image of a more credible and sincere Stanley. No doubt, directorially speaking, Tandy's excessive lugubriousness was a sign of Blanche's need to feel superior and her inevitable realization that the "Tradition" she venerated would neither protect nor justify her. In one of the most critical reviews, Kappo Phelan investigated the consequences of Tandy's excesses: "Miss Tandy is all sly, sick; she never moves. It is true that she is wonderfully skilled and at ease . . . traveling from tears to shock and back expertly, but here again I quarrel. Her teariness is too often."

Tandy's portrayal of Blanche's madness in particular raised one of the leading questions haunting any actor playing Blanche, and the director guiding her: at what point should Williams's heroine show signs of madness? In over fifty years of *Streetcar* productions, audiences have seen a variety of interpretations. In some, Blanche's mind goes only after her horrific rejection by Mitch, but before Stanley rapes her. In other productions, actors show Blanche as going slowly mad from her first appearance. "From Kazan's point of view, the elements of Blanche's psychic disintegration were in her at the beginning of the play, and indeed long before it. His Blanche was constantly just on the edge of losing control . . ."[68] Eric Bentley claimed that in 1947 audiences saw a "Blanche who was more or less mad from the start." As Atkinson observed near the end of Tandy's long run as Blanche, "Blanche's mental collapse was closer to the surface throughout the play and the agony of the last act was implicit in the preliminary scenes. Blanche had slipped into the limbo of the psychopathic world before the time of the play" (12 June 1949). A vital part of Blanche's madness, as interpreted by Tandy, involved a theatricalizing Blanche who performed the hysteria of her character by writing, directing, and producing her own script.[69] According to R. E. P. Sensenderfer, Tandy "had studied and mastered the intricacies of neurosis." In rehearsals Williams admitted: "[Tandy] has already demonstrated she knows how to play my hysterical women."[70] Ophelia had come to Broadway.

Kazan scripted poignant stage business to signal Blanche's continuing loss of control. In Scene 4, he directed Tandy to "fling the coins under the dressing table, emphasizing her desperation and barely controlled volatility"; when Stanley berated her for being in the bathroom so much, she screamed at him and pounded on the table, "signifying that her control was giving out at the fear of losing Mitch"; after Stanley presented her with a bus ticket back to Laurel, Tandy "ran into the bedroom sobbing sharply. She paused in the middle of the bedroom, not knowing which way to run, and finally ran into the bathroom with shaking sobs, slamming the door shut"; and after Mitch rejected her as a bride-to-be, Tandy fled "into the street with her gowns and jewels." The rape forever sealed her in insanity.[71]

Tandy's Blanche was immersed in the hysteria so deeply that she blurred reality and insanity, paradoxically bringing the actor both praise and criticism. But beyond question, one of Tandy's strongest traits was turning madness into nobility, nowhere more triumphantly represented than in Blanche's exit in Scene 11. Chapman claimed: "there is heartbreak . . . when burdened but ever so gallant, she is led away" to the madhouse. Susan Spector carefully documented Tandy's representation of Blanche's madness: "Tandy's Blanche, under Kazan's direction, left audiences feeling that a madwoman had entered an alien world and, after shaking that world, had been successfully exorcized."[72]

While many critics like Howard Barnes characterized Blanche as a nymphomaniac, a "boozy prostitute," Tandy emphasized Blanche's sexual desires without flagrantly crossing the threshold of propriety. Tandy's frail gentility colored Blanche's sensuality. In her interpretation, Blanche's sexual sins remained more egregious in the script than in performance. In this regard, John Mason Brown's comments cry out for emendation: Tandy "dislodges none of the exposures of the text." The reviewer for *Newsweek* (15 December 1947) perceptively intimated that Tandy's Blanche, while powerful, did not square with the image of Williams's character: "Offhand it is not easy to consider Jessica Tandy cast as a nymphomaniac with a Southern accent and a peg of whisky in free hand, but she achieves a characterization that is a triumph of acting over apparent miscasting." Euphemia Van Rensselaer Wyatt aptly described Tandy's more delicate Blanche as "a lily with a rotten calyx." In performance, Tandy's Blanche was seductive without being scandalous, more a desperate, fallen woman than a brazen trollop. Her Blanche was the faded, not scarlet, belle, closer to such literary ancestors as Camille (with whom Blanche jocularly compares herself before the un-literary Mitch in Scene 6), also known as Marguerite Gautier (whom, ironically enough, Tandy played in the 1970 revival of *Camino Real*). Theodore H. Parker complimented Tandy for this "exact balance between the tawdry and the beautiful." And Elliot Norton of the *Boston Sunday Post* (9 November 1947) also put Blanche's sexuality into this helpful perspective:

> Blanche is a . . . jaded belle on the verge of mental collapse. Miss Tandy makes her a pretty coquette in some scenes, a giddy drunkard in others.

In one sequence, she flares into rage against her supine sister for living with the man-beast . . . In the final scene, she cracks your heart . . .

Consistent with her portrait of Blanche as a "pretty coquette," Tandy refused Williams's request to pose for a promotional photograph in a see-through slip such as a more lascivious Blanche wore in Thomas Hart Benton's painting of the play. She did not want to encourage the audience to co-script *Streetcar* as "a sexy, salacious play." In a protest letter to Williams, she emphasized, "I don't want to do anything that will lead future audiences to think that they are going to see sex in the raw."[73] Audiences, of course, thought what they liked. Sadly, too, as *Streetcar* ran closer to its 855th performance, Tandy "had to fight with the audience every night because in time [it] got less and less sensitive," undercutting Tandy's seriousness with laughter.[74]

To suggest Blanche's sordid past, though, Tandy bleached her dark hair blonde and wore Lucinda Ballard's flowing gowns, "rich with folds and airy in texture" *(N 374)*. A blonde Tandy reminded Linton Martin of Jeanne Eagles, who starred as Sadie Thompson in *Rain* twenty-five years before the Boston *Streetcar* tryouts. Working with Kazan, Tandy developed appropriate stage business and props to project Blanche as a fallen belle compelled to attract a man – any man – for security. Tandy seductively sprayed perfume on herself and on Stanley in Scene 2 to arouse him. Throughout *Streetcar*, she used a cigarette to woo men's attention – Stanley's in Scene 2, Mitch's in Scene 3, the paperboy's in Scene 6 – by flirtatiously asking for a light. Kazan and Tandy added details to Williams's script, especially in Blanche's attempt to ensnare Mitch. In Scene 3, for example, "Blanche dazzled Mitch by waving her cigarette holder around, fitting the cigarette into it, and taking a light from him with aristocratic elegance."[75] In Scene 3 again, "as Mitch started tying his tie . . . eating Sen Sen in preparation for meeting her, Blanche arranged her chair in the light and began combing her hair seductively." Subsequent Blanches – e.g., Uta Hagen, Ann-Margret, Blythe Danner – would be far more explicit, even risqué, in representing Blanche's sexuality.

However stirring, Tandy's performance did not accomplish Kazan's original goal of having the audience switch allegiance from Stanley and then, as the play progressed, back to Blanche. Tandy lost ground; Brando gained. As Kazan recalled, "The audiences adored Brando. When he derided Blanche, they responded with approving laughter. Was the play becoming the Marlon Brando Show? . . . What would I say to Brando? Be less good? Or to Jessie? Get better?"[76] In his autobiography, Brando surprisingly confessed: "I think Jessica and I were both miscast, and between us we threw the play out of balance . . . she was too shrill to elicit the sympathy . . . the woman deserved. This threw the play out of balance because the audience was not able to realize the potential of her character, and as a result my character got a more sympathetic reaction than Tennessee intended."[77] From her feminist reading of history, Anca Vlasopoulos located Stanley's ultimate triumph in patriarchal privilege: "authority within the play moves from Blanche to Stanley precisely because society legitimizes his masculine history over her feminine one."[78] In his highly critical review of Kazan's direction, Harold Clurman concluded: "The play becomes the triumph of Stanley Kowalski with the collusion of the audience . . . this is natural because Miss Tandy is fragile without being touching" while Brando's Stanley "was touching without being irredeemably coarse."[79] Tandy was the first in a long line of soft and shimmering Blanches.

Marlon Brando as Stanley

Marlon Brando and Stanley Kowalski have become synonymous in world theatre. Williams even remarked that Brando ruined the role for other actors. When filming the teleplay of *Streetcar* in 1983, John Erman heard one passerby ask: "Who's playing Marlon Brando?" (*People Weekly*, 15 August 1983).[80] Surprisingly enough, Brando was not the first choice to play Stanley. With her Hollywood background, Selznick wanted John Garfield, but Garfield made excessive demands including leaving the play at his, not the producer's, discretion, and then when news prematurely leaked he had accepted the role, he withdrew entirely from the project. Moreover, according to Thomas H. Pauly, Garfield turned down the role of Stanley "because he felt Blanche dominated the play."[81] When Burt Lancaster, Selznick's other choice, was not available, Kazan went to Clurman at the Actors Studio who recommended the young Brando, then enrolled in Robert Lewis's acting class. Brando had appeared as Lars in *I Remember Mama* and alongside Katherine Cornell in *Candida* and turned in a powerful though brief performance in Maxwell Anderson's *Truckline Café.*

Brando's age helped Kazan achieve his own concept of Stanley. While Garfield would have been "perfect for portraying Stanley's toughness and animal energy,"[82] he was much older (thirty-five) than Brando (twenty-five). As Kazan reasoned, "I'd always thought of Stella and Stanley as a young couple in their early twenties, Blanche a good deal older . . . I thought if Williams could see the casting that young, it might work . . ."[83] It did. Kazan sent Brando to see Williams, who was vacationing on Cape Cod, and when the young actor arrived, he fixed the playwright's faulty plumbing and electrical wiring and then read for the part. Williams was ecstatic and "let out a 'Texas Tornado' shout. 'Get Kazan on the phone right away! This is the greatest reading I've ever heard . . ." [84] Although some like Selznick objected to Stanley being so young, Williams concurred with Kazan's decision and wrote to Audrey Wood on 29 August 1947: "It humanizes the character of Stanley in that it becomes the brutality or callousness of youth rather than a vicious older man. I don't want to focus guilt or blame on any one character but to have it a tragedy of misunderstanding and insensitivity to others."[85] Not only was Williams overwhelmed by Brando's powerful reading but, as Kazan speculated, "he seemed enraptured by the boy" himself.[86] Stanley was born.

Brando bristled at the suggestion that he and Stanley were alike, that Brando was playing himself. "I was the antithesis of Stanley . . . sensitive by nature and he was coarse with unerring animal instincts and intuition. Later in my acting career I did a lot of research before playing a part, but I didn't do any on him. He was a compendium of my imagination, based on the lines of the play. I created him from Tennessee's words."[87] Undoubtedly, Brando's imagination was synchronous with Williams's script. The hallmarks of Brando's Stanley – "a mosaic of sexual insolence, sullen moodiness, puckish good humor, and terrifying rage"[88] – were indeed "a compendium" of Stanley's character. Irwin Shaw hailed Brando as "the best young actor on the American stage . . . always . . . on the verge of tearing down the proscenium with his bare hands." Reinforcing Brando's assertion that the role came from within him, Kazan declared that Brando's "every word seemed not something memorized but in the spontaneous expression of intense, inner experience" and, in short, pronounced Brando a "performance miracle . . . in the making."[89]

In build, stance, and body language, Brando looked like Stanley – a street brawler, muscular and predatory. He intentionally cultivated the image of Stanley as the fighter ready to explode, eager to do any opponent harm, a legacy almost mandatorily bequeathed to future Stanleys in theatres around the globe. John Mason Brown appropriately commented that Brando is "all force and fire; a Rodin model; a young Louis Wolheim with Luther Alder's explosiveness." He kept a punching bag in the boiler room of the Barrymore and when he was not on stage he would spar with his understudy, Jack Palance, or with Nick Dennis who played Pablo.[90] Encoding Stanley's violence, Brando frequently displayed his pugilistic talents, all of them intensified through Kazan's direction. He opened the play by throwing a blood-stained package of meat to Stella; at the end of Scene 3 he challenged all of his poker-playing buddies in a grisly fight; in Scene 7 he malevolently cleared his place at Blanche's birthday dinner, hurling food and dishes all over the stage; and he overpowered Blanche in the rape scene. Speaking for many critics, Thomas R. Dash observed: "Brando can explode in a convincing fit of temper" and in so doing terrify the audience.

Even the way Brando stood reinforced his "tough guy" image. John

Gronbeck-Tedesco has argued that Brando's "physical style" was marked by "diagonal and serpentine spinal alignments together with the contrapposto torque of one large muscle group against the other . . . a signature of the central actors in Williams's plays and . . . [displaying] a weight distribution that . . . asserted a heightened athleticism and coordination." In the rape scene, for instance, "Brando placed himself in a serpentine posture with one shoulder moving downward and the other upward. The upper torso twisted against the pelvis and legs, and the neck extended upward even while [Stanley] was looking down at his victim." Jessica Tandy sat "in a chair recoiling from Stanley. Her body . . . leaning diagonally far beyond the boundary of support provided by the legs and the chair . . . a feat of virtuosity."[91]

In addition to Brando's physique, his good looks transformed Stanley into a sexual icon, a new male sexual hero arousing women in the audience as no actor on the American stage had done before. Yet Charles Higham insightfully pointed out the paradox of Brando's sexuality: "Women in that more inhibited age felt tense and awkward at being actually aroused by Marlon; men were rendered uncomfortable, made to identify with an ignoble savage. Williams had taken the daring step of insulting both sexes by inference: women for clinging to romantic daydreams and men for lacking romanticism in their bluntly physical approach to sex."[92] Seeing Brando's sexuality in light of Williams's own agenda, Carla McDonough stressed that the "'sensual brute' Stanley, Blanche's husband Allan, and the naive Mitch together epitomize the conflicting masculine identities in Williams's stage world."[93] Beyond doubt, in performance Brando's raw sexuality – his sexual magnetism – reflected "the confidence of resurgent flesh" that Kazan called for.

True to Method Acting, Brando uncannily fulfilled all the requirements of Williams's *gaudy seed bearer*," as articulated in Kazan's *Notebook*. He appeared half naked – with his shirt off – in Scene 2 when Blanche meets him and in Scene 10 when he prepared to change into his celebratory red pajamas. Even with his clothes on, Brando exuded priapic splendor. He wore a soiled T-shirt, which became the trans-national symbol of Stanley's ethos, to reveal his manly biceps. Carlo Fiore, one of Brando's closest friends, crudely remarked that "to show he had a perpetual hard-on, he wore tight jeans to outline the bulge of his genitals."[94] As Kazan emphasized to Brando, Stanley "conquers with his penis" (*N* 371). Although writing in scorn of the role, Mary McCarthy nonetheless clearly identified Brando as "the realist of the bladder and genitals, the monosyllabic cynic, made to apostrophize sexual intercourse in a kind of Odetsian poetry." Not without cause did George Jean Nathan christen *Streetcar* "The Glands Menagerie."

Further visualizing Stanley's sexuality, Kazan emphasized "he sucks on a cigar all day because he can't suck on a teat" (*N* 375). Although the cigar was omitted from the final acting script, Brando memorably incorporated the rhetorical power of orality into the role through a host of gustatory and phallic gestures. He chewed gum in Scene 2, sucked on a coke bottle in Scene 4, and on a bottle of beer that he shook and sprayed all over the stage in Scene 10. Further valorizing the oral, Brando's Stanley ate with his fingers – his "cold supper" in Scene 2 – picked his teeth, and savagely licked his fingers and lips at Blanche's ruined birthday dinner.

Brando's delivery may have been the most distinctive part of Stanley's character, another often imitated signature of the actor's style. True to Stanley's personality and background, Brando's Stanley proved "I never was a very good English student" (Scene 1). Critics accused Brando of mumbling and slurring his speech; yet such verbal traits suited an illiterate, lower-class Stanley more interested in comfort than communication. (Stanley's motto is "Be comfortable.") As Brando told Kazan, "Guys like Stanley [are] so muscle bound they can hardly talk. Stan doesn't give a damn how he says a thing. His purpose is to convey his idea. He has no awareness of himself at all."[95] Yet while Brando's ideolect for Stanley – a patois that subsequent Stanley's invariably imitated – clearly was the antithesis of Blanche's language of Southern gentility, it was perfect for Stanley's own struggles. Stanley's speech was as jabbing and sleazy as the blues played at the Four Deuces. Gibbs aptly labeled Brando's verbal humor as "savage and obscene." Stanley's most memorable poetry – shouting "Stella" at the end of Scene 3 or reminiscing about "colored lights" – became indelibly stamped with Brando's subtext, a verbalization of the actor's own emotional Stanislavskian center.

Most importantly, Brando readily (re)solved a major problem that Williams and Kazan saw in the role. Stanley had to be "attractive" to Stella and even though he ultimately crushes Blanche, "he should not be hated for it."[96] Brando's Stanley was too complex, too ambiguous to be the "black-dyed villain." The actor easily gave the lie to Gibbs's misleading, unjustified criticism that Stanley was "almost pure ape." In a number of scenes displaying Stanley's conjugal love, Brando developed a kinder, gentler side of Stella's husband. Sensenderfer detected a softer Stanley: "Mr. Brando's role as the sister's husband is much less complicated yet it has its facets. His transition from animal brutality to a sort of crude affection are flowing, convincing, never jerked." According to O'Brian, Brando's Stanley was "alternately brutally rough and tenderly solicitous of his wife, and makes a paradoxical role believable." Eric Bentley memorably recorded that Brando's Stanley was "an Odets character" who wore "the mask of a suffering soul." Most insightfully, Clurman found that Brando's "combination of an intense, introspective, and almost lyrical personality under the mask of a bully endows [Stanley] with something almost touchingly painful."[97]

In directing Brando, Kazan repeatedly stressed that true to the spine of his character, when Stanley's home, his wife, his way of life were being threatened by Blanche, he had to confront and contain this outsider. Kazan recognized the feminine side of Brando's portrayal of Stanley, too, which helped the character come across as less of a villain and more of a protector. Interestingly enough, Brando's Stanley shared many traits in common with Tandy's Blanche. Like her Blanche, his Stanley was a performer. Carla McDonough convincingly linked Stanley's "posturing" to Blanche's:

Although Stanley calls Blanche's bluff concerning her performance as a chaste lady, he remains unaware that his own posturing is every bit as calculated. Like Blanche, Stanley has his own costumes, particularly the sweaty T-shirt and the gaudy silk pajamas. Like her, too, he performs his sexuality in gesture and movement. Blanche cringes from lights and plays up her physical delicacy. Stanley smashes lights (and tables and bottles) and plays up his physical strength. Blanche pretends innocence and ignorance, while Stanley pretends experience and intelligence.

In short, "Stanley's masculinity is simply another 'masquerade' " in *Streetcar*,[98] the ultimate deconstruction of this idea being realized in the camp *Belle Reprieve*. Finally, as Kazan moved further into rehearsals, he also discovered that "Stanley is fundamentally as neurotic as Blanche. In countering her behavior with one that is radically different yet no less strange, [Brando] rival[ed] [Tandy's] demands for audience attention."[99]

Karl Malden as Mitch

Chicago-born Karl Malden was perfectly cast as Mitch, the burly, awkward and gullible beau Blanche tries to entrap. Before his acting career, Malden held jobs as a steel mill worker, truck driver, and milkman, all occupations whose blue-collar genuineness he projected on stage through Mitch. Like Brando, Malden had been a member of The Actors Studio and had appeared in *Truckline Café,* and like Brando and Kim Hunter, he launched his career with the Academy Award he won for *Streetcar.* Malden's Mitch was an early example of Williams's ill-fated and comic gentleman caller, an unsuitable suitor, a line that Williams continued with Mangiacavallo in *Rose Tattoo*, Kilroy in *Camino*, and Archie Meghan (whom Malden also played) in *Baby Doll.* The critics found Malden's Mitch impressive. Richard Watts, Jr. honored him as "one of the ablest young actors extant"; and Ward Morehouse endorsed Malden as "tremendously effective as the gawky, naive suitor who is agonized by the revelation of Blanche's past." Under Kazan's direction, Malden magnificently captured

Mitch's pained life as a mama's boy whose manhood was constantly at stake and under attack. The harder Malden's Mitch tried to be a suitor, the more pitiful and unfulfilled his character appeared.

Mitch's sexual desire in particular was undercut by the expression of it. As Murphy indicated, "To encode the connection between Mitch's awkwardness and his sexual desire, awkward gestures and movements were emphasized at potentially romantic moments, making Mitch . . . tentative about his masculinity."[100] Seeing Mitch in comic terms, Kazan physicalized the role through appropriate gestures, props and costume. At the end of Scene 2, for example, the husky Malden looked foolish as he swayed bear-like to music coming from Blanche's little white radio. In Scene 6, when Blanche and Mitch return from the amusement park, Kazan had Malden carry a Raggedy Anne doll (instead of a statue of Mae West, as Williams had indicated in the script), further calling attention to Mitch's naive and tattered behavior in love. Malden's Mitch was blind to the Mae West side of Blanche. Whenever he tried to express his feelings for Blanche, Malden was "eloquently unrelaxed" (Hawkins, 4 December 1947). When Mitch returned to Stanley's to "get what I've been missing all summer" in Scene 9, he was dressed in dirty work clothes, his truer métier, as opposed to the suit and tie he uncomfortably wore in Scenes 2 and 6. Malden's greatest achievement, though, was that his Mitch offered not only comic action, but also, as Gibbs observed, "a queer touching blend of dignity and pathos." Malden persuasively enacted Mitch's ultimate tragedy, according to Kazan, of having no woman to go home to except his dying mother.

Kim Hunter as Stella

Before starring as Stella, Kim Hunter had played ingénue roles in little theatre in California and was in motion pictures in England (*Stairway to Heaven*) and in America, where she was under contract to David O. Selznick for *Arsenic and Old Lace*. Selznick herself cast Kim Hunter as Stella, and the critics enthusiastically endorsed her choice. According to William Beyer, Hunter was "a lushly beautiful and intriguing actress . . . perfect as Stella, warm, sensuous, and thoroughly likeable." Recognizing Stella's pivotal role, Hawkins applauded Hunter for being "mellow and philosophical as the devoted sister who tries to synchronize two impossible loyalties." While Richard Watts, Jr. quickly categorized Stella as "the less complex sister," Shaw more accurately pointed to the difficulties the character posed for Hunter: "Stella's is a . . . forgotten role . . . a neglected character . . . she has willfully and delightedly allowed herself to become the slattern her husband can desire. But the development of [the character] is skimped, neither the slattern nor the belle is convincing . . ."

Stella's "narcotized" sexuality was at the heart of Williams's character, and also the source of her problematic status in the script. Hunter's Stella looked to Stanley for the support and sexual fulfillment that Blanche sought, yet Stella had to pay "a terrific price," according to Kazan, to please Stanley: "She keeps her eyes closed, even stays in bed as much as possible so . . . she won't feel the pain of this terrific price . . . She walks around . . . as if in a daze . . . waiting for the dark when Stanley makes her feel only him . . . She is drugged" (*N* 372–73). Stella was forced to deny the world of culture and refinement she knew at Belle Reve and revel in the carnivalesque, the "cheerful squalor" (Rosamund Gilder) of Stanley's world, accepting the antics of her neighbors the Hubbells and tolerating the violence erupting precipitously around her. The couple's passion, according to Richard Cook, explained away any problems over Stella's coping in New Orleans. "It is a match whose physical passion overshadows the differences in backgrounds and tastes of husband and wife." The love scenes between Hunter and Brando were intensely passionate, signs of the young couple's pleasure as well as reminders of what Blanche would not have. The most memorable event in the play for many audiences occurred at the end of Scene 3 when a penitent but bestial Stanley plaintively shouted for Stella to come downstairs, a visualization and recapitulation of Stanley's boast that when he first met Stella he pulled "her down off them columns and [she] loved it."

Hunter experienced problems in developing Stella's character in production. The actor's innate enthusiasm ran counter to the character's "drugged" presence. Seeing a lively Hunter in the first scene during rehearsals disturbed Williams so greatly that he characterized her as "a co-ed on a benzedrine kick."[101] But, as rehearsals continued, Hunter became more sedate, better attuned to the slower rhythms glorifying Stella's earthiness and her narcotized acceptance of life with Stanley. In Scene 4, for example, Hunter lounged in bed, surrounded by comic books, a tableau of domestic indolence and her self-defining pregnancy. At the conclusion of *Streetcar*, Hunter stood gently sobbing as Stanley attempted to console her as Blanche departs for the asylum.

STREETCAR ON TOUR

For two years, *Streetcar* made headlines across the nation, and was sought by every major theatre in America. A national tour was both inevitable and enormously profitable. To meet the national demand to see *Streetcar* Selznick signed two tour companies. One of these companies starred Uta Hagen as Blanche and Anthony Quinn as Stanley; the other featured Judith Evelyn and Ralph Meeker. The Hagen–Quinn team received far more attention. Hagen, who had several Broadway credits to her name, had won critical acclaim for such Broadway productions as *The Whole World Over* and *The Sea Gull,* and as Desdemona opposite Paul Robeson's Othello in Chicago in 1948. Blonde, stately, and twenty-nine, Hagen won the critics' hearts as Blanche DuBois. Not only did she tour with *Streetcar* but she had the distinction of being the second actor to portray Blanche on Broadway.

Hagen's itinerary was demanding. She started playing Blanche in New York from 3 July through 11 August 1948 while Tandy was on vacation. For the first two weeks Hagen played with the National (touring) Company – Anthony Quinn (Stanley), Mary Welch (Stella), and Russell Hardie (Mitch) – and for the next four she appeared with the original *Streetcar* company. Then the National Company, directed by Clurman even though Kazan's name remained on the playbill, went on a ten-month tour, beginning with a five-month stay (21 September 1948 through 26 February 1949) at the Harris Theater in Chicago. Returning to New York on 12 June 1949, Hagen and the National Company played on Broadway until 17 December. Then she continued with *Streetcar* on tour with appearances in Philadelphia, Rochester, Toronto, Buffalo, and Boston. Hagen wound up her performances as Blanche at the City Center in New York for the 1949–50 season (23 May – 11 June 1950).

While Hagen came close to Tandy's 855 performances, she offered a provocatively different interpretation of the role, and the play as a whole, all with the approving assistance of Clurman. As Brooks Atkinson stressed: "Hagen is giving an original performance that is thoroughly her own and that is overwhelming . . ."[102] To avoid any imitation, Hagen refused to watch Tandy's Blanche "until she spent six weeks working on her own interpretation of the part and had gone into rehearsal," as Clarissa Start recorded. Tandy enthusiastically commended Hagen for her new, effective interpretation: "It was like re-discovering the play. I had a wonderful time watching Uta . . . she came to [the role] with a fresh approach. She didn't copy me, but I intend asking if I can steal from her. Take the way Blanche accepts the train [sc. bus] ticket . . . The way I accept that ticket it's an internal emotion, expressed. But the way Uta handles it, it's dramatically external, you can see stark futility, helpless rage, mount on her face . . ."[103] This one action dramatically pinpoints the world of difference between Tandy's Blanche and Hagen's – Tandy's focus on frailty and madness (interiority) as opposed to Hagen's externalized pain and suffering (physicality).

Although Atkinson confessed that it was "an impossible decision" to "decide which actress gives the better performance," reviewers were clear about how and why such differences existed. Atkinson easily admitted that Hagen was "sturdier physically than Miss Tandy," a fact brought out in the advertisement from the *New York Times* bidding Tandy farewell and Hagen welcome with the two actors dressed as Blanche on opposite sides of the page. Highlighting Hagen's "artistry," Robert Garland observed: "Healthier and heftier than Jessica Tandy's, Miss Hagen's Miss DuBois manages to break your heart in two." Director Clurman perceptively linked Hagen's larger build to her less frail representation of Blanche – Hagen offered "robust and sensuously potent elan . . .a fierce will to expression and histrionic facility."[104] George Eells and Claudia Cassidy both saw Hagen's Blanche as a powerful interpretation equaling the work of Laurette Taylor, having the "same inner, unerring brilliance" (Cassidy). Hagen told Clarissa Start: "I found when I got into 'Streetcar' that I felt so free and limber, almost as if I had been doing sitting-up exercises." Hagen's gestures, movements, and speech cadences established a more assertive, less pathetic Blanche than Tandy's. William Hawkins earnestly reported that when Hagen yelled "Fire" in Scene 10, "one is prompted to look for a near exit, not to escape conflagration but to flee from her wildness." Accordingly, Hagen was less intimidated in the face of Stanley's challenges. As Myles Standish pointed out: "Uta Hagen as Blanche is superb. Each writhing, wracked emotion of the woman's tangled mind is graphically projected, and she can reach deep for the reserves of power." Where Tandy withered in agony, Hagen recoiled in wilfull submission.

But perhaps one of the most significant shaping differences between the two Blanches was that, under Kazan's direction, Tandy came into the play already suffering from hallucinations, not able to distinguish reality from fiction, while Hagen went mad precisely because of Stanley's attacks, verbal and physical. As Eric Bentley noted, "Miss Tandy's interpretation may fit the ending better . . . but Miss Hagen's fits the main body." Once again, Atkinson insightfully described Hagen's style in representing Blanche:

> Miss Hagen is an actress of strength and power who had constructed the part with lucid deliberation, carefully underscoring the meaning of individual scenes. When malevolence of the world tortures Blanche beyond the point of endurance, Miss Hagen reaps the reward of her method and vividly describes the agony, fright and loneliness of a woman who has been pushed out of human society into the pitiless seclusion of madness.

Expressing a contrary view, Richard Watts, Jr. maintained that "If Miss Hagen is less impressive than Miss Tandy in showing the collapse of Blanche's neurotic mind, she is much more believable in suggesting the girl's Southern background." This was the essence of Hagen's Blanche.

Hagen's method – described in her *Respect for Acting* – was responsible for another major difference between her interpretation of Blanche and Tandy's. While Tandy portrayed Blanche as the frail butterfly searching for protection, Hagen was the romantic and elegant lady eager to satisfy her needs. If dependence was Tandy's Kazan-developed spine, then needs, all manner of them, shaped Hagen's portrayal of Blanche. Although Hagen's method led her to find correspondences between her life and Blanche's, she also realized that "the earthy, frank, gutsy child of nature" that she was demanded that she "hunt" for substitutions to develop the role. As Hagen explained,

> I have to hunt for an understanding of – and identification with – [Blanche's] main needs: a need for perfection . . . a romantic need, for beauty, a desire for gentleness, tenderness, delicacy, elegance, decorum; a need to be loved and protected, a strong sensual need; a need for delusion when things go wrong.[105]

Where Tandy was caught in the maelstrom of madness, Hagen inhabited a larger and more contoured world in which Blanche struggled, in a variety of circumstances, for fulfillment. Hagen offered a broader spectrum of psychic realities than Tandy did.

Uta Hagen played magnificently opposite Anthony Quinn's Stanley. When Kazan chose Quinn for one of the touring companies,

2. Uta Hagen (Blanche) and Anthony Quinn (Stanley) in the road company production of *Streetcar* (1949)

Quinn had very little stage experience, although he had appeared in more than fifty Hollywood films, mostly as "gangsters and Mexican bandits."[106] His New York debut came in 1947 in an easily forgotten play, *The Gentleman from Athens*, which opened the same time as *Streetcar*. Quinn seethed with rivalry with Brando: "I took Brando's triumph [in *Streetcar*] as a personal affront. It had to come from somewhere . . . it came out of my hide." When Quinn joined the cast of the National Company, Kazan was still directing the play and "so he naturally looked to mirror the original in as many ways as possible." Unlike Hagen who did not want to be influenced by Tandy, Quinn studied Brando's every gesture. "At first I tried to avoid Marlon's Kowalski. I knew I would follow him in the role, but his pull was too strong. I would be lost without his performance as a reference point." But when Clurman took over from Kazan, Quinn "put his own stamp on the role."

Though the second actor to play Stanley, Quinn had the unhappy honor of being the first actor to falter in Brando's shadow. The second Stanley Kowalski was unquestionably less versatile than the first. Richard Davis at the *Milwaukee Journal* claimed that Quinn easily captured Stanley as "the lusty, vulgar man of strength whom the play contrasts" with Allan Grey . . . [but] added the "robust Quinn is not a virtuoso." Kahn at *Variety* more bitterly declared, "Miss Hagen gives a performance that mounts constantly in her portrayal of the school-teacher tart, though the same cannot be said of Quinn . . . [who] hasn't the intensity, the shading or the sensuousness suggested by Brando . . ." Similarly, Myles Standish reported that Quinn "brings out the brutishness, ruthlessness, and primal emotional makeup of Stanley by deft and studied underplaying," hardly a Brando trait. While critics may have faulted the illiterate Quinn for lacking Brando's cunning and excitement, Richard Watts, near the end of the City Center engagement in 1950, applauded Quinn: "His Stanley Kowalski is a little less petulant and sulkily spiteful and more a man of frank and natural animal instincts, honestly revolted by Blanche's airy pretensions. His toughness never for a moment seems mannered."

Taller than Brando, Quinn physically complemented Hagen's Blanche, who was taller and more in command than Tandy's. Hagen and Quinn cut a striking pair on stage, recreating a much less imbalanced set of adversaries than Tandy and Brando did. William Hawkins described the way Quinn made his imprint on the role:

"Quinn is in many ways a natural for the role of Stanley and he understands the balance between crudeness and simplicity in the character. When he first accosts Blanche, in a long appraising stare, he plots the whole progress of their scornful and lustful relationship." Recalling a performance in San Francisco, playwright James Schevill saw Quinn overshadowing Hagen:

> My first impression of *A Streetcar Named Desire* was of the powerful presence of Anthony Quinn . . . He completely eclipsed Uta Hagen as Blanche . . . Quinn was the epitome of macho strength, a sexual force driven by irresistible natural energy. The audience marveled at his unique physical grace, and was almost sympathetic when he raped Blanche – after all hadn't she teased him with her southern flirting and her aristocratic pretensions?[107]

The battle for dominance between Blanche and Stanley was also played out between the actors in *Streetcar*'s early production history.

Later performances of Williams's play inevitably located themselves in relation to the defining Stanley of Marlon Brando and Jessica Tandy's Blanche. The way these two actors interpreted Williams's characters – in costume, gesture, movement, speech, and intent – valorized the acting methods Kazan promulgated and Williams's script substantiated. The Broadway premiere, furthermore, memorialized the artistic teamwork that made the *Streetcar* premiere possible. Brando, Tandy, Hunter, Malden, Kazan, and Williams created an icon in 1947–48 that has been venerated, adapted, or challenged in more than fifty years of performances.

CHAPTER TWO

STREETCAR ON THE WORLD STAGE: THE NATIONAL PREMIERES, 1948–1953

Streetcar took the world stage by storm. In the late 1940s and early 1950s a cavalcade of national premieres propelled Williams's play into Europe's leading theatres and continued well into the 1980s to other theatres around the globe. *Streetcar* was a *cause célèbre* with theatre companies and audiences clamoring for productions. Documenting the dates and economics of these earlier premieres, Audrey Wood, Williams's longtime agent, maintained meticulous correspondence with theatre companies about foreign rights, fees, dates, and even receipts.[1]

The first production of *Streetcar* outside the US was at the Pronato del Teatro's Salia Talia in Havana in July 1948 – while the play was in its seventh month on Broadway – and directed by Modesto Centeno who would stage *Streetcar* twice more in 1957 and 1965.[2] Subsequent premieres in Spanish-speaking theatres occurred in Argentina in September and in Mexico in December 1948.[3] Also starting in late 1948 was the glittering array of European premieres with *Streetcar* coming in October to Brussels and Amsterdam; in January 1949 to Rome; in March to Sweden; in October to London and Paris; and on 10 November to Zurich. The German premiere in Pforzheim on 17 March 1950 was performed at the Stadttheater (then controlled by the occupying American forces) through a translation, made by Berthold Viertel, steeped not in Williams's magic but in grating realism.[4] Viertel's translation was also used in the Austrian premiere at the Akademie Theater in Vienna in April 1951. The Swiss premiere was at Basel in 1951. Williams's hope – lamentably unrealized

– was to have *Streetcar* produced simultaneously in eight European capitals.[5] *Streetcar* entered the Pacific Rim with an Australian premiere in Melbourne in 1950; in Japan in May 1953; and in Seoul in October 1955. The first professional production in New Zealand was not until August 1975.

Streetcar's delayed Spanish debut – January 1961 – was as much a result of strained relations between the US and Generalissimo Franco's "pariah" government as it was of cultural conflicts over *Streetcar*'s content.[6] For similar reasons, *Streetcar*'s premieres in Communist countries lagged behind Broadway by many years. In Poland, twin *Streetcars* premiered on the same day – 21 December 1957 – at Teatr Zieni Pomorskiej in Torun and at Rozmaitosci Teatr in Wrocław, with the Warsaw opening following in April 1958.[7] The Czechoslovakian debut came in November 1960 in Ostrava, Moravia. *Streetcar* did not arrive in Moscow until 1971, when it was directed by A. Goncharov.[8] Perhaps the latest *Streetcar* premiere was at the Tianjin People's Art Theatre in Mainland China on 21 October 1988, with British director Mike Alfreds, who claimed his production opened an "artistic new continent."[9] No one country, no one culture ever owned *Streetcar*.

These national premieres are a significant record of *Streetcar*'s immense popularity as well as a tribute to the directors (e.g., Olivier, Visconti, Bergman), scenographers (Zeffirelli, de Nobili, Strom), and actors (Vivien Leigh, Arletty, Karin Kavli, Vittorio Gassman, Rina Morelli, Marcello Mastroianni) who mounted the play. Not wanting to replicate the work of Kazan and Mielziner, these directors provided new, provocative ways of performing Williams's play, expanding the script by incorporating their own cultural symbols, values, anxieties, and idioms into production. But *Streetcar* reciprocally changed world theatre, too. Productions radically transformed the way actors were trained, in non-English-speaking countries especially. Unaccustomed to Williams's plastic theatre with its expressionistic techniques, actors were required to learn a new style of performance. Many actors worldwide – Brando, Malden, Mastroianni, Wolf Ruvinskis – got their start in *Streetcar*. Moreover, actors brought different subtexts for their characters from those found in the Broadway production. *Streetcar* also introduced new possibilities for set design and staging, encouraging scenographers to adopt a less linear and far more fluid style radically departing from staid realism or deterministic natural-ism. Audiences worldwide changed, too, because of *Streetcar*. One of the most revealing accounts of how *Streetcar* affected audiences comes from a letter, dated 5 October 1955, from Elizabeth T. Fraser of the Korean American Foundation to Williams about the Korean pre-miere. "When one knows the type of theatre Korea has been used to seeing, and the ultra-conservatism, particularly in regard to women, it is truly amazing that the cast could interest audiences in *Streetcar* so well . . . this was the first time Korean audiences saw a kiss on stage."[10]

The following six representative national premieres of Williams's play illustrate the significance and diversity of *Streetcar*'s entrance into world theatre.

Mexico City, December 1948; May 1949

Un Tranvía Llamado Deseo was first performed nine times, from 4 December through 12 December 1948, at the Palacio de Bellas Artes in Mexico City by a semiprofessional, experimental company, the Teatro de la Reforma, under the direction of Japanese-born Seki Sano. Efrain Huerta pronounced their *Streetcar* "the most important theatrical play ever staged in Mexico."[11] It is one of the ironies of theatre history that a Japanese director premiered an American play and transformed Mexican theatre in doing so. Mounting *Streetcar*, Sano also helped to "introduce Stanislavski's and Meyerhold's tech-niques to Mexico" and to revolutionize the way actors rehearsed and delivered their lines on the Mexican stage.[12] A member of Stanislavski's staff in Moscow, Sano was honored as "the fourth direc-tor of theatre in the world" by Luis de Cervantes. Using Stanislavskian techniques to embed his actors intimately in their roles, Sano molded such students, or disciples, as Ricardo Montalbán, Miroslava, Lillian Oppenheim, Reynaldo Rivera, Wolf Ruvinskis, and María Douglas, the last four of whom starred in Sano's *Streetcar*. Sano won the Mexican Theatre Critics' Director of the Year Award and the high praise of one of Mexico's greatest cultural heroes, Diego Rivera, revered painter, stage designer, and also a patron of the Teatro de la Reforma.

Cross-cultural cooperation was responsible for the translation of Williams's play done by Lillian Oppenheim, who played Stella, Reynaldo Rivera, who was Mitch, and Sano. This first translation of a Williams play into (Mexican) Spanish met with contradictory assessments. Armando de María y Campos exulted: "The translation . . . is perfect, and ideal of what is contained in English – it employs slang from New Orleans usefully to give strength to the characteristic linguistic expressions of the environment it invokes" (11 December 1948) yet Luis Suárez del Solar protested that it all sounded "false in Spanish . . . Because some of the actors were foreigners, they were made to speak unnaturally slowly."

Sano's "apprentice actors," however, reached great heights thanks to *Streetcar*. Six months after the short-lived premiere, the Teatro de la Reforma staged a second run of the play for 100 performances – from 4 May 1949 until 1 August 1949 – moving to the larger Teatro Esperanza Iris. The fledgling company even read the play on Mexican radio "in the apartment of novelist Julia Guzmán" (Huerta). This second *Streetcar* production was possible in large measure because of Sano's talents, as acknowledged in a letter from Audrey Wood, dated 10 January 1949, which he included in the playbill:

> Norman Rothschild came to see me bringing all the photographs from your production . . . His enthusiasm was so great that . . . it seemed that your production was even better than the original. Personally, I am disposed to allow the repetition of staging this play in Mexico, provided that the cast continues to be as good as it was at the premiere, and that you continue to be the director.[13]

Wood no doubt knew of Williams's sentiments quoted in the Mexican press: "My play was represented better in Mexico than here in New York" (Luis de Cervantes).

Reviewers enthusiastically compared Williams to Eugene O'Neill. Contrasting *Streetcar* with *The Glass Menagerie*, Armando de María y Campos found "*Streetcar* has achieved a dramatic intensity and psychological depth . . . it is one of the most beautiful achievements of North American theatre since O'Neill" (4 December 1948). Mexican critics also lauded *Streetcar* as highly realistic theatre. The anonymous reviewer in *Ultimas Noticias* extolled Williams's "super-realism which gave the impression of being more real than reality itself." María y Campos also respected Williams's "brutal tenderness and poetic realism" (16 December 1949). Some reviewers, however, branded Williams's realism "rude" and "brutal." Manuel Altolaguirre, for example, objected to Williams's "offensive realism," and he did not want to see the "brutal gestures of a man hitting his wife after a game of poker, filthy with rum and obscene phrases on his lips." Articles in *Hoy* for 14 May and 4 June 1949 playfully reported on the scandal associated with Stanley Kowalski wearing boxer shorts and Blanche and Stella parading on stage in intimate apparel. Years later, Dolores Carbonell and Luis Mier Vega charted the effect of the play on Mexican theatre and culture: "Some who were watching in the 1940s were scandalized. Topics such as alcoholism, drug addiction, homosexuality, sexual frenzy, and madness, which the North American author of *Streetcar* opened so plainly in his drama, shocked the theatrical community . . ."[14]

Sano chose María Douglas, his protégée at the beginning of her career, to play Blanche. Douglas was exactly right for her role with her blonde hair and "a well-cut figure, a voice with a graceful tone, a pure dramatic temperament, and with ample experience in the theatre of realism" (Esquivel). Arturo Mori proclaimed her as "an exceptional dramatic actress" and chastised those who wrongly searched outside their country "for what they already have at home in María Douglas and have not yet been able to discover." Twenty years after Sano's premiere, Beatriz Sheridan, "considered one of Mexico's finest actresses,"[15] and the second Mexican Blanche DuBois, was asked, "What were you most afraid of when they offered you the role?" She replied: "I was afraid of the fans that María Douglas had."[16] Ironically, Douglas received no award for her Blanche in 1948–49, but did star in four more *Streetcar*s directed by Sano, the next being in April 1953.

The spine of the role for Sano was to present Blanche as an arrogant and flirtatious woman who because of her vulnerable obsessions becomes a victim. Under Sano's direction, Douglas confidently entered the play with pride and snobbery. As Rafael Estrada noted, "Proud Blanche DuBois tries to create 'an immediate proximity to God,' invoking the principles of the spirit and the intelligence . . . but is driven into the madness of her own negation." For María y Campos, Douglas's Blanche was "wounded fatally in puberty and attached herself to on old decaying order. She is destroyed in her dreams and illusions" (7 December 1948). Antonio Magaña Esquivel traced Blanche's problems to being "an alien in a New Orleans inhabited by primitives. With her dreams on her back, Blanche throws this world into imbalance, yet she does not achieve her goal but becomes her own victim," thus foreshadowing a Foucaultian reading that censures Blanche as the poisoned disrupter.[17]

Perhaps Sano's most innovative interpretation of Blanche came in her exit to the madhouse. Since there was no essentially physical barrier separating actors from audience at either the Bellas Artes or the Esperanza Iris, Douglas's Blanche was able to walk right through the audience, as Ceferino R. Avecilla claimed:

> The moment in which Sano reaches his greatest success is in the final scene where the martyred protagonist crosses between the spectators and follows, across the hall, the same road that they will take moments later, when the curtain falls, guillotined by time. In that final moment, what might appear to be dramatic excess turns out to be not only justified but poignant . . . Having the audience at her mercy, Douglas makes them tremble with emotion to see her pass so close to them . . .

3. María Douglas (Blanche) and Wolf Ruvinskis (Stanley) in the Mexico City premiere of *Streetcar* (1948)

Because of such staging (and Douglas's powerful performance) Sano retheatricalized Blanche's tragic experience, implicating the audience as both onstage witnesses to and participants in her tragedy.

If Douglas was the soul of Sano's *Streetcar*, then Wolf Ruvinskis (age twenty-six) as Stanley Kowalski was its brawn. Another Sano student, Ruvinskis debuted in *Streetcar*, and went on to appear in more than 150 films and numerous plays in Mexico, Argentina, and Spain. He appeared as Stanley Kowalski again in Sano's 1953 revival as well as in the Spanish premiere in 1961.[18] Boxer turned actor, Ruvinskis had numerous professional fights in Mexico, California, and Oregon in the late 1940s. Using his Stanislavski-based methods, Sano tapped into Ruvinskis's fiery temper to elicit the aggressiveness the role demanded. In Ruvinskis, Sano saw the raw realism he prized in Stanley and in the play in general – violence, brutality, explosiveness. Ruvinskis played Kowalski with Hispanic passion – hitting Stella, exploding into rage with his friends, and brimming full of oaths. Appropriately for a Mexican Stanley, Ruvinskis drank rum, not Southern Comfort or Jax beer. Ruvinskis also captured a lecherous Stanley who took delight in sexual power, as can be seen in Figure 3. But his Kowalski was also unrelentingly brutal in mocking Blanche and in enjoying torturing her as his victim. In Scene 2, for example, Ruvinskis outdid Brando in taunting his sister-in-law by wearing Blanche's tiara himself as he balanced her pearl ropes in one hand and an open jewelry box in the other. Several critics still found the actor too much the blunt pugilist. Francisco Monteverde, for example, protested that Wolf Ruvinskis sometimes stressed in Stanley "the traits of a villain in melodrama or in movies through his character governed by instincts." But by *Streetcar*'s second run, Ruvinskis's problems as an actor were under greater control. And Sano had made theatre history.

Rome, January 1949

The Italian debut of *Streetcar* (*Un tram che si chiama desiderio*) was performed by the Rina Morelli-Stoppa Company at Rome's Eliseo Theatre on 21 January 1949, "the most sensational society event in Rome's theatre life this season" (*Il Paese*).[19] The production, which stretched four hours, or until 1:00 a.m., succeeded because of the creative energies of some of Italy's (and later America's) most notable figures in the world of cinema. Director Count Luchino Visconti, whose films *Ossessione* (1942) and *The Leopard* (1963) won him international fame, did such an extraordinary job directing the Italian premiere of *The Glass Menagerie* two years earlier that Williams himself gave the Italian rights to *Streetcar* to him.[20] According to Williams, Visconti's *Streetcar* was "the best European version of his play."[21] Franco Zeffirelli, one of Visconti's protégés, made his debut as scenographer. Two other future Hollywood celebrities played the lead male roles in *Streetcar* – Vittorio Gassman as Stanley and Marcello Mastroianni as Mitch. Anna Magnani, one of Williams's favorites, whom he christened the "Tigress of the Tiber,"[22] was scheduled to play Blanche, but did not either because of a personality clash with Visconti or because of her other commitments.[23] Although never becoming a film star of the magnitude of Gassman, Mastroianni, or Magnani, Rina Morelli, a long-time Visconti associate, created a Blanche who was memorable though far different from the one American audiences saw. The Italian premiere lasted a little over a month, with Williams attending the opening night. Visconti offered a second Italian *Streetcar* in Milan in 1951 with Morelli again playing Blanche but with Mastroianni replacing Gassman as Stanley.

Visconti's *Streetcar* aroused immense and long-lasting interest. Several Italian reviewers seized the opportunity to criticize *Streetcar* in particular and American drama in general. As Monica Sterling points out,

> Italians found Tennessee Williams . . . one of the most exciting of the new generation of American writers whose work was beginning to reach Europe. But as the horrors of war were forgotten, particularly by those who had not experienced them, a spurious sense of propriety returned. So *A Streetcar Named Desire* not only excited, but also shocked, causing . . . tongues to wag.[24]

The two chief complaints about Williams's play heard in Italy, previously voiced in America, too, were that its language was vulgar and that its plot was "shapeless," "episodic." Carlo Trabucco, who found *Streetcar*'s language "coarse, uncouth, and unnecessary," hoped that

"Tommaseo's dictionary of synonyms would offer the translator Gerardo Guerrieri some other words to substitute for the coarse ones." "M.C." also faulted the dialogue: "The little episodes that follow one another without any psychological connection . . . are at the level of the cinematic; *Streetcar* offers only a series of notes, random aspects of an environment colored too often by banal dialogue and by useless vulgar language." Although Giovanni Calendoli conceded that "the episodes are drawn with sharp psychological insight," he protested that *Streetcar* "lacked any poetic strength," which may be attributed to a flawed translation. Harsh opinions about the *Streetcar* plot were counter-balanced by other critics who, like A. Fratelli and Rosso di San Secundo, respected Williams's script for its "spontaneity . . . [for being] a real document of life on stage." Vito Pandolfi celebrated "the unity that lies in the magic of the play."

Visconti left his mark everywhere on the production. Though "some critics accused him of imitating Kazan's realism,"[25] Visconti assiduously distanced his *Streetcar* from the Broadway production as much as possible according to Zeffirelli.[26] Judging by the reactions of the Italian press, Visconti created a masterpiece. "Three-quarters of the success of the production should go to Visconti and only one-quarter to the playwright," claimed M.C. Elio Talarico also lavishly praised Visconti, who "gave a nearly perfect interpretation of *Streetcar*" by introducing a new type of drama to the Italian stage with Williams's plastic theatre. Visconti's realism was right for the times.

But Visconti heavily politicized Williams's script and, purportedly, with the playwright's approval. Rejecting a psychological interpretation such as Kazan's emphasized, Visconti instead was guided "by a pervasive desire to present burning social issues and existential content where political meaning was expressed through exaggerated realism."[27] The critics repeatedly foregrounded "the burning social issues" of Visconti's *Streetcar*, particularly those on class struggle and the disparities between a fading elite European and a primitive American culture. M.C. found Visconti's views compatible with Williams's. "In *Streetcar* Williams wanted to portray that humiliated category of people standing between the middle class and working class, aiming for psychological escape yet condemned to a pitiful contemplation of the failure of their existence." Visconti, for example, embroiled Stanley in the maelstrom of class warfare as a symbol of the working class. As M.C. noted, Stanley "displayed the fierceness of instinct, the almost beastly primordiality of a worker so overwhelmed by misery and work, sunk in an atmosphere full of vapors and tormenting mortifications." Achille Fiocco, however, argued that such dramatic realism was actually compromised by Williams's and Visconti's political agendas:

> Williams could not stop stressing the contrast of classes, aristocracy and plebs, and by catching a Strindbergian echo, he made them [the contrasts] more complicated, giving the male an inferiority complex in which he is blindly determined, forgetful of any idea of humanity. He is forced to destroy the hated yet desired simulacrum of diversity, and after crushing it, to possess it.

Like other critics, Fiocco found Visconti valorizing Blanche but devaluing Stanley's sexual *élan vital*. Expressing the most Eurocentric view of Visconti's realism of all the Italian critics, Raul Radice minimized the innocence or realistic allure of American culture: "Williams wants to present a country made up of the dregs of European society." Visconti's view of America inscribed in *Streetcar* was anything but an Edenic melting pot.

Inseparable from the "burning social issues" in Visconti's *Streetcar* was his obsessive reproduction of reality, his hallmark. As Fratelli and di San Secundo remarked, Visconti "uses rare strength, uses everyday language to express joy and sorrow, vulgarity and poetry, where reality is reality yet not realism." Nowhere was Visconti's verisimilitude more powerful than in his representation of New Orleans. "Luchino spoke of the city as if he came from there," exclaimed Radice. New Orleans was the centerpiece of his *Streetcar*, the focal point of Visconti's interpretation of America. Scouring several markets to find New Orleans-like furniture, draperies, and costumes, Visconti, according to Gian Domenico Giagni, went to the Campo de' Fiori . . . and searched among hundreds of beds, tools, furniture, glass, overalls, rags, candles, looking for New Orleans, the southern city in the USA. It was South like Marseille and dirty, trafficking, a harbor city, and also shady like Marseille. He found the bed, the flowery dress and the straw hat for the black woman . . . the tiles, the tables, the wardrobe, the handbag for Rina Morelli, a check shirt, street lamps . . .

But Visconti's New Orleans projected little of the "lyricism" or "raffish charm" located in Williams's script. Instead, Visconti exacerbated the city's darker shadows, emphasizing New Orleans as the locus of moral decay. According to Talarico, Visconti's *Streetcar* "vibrates with allusions, suggestions of underground human contacts, almost to the point of surrealism and pathology." Vito Pandolfi masterfully explicated the sinister side of Visconti's New Orleans:

> The curtain opens up on New Orleans. Do you know what New Orleans is? The South and the sea leading to decay, with a wave of sounds, the evil of freedom. European man landed there to destroy himself, drowning in alcohol and losing, step by step, any reason for life in the dirty beds of the mestizos' brothels. The legend of Jazz sang all this . . . The white man is at the limit of his civilization in those stormy skies. His instincts reach the end of the course, in violence and horror . . . So say the songs that Negroes collect in New Orleans . . . the white man goes adrift because only this is clear in his conscience: to be condemned to evil by evil. He would like to reach the bottom as far as the limit of any possibility, of instinct, of sex, possessing and destroying him.

Rather than celebrating the ethnographic vitality of New Orleans – "The easy mingling of the races in the old part of town" – Visconti represented the city as a place of temptation, an inferno for anyone succumbing to its Circean vices.

As in his films, Visconti read *Streetcar* through a dark, brutally realistic prism. Interpreting *Streetcar* far more pessimistically than Kazan did, Visconti concentrated on spiritual bankruptcy, and the disintegration of the home and family. Desire in Visconti's *Streetcar* was neither illusory escape nor romantic ideal; it was destructive appetite, "carnal slavery" according to Silvio D'Amico. To project such desire Visconti renegotiated one of the original props with even greater dramatic power. A signature symbol for the Kazan production was the Chinese lantern Blanche puts over the naked light bulb in Scene 3. In Visconti's *Streetcar*, however, the Kowalski bed became the dominant visual metaphor. As Radice reminded Italian audiences, the "history of Visconti's direction can probably be called the history of the beds," since these symbols appear prominently in his film and stage work. Reeking with the "smell of foul and dirty sheets" (Radice), the bed and sweaty bodies emblematized the carnal desire Visconti saw infusing the vulgarity, sex, and primitive instincts of the residents of the French Quarter, an American Marseille.

Historically, the Italian *Streetcar* may be remembered as much for the contributions of its designer, trained architect Franco Zeffirelli, as for its director. Influenced by American realism and European films (he spent his boyhood watching films in Florence movie houses), Zeffirelli created a far more realistic set than the illusory streetscape of Mielziner's scrims. As Zeffirelli explained in his *Autobiography*,

> Kazan's production had used scrims, painted gauzes to change the mood, while I used a building whose façade rose or fell as necessary, creating a once elegant, though now dilapidated, New Orleans street or the ramshackle interior of the house. I think this added a necessary realism to the play, and certainly Tennessee Williams, who came over for the opening, thought so.[28]

Zeffirelli's stage was dominated by a two-story house with typical New Orleans decorative iron railings and a winding side staircase. Removing the fourth wall – the façade – Zeffirelli showed the interior of the Kowalskis' shabby, two-room apartment – messy, drenched in filth, an appropriate *mise-en-scène* for the infamous, lustful bed dominating the production. He turned "Stanley's house into a main character, the environment existed for itself," according to Calendoli. Flanking the Kowalski house were two narrow side alleys leading to a maze of streets and cramped flats, symbolizing the claustrophobic, nightmarish atmosphere of Stanley's New Orleans. In Pandolfi's view,

"The effect of the walls of the house closing up and the side streets plunged in haze powerfully shows the dreariness of life." Ermanno Contini recalled that "the exterior effects of Zeffirelli's set depicted a photographic immediacy of crude facts." Yet, ironically enough, reviewers judged the set to be romantic and primitive at the same time, which may have been Zeffirelli's greatest challenge and accomplishment.

Zeffirelli captured the sights and sounds of New Orleans with the following apparatus, as described by Giagni:

> I was allowed to get a look behind the scenes, to see the backdrop for Kowalski's poor house. It was unbelievable: rickety stairs, ladders, a host of instruments, an oxygen cylinder (for the whistle of the streetcar), as well as a record of a streetcar, a large piece of tin with scrap iron (shaken and dented to create the sound of ten lunatics) when the cylinder whistles.

Zeffirelli clearly associated the cries of the city – the nightmare world – with Blanche's madness. The streetcar in particular afforded him an evocative vehicle to signal her disintegration. Its rattle and clang realistically reminded the audiences of New Orleans as well as encroaching danger and the death of Blanche's desire.

Accompanying these frenetic sounds were musical strains provided by the Trovaioli Quartet and a Hammond organ which echoed the pulsating passions of the French Quarter. The Roman *Streetcar* projected "endless jazz variations and sharp and hoarse voices" and through these sights and sounds Zeffirelli and Visconti "wove a wide weft of starts and emotions ranging from coitus to craziness" for Pandolfi. Calendoli insightfully commented on the links between music and scenography:

> Blanche's madness was brought to completion in the long mimic intermezzos under clever direction while music and light invaded the stage like an excited and intense dialogue intelligible like speech . . . this stage consistently expressed Visconti's leading principle that effective theatre offers a synthesis of all the arts – music, choreography, pantomime, and dance.

Almost forty-five years after the Italian *Streetcar*, Zeffirelli recollected that "if there was one play that cried out to be made into an opera, it was *A Streetcar Named Desire*. One marvelous mad scene from beginning to end – a perfect vehicle for a lady. *Butterfly* is nothing compared to it."[29]

According to the Italian critics, Rina Morelli was the perfect Blanche. When she starred as Blanche, Morelli was forty-two, older than any of the American actors who played the part up to that time. Morelli's reputation was justly based upon "intensity and imagination, truth and lyricism" (A. Possenti). Pandolfi extolled her performance claiming that "she puts her own person as a symbol into the play." Her size distinguished her from previous Blanches and from almost all future ones – she was only five feet tall. Many Italian reviewers commented on her size – e.g., "she is tiny and even lost five kilos during Visconti's grueling rehearsals" (Radice) – especially as it affected her and their interpretation of Blanche. Unquestionably, her size recruited sympathy for Blanche and became a reflection of Blanche's tragedy. As D'Amico spelled out, her "heroic little body broken by a tragic blow bore a superhuman fatigue." Next to Gassman's towering and muscular Stanley, Morelli's Blanche was perceived as more sinned against than sinning. Her Blanche became the tragic victim, not the seductress. Contini observed that Morelli "shows all of her exceptional resources – suffering, anxiety, anguish, dreary despair – that move her character, making her struggle like a wounded beast. All these emotions are found in this very sensitive actress's fragile strength." The diminutive Morelli successfully scaled Blanche's tragic heights.

But Morelli's performance was one-dimensional. She did not bring out Blanche's sexual promiscuity or the humor that would dominate later productions of the play – e.g., with Tallulah Bankhead, Ann-Margret, Blythe Danner – but focused instead on Blanche's tragic plight in Stanley's world of sexual fury. Unlike American or British Blanches (Jessica Tandy, Uta Hagen, Vivien Leigh), though, Morelli's Blanche escaped critical censure for lustful behavior or selfish intrusions. The Italian critics did not publicize Blanche's sexual sins, as their American and British counterparts did, nor did they express sympathy for Stanley's plight. With her "flashes of inspiration," Morelli "discovered in Blanche . . . the universe of human conscience subjected to endless intrusions of what is external, a force which invaded her and consumed her with desire . . . Her tragedy is that of the world surrounding her," claimed Pandolfi. Morelli perfectly embodied "the death of illusion" for Calendoli.

Vittorio Gassman's Stanley was electrifying. His "athletic figure, perfectly modulated voice . . . romantic flair, and enormous talent" served him well as a violent and sensual Stanley.[30] Fratelli and di San Secundo emphasized Gassman's "frenetic impetuosity in the role," and Talarico likewise stressed that he was "impetuous, harsh, spontaneous-acting, always moving around, always keeping on the go." At one point, Gassman became so agitated it "looked like he was having an epileptic fit"(Radice). Ironically, Gassman's Stanley may have been more dangerously aggressive than Brando's, intensifying the violence of the Broadway premiere, breaking an average of five bottles a night on stage, and angrily fuming with his friends, who, collectively, smoked about 120 cigarettes each performance (Giagni). But there was little cunning in Gassman's Stanley, indicating perhaps that the actor's subtext, as articulated by Visconti, was primal, sexual energy. Apparently, Gassman went for the jugular rather than the clever. If Gassman lacked Brando's slyness, he nonetheless convinced the Italian critics of Stanley's remarkable tenderness. Fratelli and di San Secundo identified the spine of Stanley's complex character as "hard, violent, and yet as tender and realistic." Perhaps the most eloquent appreciation of Gassman's Stanley came from Pandolfi: "He shows an aggressiveness and a bursting virility that shakes Blanche's sister's [Vivi Gioi] life; she is immersed in his power, subdued, hanging from his arms trying to draw life from him and to feel submerged in his sphere, which contains her all."

Blanche's suitor Mitch was played by the inexperienced, young (23-year-old) Marcello Mastroianni, who later achieved international stardom in Frederico Fellini's *La Dolce Vita.* His Mitch was highly respected by Italian critics and audiences alike. Calendoli celebrated Mastroianni, "whose interpretation of Mitch was cautious and convincing"; Fratelli and di San Secundo characterized Mastroianni as a "dear tender boy as Mitch," adding that "Mitch is both primitive and sincere, and is played with beautiful spontaneity by Marcello Mastroianni." Years later, Mastroianni recalled that the part of Mitch "fit me like a glove, since I came from that kind of milieu: my father had been a carpenter, and I had no real schooling as an actor. I was just being myself in that part, the nice boy from a workingman's background."[31]

However realistic Mastroianni's Mitch appeared to the Italian reviewers, it clearly was not the Mitch that American audiences saw in Karl Malden. The sexual and political dynamics in Mastroianni's Mitch were different. According to Malden's interpretation, Mitch was an older, lumbering and ungraceful bear of a man whose uncertain sexuality was the source of frequent jibes from his friends. Mastroianni's Mitch was younger, much better looking, and a more sexually desirable, potential mate for Blanche. A handsome Mitch made Blanche's tragedy seem even more desperate. Moreover, Mastroianni was a less culpable accomplice in Blanche's undoing. His Mitch was less dangerous, less tainted, the subtext for his character being the proletariat youth on the threshold of discovery and experience, reinforcing again the social context in which Visconti read *Streetcar.*

Ultimately, the Italian reviewers were more impressed with Visconti's "big show" than with Williams's script. As Carlo Trabucco boasted, "The little merit of this play is due to Luchino Visconti." But Visconti's success would have been impossible without Williams's *Streetcar,* the interplay between them verifying the cultural reciprocity of script and performance. Appropriately enough, Mastroianni observed in an interview a year before his death: "New York is a piece of Europe in America."[32] The Italian premiere of *A Streetcar Named Desire* also transported "a piece of America, suitably altered, to Rome."[33]

Sweden, March 1949

Perhaps no country in Europe was more enthusiastic about doing *Streetcar* than was Sweden. Responding to the call of Williams's Swedish publisher Bonnier to perform the play, no fewer than five Swedish stages competed in offering the first performance – Gothenburg City Theatre; Malmö's Intimate Theatre; Stockholm's Royal Dramatic Theatre; Hälsingborg's City Theatre; and Norrköping's City Theatre. However, only Gothenburg and Malmö were ready by the target date of Tuesday, 1 March 1949. Raising the curtain at 7:30 p.m., Gothenburg beat Malmö for the honor. At Gothenburg, *Streetcar* was known as *Spårvagn till Lustgården (Streetcar to Paradise)*, which ironically includes the Swedish term for Eden, while at Malmö (and Norrköping) it was *Linje Lusta*, which translates into *Train Route of Lust* (with both sexual and non-sexual meanings, as in the English word *desire*).

Swedish audiences in 1948–49 were familiar with *The Glass Menagerie*, which had been widely performed throughout 1946. Thanks to *The Glass Menagerie* and now *Streetcar* Williams was riding the crest of Swedish success and was favorably compared with Scandinavian playwrights Ibsen and Strindberg. Henrik Sjögren discerned that Williams's immense popularity in the late 1940s and early 1950s was a result not of the "fragility of illusions" in *The Glass Menagerie* but "his spicier life-like dramas, constructed in the best Ibsen tradition and in which personal conflicts arise out of a more or less sexually perverse environment."[34] For Kjell Hjern, Williams, like Ibsen, explored with grim determination the "life lie,"[35] and according to Herbert Grevenius, Blanche DuBois was a Miss Julie pulled out of her environment.

The star attraction of the Swedish *Streetcar* was Ingmar Bergman, resident director in 1948–49 at the Gothenburg City Theatre, Sweden's most technologically sophisticated playhouse. Bergman's *Streetcar* was his farewell to the city and one of his best productions. Bergman himself spoke of his mounting of *Streetcar* in superlatives: "This is the best play I have ever directed" (quoted by Erwin Leiser).

He felt a powerful attraction to the play because of an artistic kinship with the playwright. With its psychological themes, its experimental staging, and its heroine artist-victim, *Streetcar* had a haunting effect on him. What Birgitta Steene has said of Bergman's own artistic vision could be applied to the young Williams: "In Bergman's view of life, people are always seeking dominance over others and society is depicted as an authoritarian bureaucracy. In his early work, young people are often victimized; in his later work, artists and performers are usually the maligned and the prosecuted."[36] As in Visconti's *Streetcar*, the pulsating forces of dark desire in New Orleans colored Bergman's production. Stanley's threatening dominance over Blanche, the victim and artist, seized Bergman's imagination as powerfully as it had Williams's.

Bergman, however, transformed the idea behind the original American set for *Streetcar* into something more concrete yet more consistent with his representation of desire in Williams's play. Working with set designer Carl Johan Ström, Bergman uniquely adapted Williams's symbolic landscape for his Gothenburg audience by boldly rejecting the gossamer scrim and substituting his own idea of place, which while different from Mielziner's and Williams's interestingly enough complemented theirs. Bergman made symbolic and practical use of the "free, fluid . . . stage space at Gothenburg" where there was a large revolving stage with an inside and an outside stage, creating the three-dimensional stage structures, or houses.[37] The set for the opening scene of *Streetcar* showed on the left hand of the outside stage a "boarding house"; the two-story building next to it was the "drug store," and next to that structure was a "non-stop movie theater" called Desire, or the Pleasure Garden. The second story façade of the movie house was draped with a large poster that read "Night in Paradise." On the stage in front of the drug store and near the movie theatre was an apple tree that lost more and more of its leaves the closer Blanche moved toward her tragic end.

The set vividly projected Bergman's conception of New Orleans. The two-storey houses with their open porches and intricate lattice work were clearly reminiscent of New Orleans architecture. A Blanche in stockings and garter-belt stood in front of a dingy kitchen sink behind the icons of American life for Bergman – Kellogg's corn flakes, Hershey's chocolates, a fusebox, and a crank phone. The crowded street in front of the "boarding house" and cinema suggested the frenetic activity in the French Quarter. The people who flooded Bergman's stage also reflected a New Orleans ambience. Black-faced Swedes congregated outside the cinema embodying the "easy mingling of the races." Grevenius reported: "You are in the South, New Orleans, where people of color dress in all colors, in a suburban neighborhood called Elysian Fields . . . There is a flow of bright-colored people – black, white, yellow, and mixed." The character types Bergman chose to represent New Orleans also reinforced the powerful hold desire – or lust – had over the residents. A prostitute kissed a man downstage while meandering drunken sailors further symbolized unbridled passion as well as travel, two characteristics of Blanche's plight. Suspended above all this sexual energy was the cinema marquee with the word "Desire," emphasizing for Bergman the emblem of New Orleans, a desire that was feverishly non-stop yet also incessantly illusory.

In interpreting *Streetcar*, Bergman metaphorically and literally exchanged a streetcar for a movie theatre. In doing so, however, he did not try to distort or alter Williams's work. As Bergman confessed, "I cannot and will not direct a play contrary to an author's intentions. And I have never done so. Consciously I have always considered myself as an interpreter, a re-creator."[38] Yet, this change fixed Bergman's stamp on the play. Symbolic place was central to all of his work, and for his *Streetcar* he drew upon his skill as a film director to intercut from another Williams play the exact symbol of the *Streetcar* experience for his audience. For Bergman, desire – as illusion, escape, entrapment – was the key to Blanche's tragedy, unlike Visconti's depiction of desire as carnal slavery. To represent this desire Bergman read *Streetcar* through *The Glass Menagerie*. The non-stop Desire Theatre in *Streetcar* shows "Night in Paradise," which symbolically and structurally echoes the Paradise Dance Hall in *The Glass Menagerie*. Just as the dance hall in *Menagerie* was across the street from the Wingfield apartment, the non-stop theatre in Bergman's *Streetcar* was only a few doors away from the Kowalski apartment. The cinema – the movie theatre – offered both an escape into illusion and a source of danger in *The Glass Menagerie*. In Bergman's *Menagerie*-colored *Streetcar*, then, the movie being shown at the theatre – "Night in Paradise" –projected Stanley's saturnalian quest for happiness with Stella as it ironically mocked the fateful night he spends with Blanche when Stella is in hospital. It also suggested that Swedish Blanches no less than American ones desperately sought the fulfillment promised in "A Night in Paradise," but the price of admission was madness.

Further, Bergman symbolically employed the inside stage when the location shifted to Stanley's two-room flat. However, he did not completely separate the outside from the inside stage. "When the inside stage is downstage, the movie theatre is located behind it and throws out – at appropriate times – swirls of hypnotizing sounds and gurgling dark laughter" (Grevenius). Though he used different means, Bergman nonetheless accomplished a dramatic end similar to Mielziner's stage poetics. Where Mielziner used scrims coordinated with musical rhapsodies from the Four Deuces down the street from the Kowalskis' apartment, Bergman constructed buildings that filtered mood and music through their walls.

Karin Kavli played an incomparable Blanche for Swedish critics and audiences, "completely merging with the part" for J. Thin. Leiser proclaimed: "If there is anybody who perhaps doubts that Karin Kavli belongs to the truly great ones in the theatre, he will now be of another opinion." Kavli reflected Jessica Tandy's fragility while at the same time incorporating Uta Hagen's forcefulness. Her stunning performance, with its blend of moods and styles, anticipated the Blanches of Claire Bloom, Ann-Margret, and Blythe Danner. The secret of Kavli's unique yet diverse strengths for Thin was that "She expressed Blanche's hysteria and fright with shuddering reality . . . she is both macabre and touching in her coquetry." For Grevenius, too, Kavli had "managed to represent so many reflections of Blanche's loneliness, confusion, fear and sexual hunger."

While Kavli's performance may have dominated the production, Blanche's sins did not escape the critics' censure, though her misdeeds were mitigated by her tragic stature. Elis Andersson noted that "Kavli's Blanche reveals little by little how hunted she is. She lies and becomes full of false pride and torn feeling." Yet in spite of Blanche's highly calculated hunt for happiness and her lapses from truthfulness, she "catches the sympathy of the audience" (Andersson). No Swedish critic acrimoniously attacked Blanche for being a common "trollop" or characterized her life as "a squalid anecdote of a nymphomaniac's decay in a New Orleans slum," as American or British critics would.

Anders Ek, a seasoned veteran of the Gothenburg company, played Stanley but was no Brando-copy. For many critics, Ek's Stanley was the innocent primitive – conveying the image of a powerful, uncomplicated young workman. Stanley is a "handsome and outgoing male with tremendous swings between happiness and resignation, between friendliness and boorishness – a thoroughly physical man. He is played with a beaming vitality and with a great sense of humor by Anders Ek" (Grevenius). According to Hjern, "Ek's Polish-American he-man was built up with many fine and inventive traits. It was a living person, no monster that the actor interpreted." J Thin even forgave Stanley for being Stanley: "Ek as Stanley has also shown that there is more to the man – his love for truth, his openness, his virility, his devotion to his wife. For all his rough ways, he is a good pal . . ." In many respects, Ek's portrait of Stanley came close to Williams's initial intention that there be no "good" or "bad" people in *Streetcar*, just those who suffered because of "misunderstanding." But Ek did not eschew Stanley's neanderthal qualities. According to Gunn Bergman, "Anders Ek catches his wife with pure animal power . . . he is brutal . . . he was like a gorilla, looking like a highly potent male who stank of sex and was slow in speech and thought, but fast like a weasel when his rutting time comes upon him." Giving Ek his due, he doubtless was able to inject both bonhomie in the role for Thin and animal magnetism and brutality for Gunn Bergman.

Beyond doubts, Bergman read his own cultural expectations and anxieties into Williams's script. The fact that a number of critics compared Williams's *Streetcar* to Strindberg's *Miss Julie* reflected Bergman's national heritage encoded through his idea of character imparted to Karin Kavli and Anders Ek. Curiously, only a few reviewers cited the similarity between Blanche and Miss Julie. Over the years, though, Bergman was to direct several important productions of Strindberg's play and even wrote an adaptation of *Miss Julie*. *Streetcar* might plausibly be seen, then, as the American counterpart to Strindberg's play.

London, October 1949

A Streetcar Named Desire made its British debut in one of the most celebrated yet controversial productions of the post-war theatre. After tryouts at the Manchester Opera House from 27 September until 7 October 1949, *Streetcar* opened in London on 12 October at the Aldwych Theatre playing to large and appreciative audiences until 19 August 1950, for 326 performances. Opening night audiences queued for twenty-four hours and rioted when they could not all get into the Aldwych. The play was booked solid for nine months.

Despite such popularity, *Streetcar* faced fierce moral opposition. An advance notice of *Streetcar* in London's *Sunday Pictorial* for 2 October 1949 (with a circulation of over five million) fueled controversy by labeling the play "salacious and degrading." Clergy like the Revd. Colin Cattell, a vicar at Southwark Cathedral, attacked *Streetcar* from the pulpit. The Public Morality Council condemned *Streetcar* for its "abominable" content; and many in the House of Commons had enquired why, under the sponsorship of the British Arts Council, *Streetcar* was exempt from paying entertainment tax as a "non-profit, partly educational work." The Tory MP for Brighton,

Mr. A. Marlowe, quipped: "The play is only educational for those who are ignorant of the facts of life."[39] Princess Alice of Athlone, King George's cousin, with her husband, the Earl of Athlone, "refused to attend a charity performance . . . because she disapproved of the subject matter."[40] Speaking for those who found *Streetcar* objectionable, J. C. Trewin complained, "All we saw, as the night wore on, was a squalid anecdote of a nymphomaniac's decay in a New Orleans slum."[41] Of course, there were supportive voices among the British press, most notably Harold Hobson, who insisted that *Streetcar* was "strictly and even puritanically" a valuable play; ". . . far from being daring, [it] is rigidly even timidly conventional. It never departs by a hair's breadth from its text, which is that the consequence of such a life is spiritual death."

Two of England's greatest stars contributed to *Streetcar*'s success. Vivien Leigh, thirty-five at the time, played Blanche, a decade after her fame as Scarlett O'Hara in *Gone with the Wind* and two years before making the Warner Brothers film of *Streetcar*. When producer Hugh "Binkie" Beaumont asked Leigh early in 1949 to play Blanche for London audiences, her only condition was that her husband, the recently knighted Sir Laurence Olivier, direct her. Olivier also became co-producer of the first British *Streetcar*. Joining the Oliviers were Bonar Colleano as Stanley, Renee Asherson as Stella, Bernard Braden as a thin, angular Mitch, and a saturnine-looking Theodore Bikel as Pablo. Though Olivier and cast did not see the Broadway *Streetcar* with Brando and Tandy, they did have the benefit of Mielziner's sets for their production and Alex North's musical score. Lionel Collier, however, faulted Olivier for following the Broadway premiere too closely:

> Olivier's painstaking copy of the New York production, by that tormented genius Elia Kazan, is perhaps not the kindest sort. It gets in the way of our seeing the play in our own light, even seems painfully *voulu*. I am not suggesting that this is great tragedy or a pretty evening, but I wish England had anyone writing with so true a sense of theatre as Tennessee Williams.

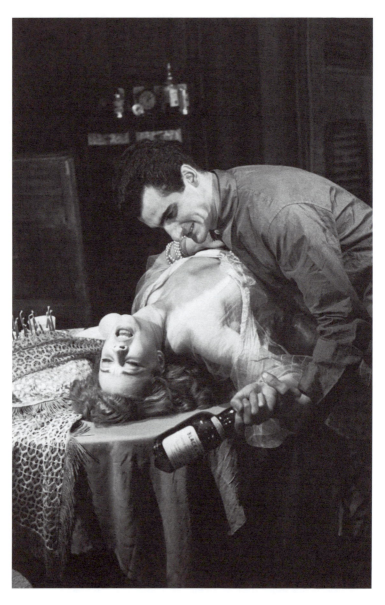

4. Vivien Leigh (Blanche) and Bonar Colleano (Stanley) in the London premiere of *Streetcar* (1949

Though Walter Hayes thought the play "offered a grim vicious American tragedy, shot through with sentiment, American style," he credited Olivier with saving the day for Williams: "Olivier's magnificent production lifts it [*Streetcar*] at times far above the intrinsic value of the playwriting." George W. Bishop offered an even more glowing endorsement: "I had the advantage . . . of having seen the play in New York. The setting is much the same, but Laurence Olivier, while he has toned down slightly one terrible scene, has added something of his own genius as a producer. I found the play even more moving at the Aldwych."

Olivier confessed that directing *Streetcar* was not all "beer and skit-tles." As Felix Barker pointed out, *Streetcar* was "the most painful undertaking" of Olivier's career. Even though Olivier determined not to duplicate Kazan's production, he realized that it "was impossible to avoid adopting a great deal of what Kazan had in mind."[42] He pored over Kazan's annotated promptbooks in an attempt to be true to Williams's meaning and concluded that Kazan had done an enviable job. Fortuitously, Kazan was in England at the time preparing to direct *Death of a Salesman,* and Olivier, apologizing for taking so much from the Broadway production, was reassured by Kazan that his London *Streetcar* would be completely different. Olivier, however, scrupulously acknowledged his debt to Kazan by indicating in the program that his *Streetcar* was "Directed by Laurence Olivier from the New York production."

Another problem haunting Olivier was *Streetcar*'s subject matter, which posed serious difficulties for the more reserved theatregoers and critics of London's West End. The Lord Chamberlain insisted on a number of changes in the script, most importantly the exclusion of any references to "the four letter word" which deprived the DuBois sisters of their plantation and other sexual references (e.g., "ruttin," Stanley's "kidneys"). Moreover, the Lord Chamberlain stressed that "There must be no suggestive business accompanying any undress-ing." But perhaps the most drastic revision demanded was in Scene 6, the reference to Allen Grey's homosexuality: "The Lord Chamberlain is of the opinion that this passage should be altered, making the young husband found with a Negress, instead of just another man."[43] Incensed at this change, Selznick wired Hugh Beaumont on 21 July 1948: "I'm for skipping England forever if it means the Grey boy must be found with a Negress."[44] In London, the Grey boy died a weak instead of a "degenerate" soul.

Firing off a brisk, handwritten sixteen-page letter to Williams in September 1949 shortly before the London opening, Olivier urged the playwright to make cuts and consider alternative "readings."[45] Filled with exhortations and explanations, Olivier's letter even included reviews from the Manchester tryouts bemoaning the play's excessive length to convince Williams to shorten the play. One reviewer attested that *Streetcar* "is of the episodic school, cut into many short pieces – surely 12 (or was it 13?) scenes are more than are needed to tell so simple a story – and it makes many of its points more than once" ("Manchester Opera House"). Recollecting Olivier's changes and his letter about them at the 1974 London revival of *Streetcar*, Williams told Philip Oakes:

> There were extensive cuts – partly on the grounds of its length, partly because of the prudery of the time. I had an 18–page letter [sic] from Olivier explaining and justifying the cuts. I can't say that I liked it. But I thought if a man takes the trouble to write me an 18–page letter then I should go along with him.[46]

And so Olivier got his way. A short review in the *Daily Herald* (28 September 1949) of the Manchester tryouts, before the cuts were made, announced that *Streetcar* "lasts for three hours, with two short intervals." Reviews of the London production mentioned that the play lasted a little more than two hours, considerably shorter than its Broadway run, and that Olivier set the play moving faster than it did in New York. Olivier's cuts apparently had a lasting effect on British *Streetcars*. Tony Church, a member of the Royal Shakespeare Company, recalled that it was not until the early 1970s that Britain saw the whole play.[47]

Aside from his artistic reasons for making the cuts, Olivier had to consider Leigh's stamina to sustain such a demanding role and determined not to overtax her. Producer Saul Colin, talking about the events that led to the final collapse of the Olivier–Leigh marriage, reminisced: "Larry's first mistake was getting involved with *Streetcar Named Desire*. His second was letting Vivien get involved."[48] Generally regarded as the best performance of her career, Vivien Leigh's Blanche was also the most devastating. Onstage for most of the play, Leigh had to re-enact Blanche's harrowing, psychically draining journey into madness five evenings and two matinees each week. A reviewer for the *Daily Mail* ominously cautioned: "This play will run for so long as Vivien can stand on her feet" ("Streetcar"). Leigh played Blanche "in more ways than just as an actress. During rehearsals she had taken on many of Blanche's delusionary colorations as her own, and soon the distinction between the stage character and the real-life woman began to blur."[49] She even imitated Blanche's mannerisms, language, and nuances away from the Aldwych. As playwright Michael Smith observed, Vivien's "own forlorn story forever interpenetrates the character."[50] On playing Blanche, Leigh herself said: "It tipped me over into madness."[51] Leigh left *Streetcar* in June 1950, after nine months.

No doubt Leigh's intensity was elicited by Olivier's directing. Unlike Kazan, Olivier was no proponent of the Method Acting associated with the Group Theatre. But since British actors and actresses were unaccustomed to outbursts on stage, Olivier had to take a more animated approach with his cast, including inspiring Leigh to passionate heights. As David Lewin observed, "It is only Olivier, I should say, who can bring out the pathos in that hard lovely beauty of Vivien Leigh. For there is a coldness in her acting. Something remote. Tonight she has had to give a warmth of the heart as well." Leigh's Blanche mesmerized audiences. Noel Coward proclaimed her "magnificent."[52] Harold Hobson rejoiced: "The best thing I saw in America was Miss Uta Hagen's performance as Blanche: Miss Vivien Leigh's is finer." Though he had denigrated *Streetcar* ("Plays in

Performance"), J. C. Trewin nonetheless affirmed that "If the play lasts in London, its good angel will be Vivien Leigh. She has never developed more power and authority, and she controls the stage finely in those last 'strong' theatrics when Blanche, her mind shivered, is on the way to the asylum" (*Illustrated London News*). Acknowledging the power of Leigh's Blanche – "She is best when conveying the nerve-wracked tension" – F. S. in *Theatre World* found her

> least convincing in persuading us that her broken marriage to a homosexual and his suicide were the real causes of her fall from grace. Her great achievement in the play was that she moved us to pity and, in spite of knowing the inevitable end, to the desperate hope that she and Mitch might find their haven.

The key to the role for Leigh was Blanche's tragic plight and guilt. According to Leigh, "Blanche was a sensitive woman who had never recovered from her tragic early marriage to a homosexual and whose loneliness may have led her eventually to decadence."[53] But two things worked against Leigh's interpretation. Firstly, since the Lord Chamberlain forbade any mention of or reference to Allen Grey's homosexuality, her audiences were deprived of this crucial information. Secondly, many London critics wrongly branded Blanche a prostitute, which impeded Leigh's hope of portraying Blanche as an "unloved woman, aware that her beauty was fading, fighting for her last slender hope of respectability."[54]

Leigh's Blanche differed from Tandy or Hagen in voice, costume, and appearance. In rehearsals, Olivier heard that "Vivien's unexpected, much deeper, much rougher voice had impressed" the company, and thought this new voice would lend her greater credibility as an actress. Olivier reasoned, therefore, that by "changing one feature one can create a whole new face" and so a "strange new person" was born.[55] Unlike Tandy's more plaintive Blanche, Leigh's Blanche was hauntingly more assertive. In the New York production, Blanche was dressed in "mothy white and faded flowered organdies," but remaining truer to Williams's script, Olivier had Leigh, costumed by Beatrice Dawson, in "a worn out Mardi Gras outfit," "fake jewelry," and a "dark red satin kimono," all of which unfortunately emphasized Blanche's sexuality more than her gentility and thus enraged the London critics. Collier labeled her "a sort of Madame Bovary of the Southern states." Further suggesting a tawdry Blanche, Leigh dyed her hair blond (giving Olivier a lock of it on opening night), and wore heavy make-up that made her look old and haggard. Clearly, Olivier chose to portray Blanche more naturalistically than Kazan had, a distinction many European directors also made.

Similarly, Olivier's Stanley – Bonar Colleano – was unlike Brando. Colleano, though, was well suited for the "new reading" of the character that Olivier advocated in his letter to Williams:

> He is fine and will be finer – he is not the bruiser type. It is a "new reading" to coin a phrase . . . Unless new readings are in order a play is not going to live. This one of yours, like other masterpieces, will continue to live and be fortified by new readings . . . Not having seen Brando's interpretation, I almost prefer this as a slightly subtler approach, damn it's more or less the way I'd have to do it myself and I do hope you wouldn't turn me down for it on that account. The idea is very simply more a Jed Harris danger than a Jack Dempsey danger. Colleano is as apelike as *he* can be, certainly as I could be.[56]

Comparing Stanley to Jed Harris, Olivier straightaway disclosed his allegiance to Blanche over Stanley, for Olivier despised the Hollywood mogul whose mannerisms he aped in creating his Richard III. Olivier's prejudices notwithstanding, Colleano played a slyer, more subtle Stanley than New York audiences saw while still retaining Stanley's volume. Most London critics approved Colleano's performance. Hobson affirmed that Colleano's "Kowalski vibrates with energy; he is the world's raw nerve and screams at a touch." Peter Fleming praised Colleano for presenting one of those "over-simplified . . . supermen [that can] make such a strong appeal to the imagination of the American male." Though faulting Colleano's inability to "give variety to dialogue," R. D. Smith caught Olivier's interpretation precisely: "Bonar Colleano was a plausible choice for

Stanley . . . virile and charming: but he has an intelligence that cuts like a razor, and it is almost impossible to think of him as a brute." Yet several critics found this interpretation unacceptable, including Kenneth Tynan, who argued that Colleano was miscast:

> Stanley should be a large, impassive, unsubtle ox – a steamroller of sex. Colleano's temperament forces him to make Stanley a lean, zingy, gum-chewing GI stationed outside Warrington; the self-consciousness of his playing . . . destroyed entirely the dumb majesty of Tennessee Williams's creation. Colleano is all that Stanley must not be: cunning, guileful, and slick as a razor.

Guilty perhaps of adjusting (or accommodating) his interpretation of *Streetcar* to the personality of his leading male actor, Olivier nonetheless deserved high marks for a bold renegotiation of the script.

Defending *Streetcar* in light of the problems that Williams's play had among the British critics, Brooks Atkinson pointedly observed: "We see and hear things in 'Streetcar' and 'Death of a Salesman' that our opposite numbers do not hear or see in England, because we are part of a national environment out of which these dramas have come." To Olivier's credit, though, he expanded the theatrical environment in which *Streetcar* continually evolves.

Paris, October 1949

Un Tramway Nommé Désir premiered at the Théâtre Edouard VII in Paris on 19 October 1949 through an adaptation by Jean Cocteau, novelist, poet, and filmmaker whose reputation for poetic flair and visual imagery dominated the production. Cocteau, who announced "We've never made so much effort or spent so much money producing an American play in France before," asserted that *Streetcar* would be even "more moving to French audiences than it was to American."[57] His rather free French translation, done with the aid of Mme. Paule de Beaumont, who earlier that year had translated Eisenhower's *Memoirs*, was peppered with salty Parisian (not New

Orleanian) argot, including numerous references to *merde*. In his program note, Cocteau described the daunting task of translating *Streetcar*: "A literary work conveys its texture, and my fingers run through it like braille. I tried my best not to lose any of its profound and twisted poetry." Cocteau's *Streetcar* ran for 233 performances.[58]

As in other national premieres, the French critics singled out native talent for honor. G. Jolly exclaimed: "For the first time we have our most treasured poet, our most astonishing director [Raymond Rouleau], and our most celebrated stage designer [Lila de Nobili]."[59] French comedienne Arletty, in her first major leading stage role, played Blanche while Yves Vincent created a primitive, Latin-looking Stanley; Daniel Invernel was "a hunky, gullible bear" as Mitch, and Helena Bossis as Stella "dominated the entire cast," according to André Alter.

If the critics appreciated what was French in the production, they nonetheless vilified the play as an occasion for scandal. Jean Jacques Gautier exclaimed that *Streetcar* "was filled with undressing, morbid events, fights, card games, enough alcohol to drown in, obscenities, and murders . . ." *Theatre Arts* announced that *Streetcar* "was greeted by the most intense critical revulsion since the days when critics and playwrights dueled at dawn in the Bois de Boulogne."[60] Jean Grandrey-Réty bristled that *Streetcar* "was a . . . fantasy-seeking play that does not go above the waistline with huge naked monkeys, climbing down trees to dance under the neon signs of advertisements." While *Streetcar* was still running in Paris in December 1950, the French road company production, with highly respected Madeleine Roberson as Blanche, was banned by ecclesiastical authorities in Namur. Other reasons for the Gallic disdain of *Streetcar* included disliking Williams's cinematographic style; a misunderstanding of the "effects of [his] characters"; and tense and sensitive "Franco-American political and diplomatic relations." Basically, "the milieu of a Williams play [was] . . . viewed through a Parisian haze of social and political preconceptions, prejudices, or patterns already established by other American authors."[61]

As Visconti had done, too, Cocteau radicalized Williams's script. Though Kazan would have agreed with Cocteau that "the characters in *Streetcar* are inhabited by dreams" (André Ransan), their directorial emphases were substantially different. Cocteau observed: "The play was written with a marvelous role for a woman but Marlon Brando . . . was so good that he overshadowed her. But here the woman's role, Blanche, which will be played by Mme. Arletty, will be more important than in the United States."[62] Arletty's Blanche triumphed over Yves Vincent's Stanley. As André Singer pointed out, "Stanley, the brother-in-law, has a greater dimension, presence in the American version. But in Cocteau's *Streetcar*, he has to let go of some of his character – his overpowering stage presence." Cocteau's Blanche was also different from the New York or London productions. She was more mysterious, wearing a black blouse under her white dress, projecting an aura of *"désir noir"* (Jean Louiguy), yet she retained her noble stature in the midst of coquetries. Blanche was both "mythomaniac and nymphomaniac" (Claude Jamet).

The most controversial element of Cocteau's adaptation was its vibrant black presence. Black belly dancers, "well endowed Negresses," naked from the waist up, gyrated in the background as Stanley raped Blanche. "Cocteau's is a dark play – and made dark especially by black male and female extras whose appearance enhances the most dramatic moments and reminds us that the play takes place in New Orleans" (*Les Nouvelles*). Ransan complained, "we are served some kind of slice of life *à l'Americaine*, a cocktail spiced with black jazz." These sexualized emendations to the script underscored Cocteau's view of *Streetcar* as both brutal and poetic. Cocteau's production confirmed that *Streetcar* was "saturated with a black synesthesia."[63] Discussing sexual ravishment and ethnicity in the script, G. Jolly astutely remarked that "After all, racial fear of the Polack is nothing but a veiled fear of a white nigger." Associating Stanley with sexualized and marginalized blacks anticipated by almost fifty years a recent provocative theory that in racializing the *Streetcar* script Williams attached the sexual and physical characteristics of Blacks to Stanley Kowalski.[64]

Rouleau's direction and de Nobili's picturesque designs aptly embodied Cocteau's vision. Rouleau's *Streetcar* was regarded as the most successful *mise-en-scène* of his career; Jamet hailed him for his "stage acrobatics." Working with a much smaller stage at Théâtre Edouard VII than Kazan and Mielziner had at the Barrymore, Rouleau and de Nobili created a fluid, transparent effect, far less nostalgic and impressionistic than the set Broadway audiences saw. Rouleau divided the locations in the script "into a series of multiple spaces that intersected and superimposed themselves on each other" (Grandrey-Réty), where events took place simultaneously in and through the Kowalski apartment and beyond into the "bizarre" city of New Orleans (*Paris Match*). Although some critics found the stage too crowded and at odds with the erotic, poetic atmosphere of the city or contended that "New Orleans dust resists all attempts to be made lyrical" (Alter), many reviewers lauded the production for capturing the "tropical environment and the human shapes full of sensual anguish" ("M.A.").

Essential to creating such an environment were de Nobili's "diaphanous" backdrops made of "light gauzes, tulles, spiraling fabrics and glossy sheers to achieve transparency" (Singer). Max Favelelli observed that these "gauzed drapes" looked as if they were "meant to catch butterflies," alluding to Blanche's reference to "butterfly wings." Behind these transparencies were superimposed key symbolic images, e.g., a plantation suggesting Blanche's lamentable past to remind the audience hauntingly of the lost world from which she was forever banished. Other tableaux behind de Nobili's gauzes enacted the penalties of desire: "At critical points in the play . . . actors are almost blacked out while behind a gauze curtain at the back quick little pantomimes are acted out – a near-rape on the street, a sidewalk shooting . . ." ("Tale of Three Cities"). The pantomimed rape anticipated Stanley's rape of Blanche. While de Nobili's sets and scrims were "sleazy and lavish" at the same time (*Le Figaro*, 2 January 1957), her "decor" was the quintessential Gallic *trompe l'œil* – to "mime desire," as Singer eloquently put it. Yet, unfortunately, the critical consensus was, as Alter observed, that "all the scenery, the lights, the

5. Arletty (Blanche) and Yves Vincent (Stanley) in the French adaptation of *Streetcar* by Jean Cocteau, Paris (1949)

shimmers, the play of shadows in the decadent charm of Lila de Nobili's design still can't fill up the frightening emptiness, shallowness of the play itself."

Blanche was Arletty's "première rôle tragique." She had seen Vivien Leigh in the London premiere and was moved by her tragic grandeur.[65] Despite Arletty's reputation as a comedienne, she was no stranger to a script with strong poetic imagery; during the war she had appeared in the French film classic *Les Enfants du Paradis*, an icon of French acting. The critics' reviews of Arletty's Blanche were supportive. Forty at the time, Arletty attempted to look regal, sophisticated, almost ethereal. Louiguy aptly analogized her to Ariel as Yves Vincent was to Caliban. Arletty's dress, her gestures, her overall composure at once struck reviewers as the sensual aristocrat fallen upon hard times. Frank Dorsey observed: "Arletty's Blanche, necessarily, is any down-at-heel aristocrat decaying in poverty anywhere – in these times she could be Russian, Polish, even Chinese." Dorsey concluded that what "the role gain[ed] in universality it los[t] in deep Southern flavor," since Arletty and her audiences could not draw from their experiences to understand the plight of the Southern belle.

Streetcar did not overwhelm Arletty. More skeptical, though, Claude Jamet observed: "Arletty is still gorgeous. . . . with her stiff silhouette, her diction, her accent, all her art and her stage presence. She is extraordinary . . . she creates a sense of mystery, the unexpected, a suspense for a revelation. But it is not her fault that in fact the revelation never comes." Arletty's Blanche captured the hysteria in the role but lacked the lyrical or (amazingly!) the comic side of Blanche. She was too rigid, her laughter too strained. As Ransan discerned, "Arletty, who usually shows a sparkling imagination, seems so ill at ease and lugubrious in the role."

In his program note, Cocteau boasted that Yves Vincent "may be closer to the character of Stanley than the prestigious Brando was." Yet audiences had little doubt that, in Cocteau's interpretation, Blanche had dethroned Stanley as the center of the play. Vincent's Stanley was suitably ape-like, a glaring contrast to the sophisticated-looking Arletty. Jolly complained that Stanley was "crude, direct." In the words of Louiguy, he "plays the gorilla . . . he will make some of the young women in the audience sigh" and "Vincent even jumps over the table to rape Blanche." Well-built and handsome, Vincent for Max Favelelli "looked more Latin than Polish." To his credit Vincent attempted to bring out Stanley's sense of humor as well.

Bossis played Stella as "seductive and sensual" for Jolly, who maintained she was "the future mother in love." According to Ransan, she was "the only natural, moving actress on stage," except, we might add, the sinuous black dancers.

Tokyo, 1953

The first Asian production of a Tennessee Williams play occurred in Japan, where *Streetcar* was performed fifty-four times from 19 March to 30 May 1953 by the Bungakuza Dramatic Company. Bungakuza, or "National Theatre," traveled to several major Japanese cities with *Streetcar* during a ten-week tour.[66] The Japanese premiere of *Streetcar* sheds light both on Williams's immense popularity and on the continuing Westernization of the Japanese theatre. Bungakuza was one of Japan's most illustrious *shingeki* troupes, a "new theatre movement, which began in 1906 and had dedicated itself to the ideal of the creation of a modern, westernized theatre, stressing the care of literary and theatrical values independently from the mainstream of commercial theatre."[67] *Streetcar* at once attracted the attention of Bungakuza founders – Kunio Kushida, Toyoo Iwata, and Michio Kato. A student of French drama, especially Copeau's work, Kushida "hoped to assume a mission in Japan as shingeki's teacher-theoretician-reformer, much as Copeau had been for the contemporary French theatre,"[68] and he saw *Streetcar* furthering such a mission.

The production of Williams's play was also a wise political choice for Bungakuza. The time for this premiere could not have been more propitious for Japanese–American relations. *Streetcar* opened about a year after the end of the American occupation, when full sovereignty had been restored to Japan. By 1952–53 Japan had already experienced, and followed in some respects, an American way of life. General Douglas MacArthur, the occupational governor-general, was highly influential in shaping, even Americanizing, Japanese society. The premiere of *Streetcar* by Bungakuza's shingeki troupe can be seen as an important extension, yet also an independent interpretation, of American culture. "Immediately after the war the American occupation authorities favored shingeki. They were distrustful of the 'feudal-istic' traditional drama of *Kabuki* and *Nō*, which were censored and subjected to special control, while complete freedom and support was given to the new westernized drama as a potential instrument of democratization."[69] Beyond doubt, too, Bungakuza staged *Streetcar* because of the enormous popularity of the film version, another bastion of American culture, released by Warner Brothers in 1951 but not seen in Japan until 1952.

In May 1952, Shirou Narumi, a Bungakuza member and transla-tor for the 1964 production, met Williams when he gave a poetry reading in Greenwich Village. The following anecdote characterized Williams's charm for Narumi:

> Looking at me with gentle and friendly eyes, he expressed positive expectations about *A Streetcar Named Desire* being performed in an unknown country, Japan. Before I left, I asked him whether there was any particular request he had. Shaking my hand firmly with his thick hand, he said with a grin, "Please make sure that it will be done in a southern accent."[70]

Narumi's story alludes to many of the problems – language, acting styles, traditions – that Bungakuza had to overcome in producing *Streetcar*. Woefully anticipating Narumi's fears about staging *Streetcar* in Japan, another Japanese critic and *Streetcar* translator, Ken Kurahashi, admitted, "In Japan our methods for staging plays are not yet fully Westernized. To perform *Streetcar* in Japanese, the director and the actors have to overcome the inadequacies and the inconveni-ences of the Japanese language to capture Williams's intentions."[71] Though some reviewers claimed that Bungakuza failed to capture Williams's lyricism fully, in part because of the problems of transla-tion, overall they applauded the company's valiant efforts.

When Bungakuza asked Ichiro Kawaguchi to direct *Streetcar*, they chose wisely. Having studied in the United States, Kawaguchi worked well with an ensemble, and used *Streetcar* as the vehicle to bring the "new drama" – with a new realistic style of acting – to the

Japanese stage. Kawaguchi's overriding concern with including every nuance extended to his view of character. Kawaguchi was a Japanese Stanislavski who also mastered Kabuki, both acting traditions that valorized the development of character over plot in a search for truth. Although he may have approached *Streetcar* too literally, missing some of Williams's subtleties and poetry, *Streetcar* nonetheless allowed Kawaguchi to showcase the best recent psychological drama. Lending itself perfectly to Kawaguchi's directorial (Stanislavskian) objectives, *Streetcar* overflowed with stories about Blanche's and other characters' pasts. Insisting that every element of his production of *Streetcar* be precisely authentic, Kawaguchi sent away to New York for Alex North's musical score.

Scenographer Kisaka Ito strove to imitate Jo Mielziner's Broadway sets and, like Mielziner, he employed scrims to signal changes and to indicate interior and exterior locations. Yet in Ito's desire to emulate the American production, he was too careful, too orderly, revealing a distinct non-Western influence surfacing in the production. Excluding the clutter and sordidness of Stanley's French Quarter neighborhood, Ito gave it an un-New Orleanian orderliness. Ohoka pointed out that the set was "so clean it changed the direction and mood of the play . . . *Streetcar* supposedly expresses the collapse of American society . . . Yet Bungakuza's staging was too neat to represent the real meaning of the play."[72] Regardless of such inconsistencies, though, Ito's expressionistic scenography cooperated with Kawaguchi's directing to bring realistic acting and the "new drama" to Japan.

Haruko Sugimura was well known in the Japanese theatre when she agreed to become Blanche, a role she played for over thirty years. Sugimura so perfected the role of Blanche that she symbolized the character for the Japanese. Remarkably, in a 1987 Bungakuza production, Sugimura at seventy-eight still convincingly portrayed a 30–year-old Blanche DuBois. Again, though, the truth that Japanese audiences readily accept an octogenarian actress as a 30–year-old says more about Asian theatre conventions than Western ones. Kabuki actors like Sugimura were traditionally able to sustain and to convince in much more youthful roles.

Sugimura received enthusiastic reviews. K. Yamawaki exulted: "Haruko Sugimura brilliantly creates the tragic character of Blanche DuBois . . . she is a figure of waning beauty and quality education, interweaving the old maid's blend of fading desire and desperation. Sugimura's rich personality, the accumulation of her long acting career, has been polished and condensed for this one role." Sugimura did not slavishly imitate Vivien Leigh's performance in the filmed *Streetcar*, but incorporated her own style and mannerisms into the role. Yamaguchi maintained that "Sugimura as Blanche is best when she sings in the bathroom. Her song, drifting across the stage on emotional waves, wrings not only Stella's heart but also the audience's. Her acting is superb, especially when she conveys Blanche's complicated nervous tension. She has mastered the acting techniques in the realistic style." Blanche's song, admirably performed by Sugimura, appealed to Japanese critics and audiences familiar with Kabuki arias similar to Blanche's rendition of the popular song of the 1930s about a "paper moon." Sugimura echoed the pathos of Blanche's wistful but tragic illusions reminiscent of traditional Japanese theatre.

Sugimura's performance also reflected the cultural stresses inherent in the production. Her main *faux pas* for the critics was overacting, perhaps vestigia of her successes in the artfully demonstrative Kabuki but also possibly a reflection of Blanche's histrionic temperament. Ohoka summed up Sugimura's problems: "She played Blanche very well, but sometimes she exaggerated her expressions too much; she needs further practice playing a character who has had so many confused, even contradictory, feelings." "K.M.O." pinpointed other flaws in Sugimura's delivery: "something more is needed in Sugimura's incorporating the lyricism of Williams's demented heroine." Apparently, Sugimura was able to suggest Blanche's extravagance but occasionally missed her verbal agility. Nonetheless, she skillfully combined different acting techniques – the stronger, more direct realistic performance with the traditional Japanese style – to develop her perceptive interpretation of Blanche.

The Japanese reviewers were even harder, though, on Blanche's character than were her American critics. There was little sympathy for Blanche. According to K. Yamawaki, "Blanche is an old woman who is tired of her life and with one last hope visits her sister. Cunningly, she forces a pure-minded man Mitch [played by Hiroshi Akutagwa] to propose to her . . . but Blanche's false life is destroyed when Stanley rapes her and she goes crazy." According to Ko, "Blanche brings ruin on herself and her family. Her fault is that she lives in a dream world that destroys her." Japanese reviewers did not absolve Stanley of his guilt; they just denounced Blanche's sins more. For K.M.O. "Blanche is a little crazy . . . she comes from the country to obtain her sister's help and displays a morbid nervousness associated with her abnormal past."

Cultural and political reasons may lie beneath the surface of the harsh reception Blanche DuBois (though not Haruko Sugimura) received from the Japanese critics. Several of them rebuked Blanche for being an unwelcome intruder, a disrupter of Stanley's household. Given the fact that the American occupation of Japan had ended a year before Bungakuza's premiere, the idea of intruders, forced visitors of any kind, surely must have been on the reviewers' minds as they assessed Blanche's behavior. For a post-war Japanese audience, Stanley's patriarchally ordered home, despite his cruelty, might have been reassuringly valorized over Blanche's hysteria. Unwelcome sisters-in-law and soldiers who have stayed too long as necessary guests bear uncomfortable resemblances, politically, if not consanguineously.

Yet another, even (paradoxically) stronger reason for the critics' less than favorable response to Blanche was that her past, her "aristocratic" origins and her quaint ways, could link her to Japan's own defeated, destructive past. Japan's culture and Blanche's past, real or imagined, suggested parallel states. Blanche the violated is like Japan the violated. Blanche easily suggested traditional Japanese culture (with its symbolical "morbid nervousness") in full retreat/defeat in 1953. Blanche and her problems in *Streetcar*, therefore, represented, through their theatrical re-enactment, the political posturing and failures from which a post-war occupied Japan was fleeing.

Playing Stanley was Kazuo Kitamura, a far less experienced actor than Sugimura. Almost all the Japanese critics faulted his limited acting abilities. His chief error was blindly aping Brando's Stanley, not developing a character of his own as Sugimura had done. Exclusively emphasizing the brutish side of Stanley, Kitamura "exaggerates Stanley's roughness so much that he makes the audience uneasy"(Ko); he clearly lacked Brando's brawn and charisma. The actor's inadequacies may well have contributed to the one-sided critical view of Stanley. Dwelling on Kitamura's weaknesses, Yamawaki surprisingly labeled Stanley as a "supporting character." The *Shin Kansai* reviewer offered pity for Stella (yet none at all for Kitamura's Stanley) for "being very perturbed over Stanley's brutishness."

Compared with Sugimura's Blanche and Kitamura's Stanley, Tomoko Funimo's Stella was judged nearly flawless. K. Kakitani, for example, stressed: "Tokomo Fumino is perfect with her passive gentleness in wild surroundings. Fumino beautifully expressed Stella's character." In *Yomiuri*, Ko brilliantly linked the essence of Stella's behavior with Fumino's talent: "Fumino plays a woman who is angry at her husband because he tortures her sister but at the same time she feels inevitably attracted to her husband's convenience and brutality."

Bungakuza continued to include *Streetcar* in its repertoire; it became the most successful American drama ever to be presented on the Japanese stage. Their *Streetcars* played to full and appreciative houses in August 1954 and June 1955, with the same cast and director as in the 1953 premiere. It was not until 1964 that Koichi Kinoshita replaced Kawaguchi as director, though, as we saw, Sugimura remained with the play for more than thirty years. When Bungakuza staged *Streetcar* in 1969, the play ran for 320 performances, a Japanese record for Williams. The playwright came to Tokyo in July of that year to visit his friend novelist and Bungakuza playwright Yukio Mishima, but "especially to see *Streetcar* performed by Bungakuza . . . [yet] he was too ill to stay after the first act." During his brief visit to Bungakuza, there was no record of whether Williams heard a Southern accent from any of the actors.

CHAPTER THREE

STREETCAR REVIVALS ON THE ENGLISH-LANGUAGE STAGE

Reviewing the 1973 revival at Lincoln Center, Brendan Gill proclaimed: *"Streetcar* remains tenaciously unaging."[1] Williams's play may be unaging but it is not unchanging. While it is true that *Streetcar* achieved the status of a classic almost from its first night on Broadway, it continues to remain engaging because it has invited and triumphed through re-interpretations. As Stephen Farber has observed, "a great production enriches the play by discovering its secrets."[2] *Streetcar* did not reveal *all* its secrets to Kazan, or exclusively to any other director, either. In major English-language revivals over the decades, directors, actors, scenographers, and costumers have modified, expanded, and redefined the Kazan *Streetcar,* building upon and deconstructing the tradition he set in motion.

In revivals, Blanche and Stanley have evolved. In the 1970s, 1980s, 1990s, Blanche has a repertoire of character traits far different from those available to Tandy, Hagen, or Leigh. Blanches have become funnier, less hysterical, and more resilient. In some revivals, too, Blanche and Stanley have exchanged roles as victims of power and agents of disempowerment. Stanley does not always triumph in revival. Beyond doubt, Brando's Stanley was so forceful that it has haunted every actor since; yet, as revivals demonstrate, there are other un-Brandolike possibilities in representing Stanley. Rex Reed's contention that "there have been many great Blanches[; t]here have been no great Stanleys" is not universally true.[3]

New types of stages and innovative designs have replaced, even subverted Mielziner's visual metaphors. Directors and scenographers have repositioned the play to fit into much more varied acting spaces. *Streetcar* revivals have been played on smaller and larger stages than the Barrymore.

83

As revivals prove, too, the political/cultural reception of the *Streetcar* script has changed over the years. As Nancy Tischler comments, "Nothing defines an age so well as its censorship. Watching *A Streetcar Named Desire* today, we find ourselves far more shocked by Stanley's abusive behavior than by the report of Allen Grey's sexual activities."[4] Through performance, the *Streetcar* script has been responsive to the times in and for which it plays, releasing and emphasizing a host of contemporary applications to and signs of female sexuality, marriage, changing notions of masculinity, the politics of desire, and even urban violence. *Streetcar* has successfully pushed theatre beyond the conventional boundaries imposed on Kazan.

The representative revivals in English surveyed in this chapter can ultimately help theatregoers to decide how much of the *Streetcar* script is (in)destructible in performance.

New York, 1956

The first major *Streetcar* revival – some branded it a travesty – was the 1956 production with Tallulah Bankhead. After a month of tryouts at the Coconut Grove Playhouse in Miami and at the Palm Beach Playhouse in January and February 1956, the Bankhead *Streetcar* moved to Manhattan's City Center Theater on 16 February for the last two weeks of the winter season. Williams himself was going to direct this revival but instead turned it over to the young Herbert Machiz, though the program still listed the playwright as "supervising the entire production." This *Streetcar* may well be the most controversial, stormy American revival because of the throaty-voiced, brash and breezy Tallulah Bankhead, who dominated the production. John Keating aptly rechristened the play "A Streetcar Named Tallulah."[5] Not surprisingly, too, the critic for *Time* (27 February) observed that "Tallulah was heartily playing Tallulah." She was "on a dramatic binge," claimed Robert Coleman.

This revival exacerbated the long-standing love-hate relationship between Williams and Bankhead. Williams had confessed that he had originally written four parts for Bankhead, or with her in mind – Myra in *Battle of Angels*; the Princess Kosmonopolis in *Sweet Bird*; Mrs. Goforth in *Milk Train*; and Blanche.[6] In 1947, though, Irene Selznick had vetoed Bankhead since Blanche was to be both tiger and moth, and the irrepressible Tallulah was unmitigatingly the tiger. But in 1956 Bankhead got her chance, and according to her biographer – and Williams himself – she worked hard at it. She gave up cigarettes and liquor and went into intensive training.[7] Recognizing that the role was tough, Bankhead concluded it was "harder than 18 *King Lears* with a *Hamlet* thrown in" (quoted by William Hawkins, 11 February).

But after seeing her performance in Miami, Williams was shocked. When he went to her dressing room (with Machiz) to rebuke her, she asked if she had "played Blanche better than anyone else had," to which Williams snapped: "No, your performance was the worst I have seen." A controversy – and hard feelings – ensued, resulting in Williams publishing an apology in the *New York Times*, [8] denying that she had ruined his play, attributing his remarks to "barroom lingo," and lauding her extraordinary subsequent performances. After that horrible opening night, Williams admitted, "this small mighty woman had met and conquered the challenge" and displayed "a woman's great valor and an artist's truth, her own, and far super-seded and even eclipsed the performance of my own play." (Bankhead tersely rejoined that she was pleased Williams "undertook to sober up."[9]) Despite Williams's accolades, however, his resentment lingered over the decades. In an interview with Rex Reed in *Esquire* for September 1971, he still held that "poor Tallulah" was "the worst Blanche in the world,"[10] and in his last professionally produced play while he was alive – *Something Cloudy, Something Clear* – he attacked the "actress" (Tallulah) as "the raging tiger . . . at City Center" who "pissed on the play . . . [and] who performed a classic role in the style of a transvestite in a drag show," yet added "But – I love you."[11]

Controversy raged among New York critics over whether

6. Scene from *Streetcar* in the 1956 New York revival starring Tallulah Bankhead (Blanche) and Gerald O'Laughlin (Stanley)

Bankhead played the role faithfully or distorted it. Her detractors were severe and nearsighted. Brooks Atkinson asserted: "Miss Bankhead has a personality . . . that is antipathetic to Blanche . . . it is fundamentally comic." Arthur Bronson observed, "Despite the actress's . . . superior talent, this is palpable miscasting. Miss

Bankhead misses altogether the softer, nebulous quality essential to make the neurotic ex-schoolteacher sympathetic" (16 February). The reviewer for *Time* (13 February) charged that Bankhead "roared over the boards, always managed to be upstage, downed her liquor as if it were the real stuff, and generally hammed her way through the play in a spirit of riotous deviltry." Claiming that Tallulah made a "novelty" of *Streetcar*, John Chapman joked that she "was better endowed by nature to have replaced Orson Welles as King Lear than Jessica Tandy . . . as Blanche." Joining in the chorus of naysayers, the reviewer for *Theater Arts* concluded, "Tallulah is a natural baritone, and Blanche is at most a mezzo." In sum, Bankhead's Blanche was censured for her comedy, her voice, her assertiveness, and her distracting mannerisms.

Happily, though, Bankhead's supporters outnumbered her detractors. Praising her work in Miami, Herb Rau proclaimed: "It is unlikely that this generation's theater-goers will ever see another Blanche again like Tallulah Bankhead." Many of Rau's New York counterparts also trumpeted Bankhead's distinctive interpretation. In Hawkins's eyes, she "edits her own experience for her performance," and "as no other actress has ever done . . . understands what it means to be a Southern lady . . . through Bankhead [Blanche] has gained a decadence, tenderness and shining physical beauty" as never before (16 February 1956). Playing strong-willed Southern women fighting for survival came naturally to Bankhead, who, several years earlier, had turned in an electrifying performance as Regina, the vixen of Lillian Hellman's *Little Foxes*. The daughter of a US senator from Alabama, Bankhead was, as Williams himself pointed out, "descended from the plantation Southland" (*New York Times*, 29 December 1963). In portraying Blanche as a Southern lady, Bankhead exploded the moth and tiger totems. Tallulah's pride – the pride of a Southern aristocrat – was grossly misrepresented as "unconquerable arrogance" (Wolcott Gibbs), a sign of the Southern lady in Blanche confronting a Yankee Stanley. Rather than being miscast, then, Bankhead brought a regional panache plus a validity in the role that British-born Tandy and Leigh could not. In Bankhead's voice Williams may indeed have heard echoes of his Delta heritage.

If Bankhead did not evoke a pitiable Blanche, she nevertheless portrayed Blanche's tragic plight. As Stanley Richard stressed: "To my enchantment . . . I discovered a . . . Tallulah . . . deep and tender, violent and sufficiently insane to appear normal, moving and coy, suffering yet concealing pain." Euphemia Van Rensselaer Wyatt likewise recognized that Bankhead emphasized "less the psychotic and erotic tendencies of Blanche than her general helplessness . . . the piteousness of her last exit was shattering." Bankhead was strongest when telling Mitch about Allan Grey and trying to turn Stella against Stanley. Honoring Bankhead for a "bravura performance," Thomas R. Dash found the "combination of Tennessee Williams and Miss Bankhead a most felicitous one . . . he can delineate feminine neuroticism [while] . . . the actress knows how to breathe fire and brimstone into such an etching . . ." Bankhead captured Blanche as the steel magnolia.

Much of the controversy surrounding Bankhead's performance stemmed from the opening-night audience's reaction at Center City, indelibly imposing its interpretation on the revival. Valorizing this audience's response, Atkinson noted: "Last night the audience seemed to be familiar with all her mannerisms, and was disposed to regard Blanche's tussle with the fates as pretty funny" (4 March). As biographer Lee Israel noted, "Tallulah's opening-night audience was exultant, elegant, and primarily male homosexual. They came because they had received word through the grapevine that the performance was a 'hoot' . . . [and] were there to laugh at their burgeoning goddess from her first words."[12] These "adoring saboteurs" (William Hawkins) laughed in all the wrong places turning serious lines into epicene guffaws. They were "determined that [Bankhead] live up to her roustabout reputation" (Walter F. Kerr).

Director Machiz admitted that Tallulah's gay admirers "found her mannerisms amusing: her tremulous voice, the whiplash movement of her head as though drying her hair, the staccato, bronchial laugh."[13] Reading the audience more than the actor, Robert Coleman wrongly deduced: "She took the first act of *Streetcar* and kidded the pants off it. She satirized it unmercifully, stimulating gales of laughter among the discerning first-nighters. But she played the second stanza [sic] as though she were Sarah Siddons [as] Lady Macbeth." More correctly John Keating concluded: "These gay lads had come to see a travesty and, despite Miss Bankhead's sturdy refusal to commit one, they applauded it as though by their actions they could call it into being."

Bankhead had no intention of playing *Streetcar* as a gay fandango. She was "bewildered . . . and had no idea what the audience was laughing at" in Miami or in New York.[14] The humor she brought to the role was a rich response to Blanche's complex character, not, as Dash misguidedly interpreted, "relief to the more somber aspects of the play." For Bankhead, Blanche's humor was more than relief; it reflected her charm, sacred and profane at the same time. That humor, radically departing from the Blanches of Tandy, Hagen, or Leigh, emancipated Williams's script from stylized rigidity and encouraged audiences to discover another secret about Blanche not foregrounded in earlier productions. Bankhead's rendition of Blanche's humor anticipated revivals starring Faye Dunaway and Blythe Danner. Most important of all, though, Bankhead's powerfully individualized interpretation unsuspectingly prepared the way for more radical *Streetcars* in the 1980s and 1990s where issues of class, gender, genre, and stylization have been interrogated and realigned.

Less than a year before Bankhead's performance, Maria Brit-Neva (later Countess St. Just, Williams's self-appointed literary executor) starred as Blanche in a little-noticed revival in an Originals Only production at Sheridan Square in New York. Slavishly following earlier Blanches, Maria Brit-Neva was pummeled. The "English actress" was "not able to express the inner tensions of that haunted gentlewoman," nor could she "bring those terrors to the surface of Blanche's personality."[15] Williams's *bête noir* Bankhead had no such problem but instead represented Blanche's terrors through tears as well as self-protective laughter. As John McClain affirmed, she was incapable of "being anything but Tallulah."

The rest of the City Center cast wilted by comparison with Bankhead. Keating claimed that the cast was "just about up to summer stock level." Gerald O'Laughlin's Stanley (the actor's Broadway debut) was roundly criticized for being too "calm," "weak," "ineffectual." Again, Keating spoke for most reviewers; "he avoids any suggestions of Marlon Brando in the role. He is equally adept in avoiding any suggestions of Stanley." Retrospectively, Williams admitted that O'Laughlin was miscast: "The part [of Blanche] must be played opposite an actor of towering presence, a Brando or a Tony Quinn, to create a plausible balance, but circumstances necessitated her playing it opposite an actor who would appear to best advantage as the male lead of a gently poetic play such as something by Chekhov, Synge, or Yeats" (*New York Times*, 29 December 1963). O'Laughlin looked like but did not act like James Cagney for George Bourke. Whatever "brutishness" O'Laughlin did possess had "no special sting" for Kerr.

Capturing a "wholesome" Stella (for Atkinson) and an "honest and simple one" (for Hawkins), Frances Heflin appeared in stark contrast to Bankhead's Blanche. Caught between sisterly loyalty and Stanley's sexuality, Heflin "capably portrayed Stella's dilemma" for Dash. Yet Stella's sexuality was rebuked in some critical quarters: "Stella's hearty if legalized sensuality seemed as repugnant as Kowalski's" (Wyatt), perhaps revealing in Heflin's response another impact of Bankhead's influence on the production.

No stranger to the script, Rudy Bond, who played Steve Hubbell in the Broadway premiere, was Mitch. He was "appropriately fumbling and bewildered" for McClain. Yet for Dash, Bond admirably "mirrors the gentility and gallant courtesy," adeptly incorporating the complexities that energize Mitch. Atkinson praised Bond for a Mitch who was "cautious, naive, essentially proper in his sense of middle-class decorum."

Bi-coastal Streetcars, 1973

To celebrate *Streetcar*'s twenty-fifth anniversary, revivals were staged in early spring 1973 on both the West and the East Coasts. Williams regretted that he could attend only the revival in Los Angeles, which "coincides with my sixty-second birthday, and I simply no longer have the mobility of a jumping flea."[16]

James Bridges's *Streetcar* at the Ahmanson in Los Angeles (21 March to 28 April) was done in what Ray Loynd called "technicolor precision," an apt comparison for this Hollywood-inspired revival. The production featured Hollywood stars – Faye Dunaway as Blanche, Jon Voight as Stanley, and Earl Holliman as Mitch – and a well-known film director, all of whom were chosen by Williams himself.[17] The opening night audience was packed with Hollywood glitterati, including Rosalind Russell, Henry Fonda, David Janssen, Johnny Carson, Robert Stack, and Charlton Heston who pronounced that the production "was what every playwright would hope for – to see a play 25 years later and to see it wear so well" (Jody Jacobs). Bridges tried to "bring a fresh approach to the work" (Ron Pennington) by challenging the audience "to forget the Kazan original" (Loynd). Gone from Bridges's *Streetcar* were many familiar icons – Stanley's T-shirt, "Stella and Stanley in hot embrace at the final curtain" (J. Moriarity), and the familiar New Orleans wrought-iron balconies replaced by designer Robert Taylor Lee's telephone poles. In breaking from Kazan, Bridges also restored Blanche to a central, dominating position which, according to Stephen Farber, "was closer to Williams's original intention."

Though Bridges tried to be innovative, even daring, the production did not succeed and must go down as one of the least appreciated *Streetcar* revivals. Critics faulted Bridges, the production, and, with some notable exceptions, the acting for being ensnared in Hollywood realism. Farber accused Bridges's *Streetcar* of being "plodding, prosaic"; his directing was "depressingly literal-minded." The result was that the poetry and the lyricism were drained from this revival;

Loynd complained "I miss [the] poetic tragedy, that airy hothouse luxuriance and decadence" for which Williams was famous. Among the most damning comments about this too realistic revival was that "one never gets the feeling of the strong physical attraction between Stanley and Blanche and the tender deep love between Stanley and Stella" (Pennington), a reproach leveled at subsequent revivals, as well. As Moriarity charged, Bridges' "approach is filmic, individual scenes merit his attention, the whole landscape is slighted."

Dunaway's Blanche received mixed reviews. True to her reputation on screen, Dunaway foregrounded comedy in the script; she "gets more laughs than Stanley" (Farber). Yet, according to Sullivan, she "misses the white moth magic" that characterized Leigh's performance, and in Blanche's most hysterical moments she was "lacking credibility" (Edwa). As Pennington put it, Dunaway's Blanche was "firmly rooted in reality [and] . . . never . . . really sees or believes in . . . visions and fantasies," reflecting Bridges's overzealous literalism. Also operating against Dunaway were her looks and her age – she was seen as "too young and too attractive" to portray a middle-aged Blanche. Several critics, though, saw great promise in Dunaway's Blanche, and rated her work superior to the production in which she played a part. Ray Loynd, for example, found Dunaway "riveting" and claimed that she alone was "worth seeing," adding that though *Streetcar* was "devalued" as a poetic script in Bridges' production, "none of this is Dunaway's fault. Put her role in a vacuum tube and you have a great Blanche."

No such flattering qualifications greeted Voight's Stanley. In trying to develop a new type of Stanley, Voight "studiously attempt[ed] to underplay the role" (Farber), an interpretation even Williams deplored.[18] Voight's boyish looks, like Dunaway's youth – icons of Hollywood glamor – worked against him as did his practiced timidity. Maintaining that Voight "seemed puzzled by Stanley," Dan Sullivan argued Voight displayed no rage, no overwhelming virility. He even "throws dishes politely." His is "not so much a panther-like threat . . . as . . . a pretense" (Loynd). Dressed in a white shirt, wide collar, and a vest with a pocket full of pens, Voight "conveyed [an] . . . embarrassed intellectuality that negates the raw emotionalism that needs to singe the air" (Moriarity), as if he were dramatizing Stanley as a decadent rock'n'roller. In essence, Voight's innovation erased Stanley from the script – "Stanley almost becomes a nonentity" for Pennington.

Holliman's Mitch, on the other hand, was magnificent, stealing thunder from Voight's Stanley. The innovations Holliman poured into the role worked. His Mitch "was not as painfully shy" (Sullivan) as other renditions of the role; he was "an interesting foil to Stanley" as Blanche "releases his tenderness" (Farber). Voight was clearly out-manned by Holliman in a production that turned the tables on Stanley by presenting a stronger, more resilient Mitch.

The East Coast *Streetcar* opened on 26 April at the Vivian Beaumont Theatre at Lincoln Center and ran through 29 July for 110 performances. Directed by Ellis Rabb, this revival starred British-born Rosemary Harris as Blanche, James Farentino as Stanley, Patricia Conolly as Stella, and Philip Bosco as Mitch. This was a land-mark revival for many reasons. It was Jules Irving's last production as Artistic Director at Lincoln Center before Joe Papp, who focused more on original plays than on revivals, took over. Moreover, *Streetcar* ushered out the old regime in grand style by setting "a house atten-dance record" (Catherine Hughes).[19] Perhaps most significantly, "there was a whole generation which had not seen a strong produc-tion of the play on the New York stage – now they have that opportu-nity," claimed Edwin Wilson. A few critics, Brendan Gill, for example, had unqualified praise for this revival – "the present produc-tion of 'Streetcar' is not merely a worthy successor to the original but an illuminating companion to it." But, ultimately, this revival, as Kevin Sanders pointed out, "was an exercise in nostalgia" which mili-tated against Rabb and the cast. The spectres of Tandy and Brando hung over the production to the detriment of Harris and Farentino. Rex Reed called this *Streetcar* "a special birthday celebration" but added that "*Streetcar* is having a rotten birthday." While some accolades flowed, many reviewers acerbically thought it was "off balance" (T. E. Kalem), "eccentric" (Marilyn Stasio), and sometimes distracting.

Rabb's direction was frequently blamed for the problems. He was accused of being heavy-handed, intrusive, even distorting the play. Unlike Kazan or Bergman, Rabb strayed too far from what reviewers regarded as the *Streetcar* script. Martin Gottfried identified Rabb's error as "impatience with the play's poem quality and boorishness in dealing with its subtlety." Rabb flooded the stage with supernumeraries and incessant sounds – kids playing ball, street vendors hawking their wares, a sailor chasing a prostitute, streams of passers-by, a Black woman singing the blues, men fighting. Reed also heard and saw "Bongo drums, cathedral bells, gang wars, people getting stabbed, men carrying other men across the stage like ballet dancers . . ." As Gottfried remarked, it was "almost as if Rabb tried to write a musical out of the play by introducing the population of New Orleans in background numbers." Novick charged that Rabb's intrusions were a "pure and flagrant case of directorial egotism at the expense of the performers and the play." Williams indignantly exclaimed: "Where are all these people? I never wrote all those parts and what the hell is going on here?"[20] Rabb doubtless introduced all the activity to fill the vast spaces of the Beaumont but in opening the full stage he was accused of dissipating the intimacy that *Streetcar* calls for and envelops. Kazan, for example, successfully projected a misty, claustrophobic environment, a "crucial hothouse atmosphere" (Stasio). Almost unilaterally, Clive Barnes endorsed Rabb's decision: "Stanley Kowalski's house in the French Quarter . . . has been seen by designer Douglas Schmidt as a kind of ornate cage, while the teeming life of the Quarter is seen as enclosing it."

Rabb had other faults. According to Clurman, he injected "too much decorative symbolism" into the play. For example, rather than whisking the paperboy off stage in Scene 5, Rabb had the young man stand "outside the house, gazing at it in yearning memory of the strange woman who mysteriously kissed him." He also misguidedly cast a male actor as the Mexican flower seller in Scene 9 and so erased the symbolic connection between Blanche and this feminine threnodist, weakening the female agency of Blanche's tragedy. But perhaps most disconcerting of all, Rabb skewed the performance away from an elemental struggle between Blanche and Stanley and toward Blanche's one-sided superiority (Julius Novick). This charge, leveled at Bridges as well, may have also been a reflection of the dynamics of acting.

In some ways, Rosemary Harris's Blanche, like Rabb's directing, was too idiosyncratic, moving too far away from the way Blanche should behave, for audiences and reviewers. Beyond doubt, though, Harris's performance won high praise. George Oppenheimer, for instance, proclaimed: "She was everything Blanche should be, with her faded gentility, her frenzied attempts to be thought respectable, her compulsive deceits and her battle with her brutish brother-in-law . . ." More frequently, however, Harris's Blanche was faulted for what was missing, chiefly that "she lacks the fragile vulnerability of Blanche" (Wilson). Gottfried complained that she was "not a frail actress"; and Barnes and John Beaufort were uncomfortable with her confident shrewdness.

Harris's Blanche was strong; Stanley was no match for her. Unlike Tandy, she was not a moth; yet she lacked "the heroic bravado of Leigh" (Lillian Africano). Nonetheless, her "husky, tremulous voice created an inner delicacy" (Novick). Audiences at Lincoln Center did not see sizzling sexuality between Harris's Blanche and Stanley. As Douglas Watt commented, Harris's "cool seductiveness keeps her just outside the character." Echoing these sentiments, Kalem admitted that Harris was "not coquettish enough. She seems too exclusively fanciful ever to be emotionally vulnerable." Nor did Harris inject much humor into the role, demonstrating again that a rounded portrayal of Blanche must offer sensuality, comedy, and tragedy.

Yet for a few critics, Harris's Blanche faltered precisely because of her emotional outbursts. Clurman found Harris "too weepy" – her performance "overstresses the quivering and shaken Southern belle at the expense of the character's dramatic will." While praising Harris's accomplishments, Kerr found her too distraught from the start; she comes in "shaken and tremulous." Consequently, he complained: "To doom [Blanche] as obviously as Miss Harris does in her constant physical anxiety, her close to tears throatiness, her instantly triggered defensiveness, is to make Stanley's task all too easy and the play's progress foreseeable." In the process, Harris left out the pain and, as Gottfried put it, "she jumps the breakdown and goes haywire before the rape." Which was Harris then – too strong or too overcome? Perhaps both. In one of the most balanced reviews, Jack Kroll observed: "Pale and lovely as a wounded dyad [Harris] captures exactly the repressed rapacious gentility of one of the most beautiful losers and marvelous roles on the American stage."

Farentino played a Stanley wronged by Blanche. As he told Judy Klemesrud: "My own approach to Stanley was that he is a guy who is not necessarily everything Blanche DuBois says he is, because if he is, that makes Blanche very realistic. He must be more of a pussycat like Stella says he is, except when he plays cards." In Farentino's view, Stanley was "a very moral man; he puts up with Blanche for six months until he overhears" her calling him an ape. No ape, Stanley for Farentino was evicting an invading Blanche.

Farentino's "moral" Stanley fared better with the critics than Voight's weak one. He won a *Theatre World* award and praise from some critics. Yet for Wilson, Farentino "missed the white heat at the core of Stanley." Seeing Stanley as Williams's "wet dream," Novick wondered if anyone could ever capture his "mythic sexuality." Martin Bookspan asserted that "James Farentino can't quite summon the last ounce of animal passion that Brando brought to the role but then who could?" What Farentino brought to the role was "the body; but he has no demon. You don't feel the seductive terror" (Kroll). Perhaps this was so since Farentino's Stanley "was perhaps more intelligent and therefore more vulnerable" than Brando's (Gill). The audiences saw Farentino's naked body in full view in Scene 10, which may have been the first nude Stanley, a costuming decision Reed branded as "totally superfluous." Not surprisingly, Clurman labeled Farentino's an "unexceptionally direct performance, serving the literal demands of the part." He was judged least effective in the rape scene; Kalem found him so "mean spirited" that the rape becomes sordid rather than the cataclysmic date he and Blanche had from the beginning. Commenting on both Farentino's appearance and the tenor of his interpretation, Novick linked him to the ambience of the 1970s with his "entertainingly jaunty, cheeky street-kid quality."

Patricia Conolly – an Australian actor – was a flawed Stella. She "was too strong for her own good," claimed Wilson; "we have to take her visceral need for her husband on faith," warned Kalem. Looking "dowdy and washed out" (Novick), Conolly's Stella hardly seemed to descend from aristocratic DuBois stock. In fact, she was the "mechanical and totally undeveloped little sister" for Africano. Philip Bosco's Mitch, on the other hand, offered "a performance of perfect pitch" (Kalem). He "turns the secondary role of Mitch into a fully dimensioned character" (Beaufort). Ironically, as in Los Angeles, the actor playing Mitch commandeered more favorable attention than Stanley did.

London, 1974

The London *Streetcar* in 1974, at the Piccadilly, starring Claire Bloom and Martin Shaw, came as close to perfect as a revival could be. "It was a notable example of what the classic revival should be – well groomed, but thoughtful, expressive, illuminating" (Clive Barnes).[21] Edwin Sherin's direction was "faultless" (John Walker), "technically stunning" (Helen Dawson). Bloom's portrayal of Blanche featured "remarkable layers of vitality, tenderness." Williams was exultant – "I declare myself absolutely wild about Claire Bloom."[22] Seeing the tryouts at Brighton, Lord Olivier also pronounced the production a tremendous success. "Every review was a knockout," rejoiced Jeremy Kingston.

Running for over ninety performances, starting from 14 March, this "plush" (Robert F. Hawk) revival was produced by Bloom's then-husband Hillard Elkins, who sought "to get the classics back to London's West End" (Kingston). Any British revival had to confront two troubling facts – *Streetcar* was an American classic and it had a distinguished British history as well. It had been twenty-five years since the Olivier premiere, and comparisons were inevitable yet highly favorable. Williams was pleased that Sherin did not cut the text, as Olivier had done. Yet Bloom was up against the titanic reputation of Vivien Leigh's Blanche, both in the London premiere and in the 1951 film. Jack Tinker spoke for most reviewers: "Until now [Blanche's] steamy legend has belonged exclusively to Vivien Leigh . . . However, legends are only ever on loan and Bloom is here in London to prove exactly how much mileage is left in the old *Streetcar*." Bloom knew and respected Leigh – they worked on the *Duel of Angels* together – but in an interview with Eric Johns, Bloom steadfastly confessed that an actor "must make the part her own by starting from scratch."

Overall, the cast won enormous respect for attempting this classic of the American stage. Ian Christie asserted: "Any English cast that embarks on a production of a play so heavily American as this Tennessee Williams classic deserves a trophy for courage. By all accounts Bloom – and the other actors – handled the dialect problems smashingly. Marguerette Littman, a native of Monroe, Louisiana and a friend of Williams, worked so closely coaching Bloom that Williams regarded her as a member of the cast. Bloom delivered her lines "with a most convincing languid Southern drawl" (Arthur Thirkell). Reviewing the revival for the *New York Times*, Clive Barnes heartily approved: "I have never heard an all-English cast tackle an American play with such linguistic authority." But while Helen Dawson likewise applauded the linguistic verisimilitude of the revival, she alone took it to task precisely because it was still too British. Asking "can British actors cope with melodramatic depths of

Williams?" Dawson responded that because "the English prefer their domestic violence to be verbal rather than physical," Bloom, Shaw, and Morag Hood's Stella "look slightly ashamed of their displays of passion."

If the production of *Streetcar* changed in England since Olivier's premiere, so, too, did its interpretation. *Streetcar* was elevated to sublime prominence by Harold Hobson as "one of three greatest American plays" (with *Salesman* and *Long Day's Journey*). While not carping, many reviewers gently cautioned that *Streetcar* had aged gracefully, though "a little melodrama had set in" for Thirkell. Only Walker found that a "glibness and sentimentality in the writing" dated *Streetcar* while Tinker labeled *Streetcar* as "old fashioned." But for a majority of reviewers, this revival poignantly reflected contemporary (changing) sexual and political mores. To be sure, the strong sexual appetite of the DuBois sisters was far less shocking in 1974 than it had been in 1949. Moving beyond the sexual scandal of the late 1940s, this revival stressed gender problems, especially "sexism, and . . . the double standard that sexism imposes. Thus we have less emphasis on Blanche's indiscretions . . ." (Barnes). Also lauding the contemporaneity of the revival, Hobson discovered that *Streetcar* had "as much sociological significance as the most politically conscious underground plays" representing "a collapsing social class."

Bloom came to the role of Blanche with nearly thirty years of acting credits, in film and on stage. Beginning her career at fourteen playing Juliet, she went on to do Ophelia, Cordelia, Nora in *A Doll's House*, and other love-pained women. She was astutely aware of the parallels between Ophelia and Blanche as well as those with her own life. No stranger to the vicissitudes of love, Bloom had had two stormy marriages up to this time – to Rod Steiger and to Elkins – and liaisons with such overbearing stars as Olivier and Richard Burton. Regarding Blanche as one of the "outlets for life's unwelcome pitfalls," Bloom perceptively described Blanche's problems in light of her own:

> The ladylike behavior of the Southern woman is, in Blanche's case, a defense. Within this lies the hidden need to obliterate a transparently false façade, with the intervention of a man, in a moment of reckless passion – this was something I could well relate to. I was also aware of Blanche's extreme terror of abandonment and her craving for protection. Her neediness only brings suffering; it is accompanied by resentment, in the anger she expresses toward Mitch and Stanley; for those are no saviors.[23]

Above all, Blanche for Bloom was just like an actor – "she lives through her imagination . . . [and] carries the player along, as does the play" (quoted in Johns).

Bloom's interpretation was spectacular, winning her *Evening Standard* and *Variety* awards. Robert Cushman announced that hers was "the most moving performance I have seen this year." Her Blanche was nothing like Leigh's – "no ghost will haunt Claire Bloom's Blanche," asserted Johns. Bloom was, as Milton Shulman observed, "no vague Southern belle but a hard calculating fading beauty" out to trap a man. In her interpretation, Bloom had "all of Blanche's bitchiness as well as her vulnerability" (Walker). Blanche, as represented by Bloom, had been in training for the role for years as seen through her "obsessive sexual coquettishness" (Jack Tinker). Not an exhibitionist, though, Blanche in Bloom's performance displayed "a marvellous dazed dignity . . . a hint of flirtatiousness, and a subtler hint of priggishness and the faintest memory of faded aristocracy" (Cushman). Irving Wardle aptly summarized Bloom's approach: she "presents a totally convincing image of Blanche – hollow-cheeked, delicate, dispensing Southern coquetry over an undertow of hysterical panic. What she leaves out is the comedy." Compared to Leigh, Bloom was more calculating, less melodramatic. Not a victim of debilitating chimeras as Leigh was, Bloom emphasized Blanche's "bright neuroticism" (Ian Christie). She put reins on Blanche's madness and became "a desperate – but not despondent – figure" (Dawson). Finally, Bloom excluded from the role any swaggering bravado and comic jousting, Bankhead's trademarks.

Bloom's looks, which fascinated many reviewers, relevantly and painfully captured Blanche's tragic predicament. Forty-two at the time, the actor offered neither Leigh's porcelain beauty nor Tandy's youthfulness. Instead, Bloom displayed "the ashen face of a woman burnt out of passion" (Barnes). "The disillusionment [is] well brought out by Claire Bloom whose haggard looks and attempt to transform them into some kind of radiance are touching . . . She is a beaten thing, like an animal at bay yet keeping up the façade of gentility, faded dignity" (R. B. Marriott). Wearing a blond wig, Bloom looked "like some old movie queen" (Thirkell) attempting to recapture or at least retain whatever vestiges of beauty and allurement she could. Appropriately, Dawson saw in Bloom's stage business of Blanche primping "the loss of face behind endlessly applied make-up."

Central to Bloom's performance, of course, was seeing Blanche as a lady fighting age, poverty, the ravages of desire. Blanche's appearance was so crucial to Bloom's subtext that she altered the traditional (British) notion of how Blanche should be costumed. (Interestingly enough, Beatrice Dawson was the costumer for both the 1949 and the 1974 British *Streetcars*.) Leigh, as we saw, was roundly criticized for being dressed as a tart in red-light district outfits. In Bloom's interpretation, however, Blanche could not look like a common streetwalker. Instead, according to Bloom, Blanche "loves beautiful things and she obviously has spent a good deal of money from the family estate on clothes. Blanche is also a whore whose personal appearance is of the utmost importance to her." Apparently, Williams also conceived Blanche in terms of fine clothes. While preparing to play Blanche, Bloom asked Williams what happens to her "after the final curtain," and he responded: "No others ever asked me that question . . . She will enjoy her time in the bin. She will seduce one or two of the more young doctors. Then she will be let free to run an attractive boutique in the French Quarter . . ."[24]

Martin Shaw's Stanley documented the further evolution of the role. A different Stanley from Brando, Quinn, Voight, or Farentino,

Shaw was honored for his originality. Williams himself proclaimed: "I love his pride. He is the finest, strongest Kowalski since Brando" (quoted in "Eye"). Wardle stressed that this Stanley "was not the dumb ox one remembers from Brando but a young, fluent, ruthless destroyer." Walker insisted that Shaw played Stanley "not as a dim, baffled creature but closely related to his recent Dionysus in the National Theatre production of 'The Bacchae,' an untrammeled primitive." Shaw was no ape, which is not to say he was in any way compromised or weak. To the contrary, he exuded the pride of the male bird, with all requisite sexuality. Benedict Nightingale marveled at his "thick neck." For another reviewer Shaw was "serviceably repellent, and animalistic" (Kenneth Hurren). Even Dawson commended Shaw: "Unlike many British actors, he is not afraid to let go and . . . can make the theatre quake." Just before the rape, Shaw started to pull down his pajamas, leaving no doubt in the audience's mind of his intentions.

Shaw was more intellectually threatening to Blanche than most previous Stanleys because of his wit and insight, helping to inaugurate a line of crafty, intelligent Stanleys. In fact, Shaw's Stanley was filled with politics and class bitterness assaulting a privileged *status quo*, turning the revival into a protest play of the tumultuous 1970s. Dressed in 1970s clothing – a nylon baseball jacket and plaid shirt unbuttoned to the waist – Shaw was trim, calculating, and more dangerous than many earlier Stanleys. As J. W. Lambert observed, Shaw had the "strutting vitality . . . [and] uncomprehending sharpness" that devastated Blanche. Shaw's detractors were few – e.g., Tinker seeing him as a "caricature." Yet despite Shaw's cleverness and panache, this British revival belonged to Bloom.

Joss Ackland's Mitch was "beautifully played" (Marriott) – presenting an older, greyer, and far more sensitive Mitch than audiences on either side of the Atlantic had seen. Casting the middle-aged (forty-six at the time) Ackland as Mitch perfectly complemented Bloom's image of the fading coquette Blanche. Reviewers repeatedly cited the scenes between Ackland and Bloom as among the best in the play. Ackland was "the simple bachelor nearly netted" by Blanche (Kingston), an unsuspecting, unglamorous Rosenkavalier. Well suited to the role, emotionally and physically, Ackland refined it. His Mitch was "another of Joss Ackland's sensitive studies of the weakness of the physically coarse," as Lambert pointed out. Prior to *Streetcar*, Ackland had played such lumbering characters as Bottom, Caliban, and Long John Silver. If Blanche's totem animal was the moth, Ackland's was the lumpish bear – large, awkward, totally self-conscious. According to Dawson, Mitch's body is so massive that he feels cramped in the Kowalski apartment and "has to walk sideways [like] an intrusive stranger . . . the eternal outsider . . . [he is] a romantic boy in a man's unresponsive body, someone who joins in but is never one of the gang. Another frightening mixture of self-respect and self-disgust."

Sherin linked (and contrasted) Mitch and Blanche in their quest for love through the physical. Showing off his "imposing physique" by stressing his height and weight, Ackland interpreted Mitch as a "brawny mother's boy whose own useless form of middle-age physical vanity makes [Blanche's] seem both useful and civilized" (Wardle). When Mitch attempted to rape Blanche in Scene 9, Ackland was not as violent as Malden, Bond, or Bosco had been, revealing yet another symptom of Mitch's consuming self-loathing. In the end, though, Mitch (in Ackland's portrayal), Stella, and Blanche were all Stanley's "subdued victims" (Milton Shulman).

Patrick Robertson's set successfully captured the effect and nuances for which Sherin strived. It recalled Mielziner's scrims without evoking their impressionistic magic. Dawson described the set perfectly: "a gauzy, flimsy structure [revealing] a see-through, hearthrough shanty house in the sticky centre of New Orleans." Through the transparent back wall audiences could see "the outside steps and a perspective of the bleached, gracefully decaying New Orleans street" (Kingston). Basically, Robertson's set consisted of "a few battered shutters, transparent walls, with a frame doorway opening onto a fire escape" (Wardle). The fire escape and other stairs forming the superstructure dwarfed the characters on the crowded, open stage below. In fact, Robertson's set looked like a skeleton, or the inside of a huge cage, making privacy or escape impossible. It was the place "that leaves Blanche feeling naked" (Wardle). Walker aptly characterized the set as a "misty ghost town." Further suggesting a decayed New Orleans ambience, Richard Pillow's lighting "filled the stage with the dusty heat and velvet shadows" (Lambert). Squeezed onto the stage was the Kowalski furniture, a chair and a bedspread both covered in a gaudy, flowered pattern evoking Stanley's blue-collar taste and contrasting with Blanche's more highfalutin' trappings.

Bloom and Shaw were so successful that it would be nine years before another revival of *Streetcar* was mounted in the UK – with Sheila Gish as Blanche and Paul Herzberg as Stanley.

Johannesburg, 1975

Streetcar had been staged before in South Africa in January 1951 at Maritzburg by Brian Brooke for the African Consolidated Theatre and at the Showgrounds in Bulawayo in May 1960. The 1951 production was less favorably received because, as "N.A.F." pointed out,

> The play's unpopularity with a large section of the South African public is due partly to a lack of maturity in its appreciation of the theatre, and partly to the fact that the play is not representative of a section of normal South African city life, and is therefore not fully understood. It is essentially an American story, for it concerns conditions of life which the American city dweller knows to exist around him, and to him it represents a true, if unpleasant, slice of life. To the South African it is unpleasant but divorced from reality.[25]

No such bias greeted the revival directed by James Roose-Evans in July–August 1975 and mounted at two Johannesburg theatres – the Intimate and the Nico Malan. *Streetcar* "no longer shocks as it did when Williams wrote the early example of kitchen sink drama in 1947, but it retains its power to move in this production" (Lynne Kelly).[26] David Coleman declared that the production's "superb stage-craft . . . transcend[ed] any smear of salaciousness or pornogra-phy." The South African *Streetcar* of the 1970s could best be described as moderate, avoiding extremes in setting, casting, and effects. Kelly observed: "With taut direction and acting, it avoids over-indulgence threatening this ruthless saga of sexual violence and mental disintegration." Whether South African censorship and/or directorial choice dictated this approach, the Johannesburg produc-tion staged an equally matched and poised Blanche (Anne Rogers) and Stanley (Michael McGovern).

Rogers was more reserved than most Blanches. The reviewer for the *Sunday Times* (8 August) found her to be "a little too chic . . . too knowing and distracted for the haunted and aristocratic waif" Williams created. Instead of . . . the "broken butterfly" in conflict with the brutish Stanley, in this production "extremes [of character] are replaced by mere gradations in the social scale." The reviewer con-tinued: "Blanche's dreams are routed from the outset by reality . . . there is little magic." For the reviewer in the *Pretoria News*, Rogers put "a little distance" between herself and Blanche, "when you know she is acting, not living the part." Yet the reviewer perceptively admit-ted: "Blanche is not only unstable, she is also highly artificial. Reality and acted artificiality are hard to distinguish." Thus what essentially appeared to be a flaw in Rogers's acting became a reflection of Blanche's chief weakness, a wonderful confluence of acting style and character trait. Commenting on Rogers's body language, Kelly con-cluded that, as the production progressed, "She becomes more and more shrunken physically and mentally."

Michael McGovern's Stanley was convincing without being over-bearing. Kelly characterized him as "direct, suspicious, bestial." Yet for Coleman he was "somewhat low key." The *Pretoria News* reviewer claimed that McGovern's "Kowalski is brutal but by no means a brute. He is too dignified, perceptive, and – toward his wife anyway – com-passionate to be labelled an ape." According to the reviewer for the Johannesburg *Sunday Times*, McGovern was "Stocky and irritable, [and] does not exhibit the slow burn of Brando's film performance . . .

a man with a greed for life, lustful, contemptuous of romance but
destructively challenged by its existence." McGovern admirably captured the ambiguities of Stanley's subtext. The object of Stanley's love
– Gillian Garlick's Stella – also contributed to this more subdued
Streetcar. Kelly noted that she brought "an underplayed sensitivity to
Stella, highlighting the stability of the girl who is only momentarily
torn between sister and husband." The reviewer for the *Sunday Times*
found Garlick to be a "perambulating advertisement for the tranquil-
lizing effects of sexual satiation," being true to the character whose
"eyes and lips have [an] almost narcotized tranquillity" (*Streetcar*
Scene 4). The costumes for this production were a major draw, stunningly evocative of the 1940s. Bill Edgson found Blanche evocatively
styled in "swell-clad fluttery," while the *Pretoria News* claimed that the
costumes "sat neatly on the borderline twixt elegance and vulgarity."

Lake Forest, Illinois 1976

In what amounted to nearly a thirtieth anniversary revival, the
Academy Festival Theatre at Barat College of the Sacred Heart in
Lake Forest, Illinois, a northern suburb of Chicago, staged *Streetcar*
on 8 June 1976,which ran for three weeks. Academy Festival had won
a Tony mention two years earlier for its *Sweet Bird of Youth*. As with
previous productions, the AFT flew in major stars for this *Streetcar*
revival – the husband and wife team of Geraldine Page (Blanche) and
Rip Torn (Stanley); Jack Hollander (Mitch) and Flora Elkins (Stella).
The production was directed by Jack Gelber, one of the "New Wave"
(circa 1959) of American playwrights whom Williams respected and
whose play *The Connection* ushered the avant-garde into the
American theatre. As Gelber recalled, Torn was responsible for
getting him to direct:

> I was involved with Rip Torn in a production of *Hamlet* . . . at the Circle
> in the Square in the Spring of 1976. During rehearsal, Rip asked me if I
> would be willing to direct *Streetcar* in Chicago with Gerry playing
> Blanche. The two of them were to play *Night of the Iguana* but at the

last minute Williams rejected the idea in favor of revival with Richard Chamberlain later in the season and so he saw the Academy Festival *Iguana* as competing with that production of and approved *Streetcar* instead.[27]

Gelber's *Streetcar* was troubling for the critics because it was raw, even dangerous. It pushed the *Streetcar* script to the farthest reaches of urban violence and unabated naturalism. Bury St. Edmund complained that the AFT used real glassware instead of "breakaway glasses," putting the audience at risk.[28] Glenna Syse was "scared" and only away from the production could she "breathe a wisp of relief." Linda Winer aptly titled her review: "'Streetcar' Rides a Rough Road."

Gelber's direction won little support, though David Elliott enjoyed his "savvy that gives the performers full stretch." He was faulted for not being faithful to Williams's play. In her radio review, Claudia Cassidy attacked him for taking "a gauzily hallucinated dream play that turns nightmare and stripped it bare of all illusion . . . vulgarizing the play beyond recognition." For Linda Winer, Gelber, a former Chicagoan, had anything but a "triumphant homecoming" with his *Streetcar*, for he "drained the rich mythic metaphor out of [Williams's] wrenching drama." Gelber's sense of the play was antithetical to Kazan's or Bergman's or even Rabb's. Seeing the script as threateningly realistic, Gelber did *Streetcar* the way David Mamet might do it; he was Mametian before Mamet. With lighting designer Lowell Achziger and set designer John Wulp, Gelber projected a brightly lit, garbage-filled stage reflecting the hostile, predatory world in which Blanche finds herself. Gelber's stage was strewn with "broken dishes, meat bones, watermelon pits, and puddles of brew" (Syse) and looked like Stanley's "garbage uncollected spring, summer and fall" (Cassidy). Not only did such a set destabilize any possibility of "raffish charm," but it also delayed playing time since it had to be cleaned up between scenes.

Such a dirty world also reflected the jazzy improvisations, the drug subculture, urban squalor, and confrontational approach intertwined in Gelber's own *Connection*. A glaring ceiling light remained unextinguished throughout the production, annoying audiences and foreclosing nostalgia or candle-lit romance in Blanche's encounter with Mitch in Scenes 3 and 5. Through such a set Gelber attempted to radicalize the *Streetcar* script in the same ways that his plays did to the American theatre a decade and a half before. He essentially altered *Streetcar*'s psychological effect by immersing the audience in a total theatre experience.

Geraldine Page was "the heart" of Gelber's *Streetcar*. A Williams veteran, she began her career at the Circle in the Square with *Summer and Smoke* in 1952, under Jose Quintero's direction, and Alexandra del Lago in the 1959 premiere of *Sweet Bird of Youth;* she also starred in the two widely acclaimed film versions of these plays. Her time to play Blanche was long overdue. Several critics feared she was too old to play the part. (Page obviously did not enjoy the invulnerability of age that Haruko Sugimura did.) Yet her Blanche was original, undeniably shaped by Gelber's sense of the character. As Dan Zeff pointed out, Page played Blanche "as a tough, self-dramatizing, wily, vain, emotionally overextended woman. Other actresses may twitter and simper like a caricature of Scarlett O'Hara gone flighty and seedy. She . . . gives the character guts." Syse similarly remarked, "This is not the Blanche of butterfly wings. This is gossamer with guts." Page displayed little of Leigh's hysteria or Tandy's forlorn helplessness. "Her famous, flirty mannerisms [were] under control"; this noble slattern could "shriek with bitterness or cackle with cynical delight" (David Elliott).

In keeping with the super-charged hostility Gelber packed into the script, when Page became "angry, she sp[at] venom like an asp" (Dorothy Andries). Which is not to say that Page was devoid of sentiment. Her scene with the paperboy won rave notices. And her voice was not always so bitter; several reviewers faulted her "feathery whisper" (Cassidy), though poor acoustics also shared blame. Ultimately, though, Page's Blanche was tarred with the same brush that reviewers used on Gelber. "Like Gelber's direction, Page plays

Blanche close to the surface . . . she was a floozy, extroverted Blanche whose confidence contracts all the years of insecurity we have come to expect" (Winer). Though impressive, "she's all alone out there" (St. Edmund). Reviewers concluded that with a better director and stronger supporting cast Page could have taken this *Streetcar* to New York.

Rip Torn's Stanley was unrepentantly vulgar, totally unacceptable to the critics. His age, looks, and exclusion of tenderness vitriolically defeated him. An extension of Gelber's *mise-en-scène,* Torn "look[ed] dirty and tired without any of that animal joy that makes his love-making such . . . hot stuff" (Winer). Appearing more like a mad revolutionary than a gaudy seed bearer, Torn was doing not Williams's Stanley but Gelber's. Zeff cautioned that Torn's reputation made him better "suited to crafty sinister characters" and that "his one-dimensional roaring level" was grating. According to Elliott, he "lacks the almost feline charm" that Brando possessed. Even in his performance of Stanley's playfulness, Torn was menacing. When he overheard Blanche plot against him, Torn swung ape-like from a staircase.

New York, 1988

From 10 March through 22 May 1988, forty years after the Broadway premiere, Circle in the Square Theatre staged a revival of *Streetcar*. A "not for profit theatre founded in 1951," Circle in the Square, according to Artistic Director Theodore Mann, produced *Summer and Smoke* as "its first big hit . . . our reputation was made by Tennessee Williams . . ."[29] After receiving Maria St. Just's approval, Mann decided to do an "all Williams season" to appeal to "a new kind of audience – young people who have heard of Williams but have never had the opportunity of seeing his plays."[30] Mann wanted to begin with *Streetcar,* followed by *Summer and Smoke* and *The Rose Tattoo.* Two years earlier, he had seen Nikos Psacharopoulos direct *Streetcar* at the Williamstown Festival in Massachusetts and asked him to bring the play to the Circle in the Square. Psacharopoulos had

turned Williamstown into "something of a . . . Williams shrine." In
1986, he directed Blythe Danner as Blanche, Christopher Walken as
Stanley, and Sigourney Weaver as Stella but, with the exception of
Danner, changed the cast for the Broadway revival starring Aidan
Quinn as Stanley, Frances McDormand as Stella, and Frank
Converse as Mitch. Danner, whom Psacharopoulos had directed in
fourteen previous productions, was the unquestionable star of the
revival.

Joel Siegel misleadingly claimed that Psacharopoulos "trans-
planted" *Streetcar* "with few changes, to Broadway."[31] Yet one major
change between Psacharopoulos's Williamstown and Circle in the
Square was the latter's challenging physical playing area. Linda Winer
described it as a "long rectangle of a stage" surrounded on three sides
by the audience, while Douglas Watt compared the stage
configuration to "a horseshoe . . . seating area." As Mann emphati-
cally pointed out:

> Basically, we are a theatre of language – a theatre of visions and poetry.
> The great thing about our space is that it allows plays of language to
> flower. Because we have very little scenery and because the audience sits
> around the performance rather than looking at the theater as a picture,
> the audience becomes part of the play. This is particularly important
> for plays of Tennessee Williams.

Many critics, however, found the revival unsatisfactory precisely
because of the staging. Rex Reed stressed "The claustrophobia that
closes in on Blanche is airier and less confining when you can see
through the walls to the audiences on the sides"; and John Beaufort
likewise complained that "the awkward thrust stage, [with its] the
see-through, two-story setting by John Conklin . . . seems to lack a
dominant focal point." Douglas Watt categorically announced
Streetcar's "full intensity can be realized only on a proscenium stage."
Critics also disliked the iron railing, resembling a streetcar, that surrounded the stage.

Psacharopoulos offered a new type of *Streetcar* on this innovative stage by trading in the sociological and mythic for an intensely realistic *Streetcar*. According to Clive Barnes, he "demystified the play cutting down a few of the mythic elements, such as the Spanish woman selling flowers . . . and stressing the ordinariness . . . . [His] cool realistic insights suggest an almost revisionist view of the play." Gone was Kazan's view of the play as an epic battle between Southern gentility represented by Blanche and brutal animal desire fomenting in Stanley. For Psacharopoulos, the characters ceased to be emblems, and took life as case studies as he stressed the clinical side of Blanche's madness and not its tragic intensity. As Frank Rich succinctly noted, this *Streetcar* was not a "morality tale" but "a terrifying plunge into the madness that affects anyone, male or female, who submits to his own personal executioner – the passion so incendiary that it consumes itself." For many reviewers Psacharopoulos's "hard-edged approach" (Barnes) dispelled the "electrifying sexuality" (Douglas Watt) of the premiere. Howard Kissel even accused Psacharopoulos of offering a "tepid tourist approach to the play . . . a cold, brittle *Streetcar,* partaking more of Massachusetts than Louisiana." Joel Siegel categorized it as a "*Streetcar* without desire"; Stearns found it "curiously sexless."

Psacharopoulos determined to do a *Streetcar* that reflected and responded to issues of the 1980s rather than the 1940s. Chief among these was truthfulness in a post-Watergate America. As Psacharopoulus observed about his Blanche: "The sexual thing might not be a problem for many people today . . . But she lies, and in the 70s and 80s morality has been identified with truth and lying, more than with promiscuity. Stanley and Stella are truthseekers" (quoted by Caryn in James). Also essential to Psacharopoulos's revival was the issue of women's plight in "the post-feminist 80s." This revival consequently emphasized the conflict women feel "between modern feminist ideology and lingering stereotypes," how to be "independent as well as strong, and survive" (James). In the spirit of the 1980s, Frances McDormand asserted of Stella: "I don't think Tennessee Williams ever meant for it to appear that Stella was a battered wife . . .

I think she hits him just as much as he hits her . . . What Stella has gotten from Stanley is the right to be a fuller human being than she ever was allowed to be in Mississippi . . . She has been liberated from what drove Blanche mad" (quoted in James). Unlike Kazan, Psacharopoulos "was very reluctant to make the red pajamas scene an out and out rape" (William A. Raidy). "The suggestion of date rape [did] not seem anachronistic" to James.

Even more than in other revivals, Psacharopoulos's *Streetcar* foregrounded one of the vexatious problems a director faced in mounting the play. Chief among them was casting the right Stanley with the right Blanche. Blanche and Stanley must excite each other and the audience as well. However effective the actors playing these roles, they will not succeed without a special dynamic, a chemistry between each other. As David Lida pointed out about the Psacharopoulos *Streetcar,* "Blythe Danner as Blanche and Aidan Quinn as Stanley are individually strong, but in their scenes together they fail to generate the sexual tension that gives meaning to play's conflict." The leading question about this revival at Circle in the Square was whether that dynamic, that chemistry is exclusively dependent on sexual fireworks or might it reside in other kinds of *Streetcars* besides the one on which Brando and Leigh rode into prototypical glory.

Danner continued the tradition of a strong, less fragile Blanche, whose performance, at least as far as the critics were concerned, was lessened by a weak Stanley. A "tall and slender woman with a blonde mane and a smoky voice,"[32] Danner won an Antoinette Perry Award nomination for her Blanche. She was called the "most intuitive American actress since [Lillian] Gish" (Steven Vineberg). Otherwise panning the revival, Siegel hailed Danner's Blanche as "superb" while Reed exclaimed that she was "electrifying . . . as consummate and hypnotic a Blanche as I've ever seen." She was strongest in playing the Southern belle "with all the ladylike decorum that belies her desperate state . . . [she had] all the delicate affectations of the belle-of-the-ball flirtatiousness" (Beaufort). As Reed also noted, Danner made audiences see Blanche's "suppressed sexuality, coyness, and the ruffled flirtatious dare of Southern women when they're over the hill." Her husky voice – like Bankhead's – brought a rich complexity to the role, revealing "smoky traces of hidden panic dulled by secret boozing yet . . . pitched with girlish glee" (Reed). Danner also injected more humor into the role than many previous Blanches did.

One of Danner's greatest strengths – "her cool, contained, lovely presence" (Watt) – however, misled the critics. She was too much in control, displaying too much resilience. Speaking for many critics, Kissel reported that "We seldom sense any underlying anguish." Winer was also distressed that Danner was so "radiant." As in her Williamstown performances, Danner was "not immediately, recognizably neurotic, like Vivien Leigh" (Vineberg). She was neither eccentric nor desperate enough, for, as David Patrick Stearns remarked, audiences "see the madness" but "don't feel the compulsion behind it." Danner erred by slipping into madness too late while earlier Blanches succumbed too soon.

Aidan Quinn offered audiences a reconfigured subtext for Stanley. Like Voight, but much more successfully, he challenged a Brando-like Stanley and incurred the critics' wrath. Frozen in a Brando warp, the reviewers attacked Quinn for not resembling Brando and even when he aped some of his mannerisms (spitting food, clearing the table) for not being forceful enough. Described as a "bantam" (Frank Rich), Quinn clearly did not have the physical build of Brando, Gassman, or Farentino, and thus problematized the role by expanding it to include an actor who was not also a muscle man. "Quinn is small and wiry, without Brando's bulk, and creates a Stanley who is the animal – but with none of the animal magnetism" (Winer); "he is too slight to impress us," proclaimed Watt. Sardonically, Siegel characterized Quinn as "George Bush as Stanley . . . the wimp version." For Mel Gussow, Quinn "with his sensitive, even soulful manner . . . resemble[d] Montgomery Clift."

If Quinn's size dwarfed the accomplishment of his performance for critics, it was the core of his interpretation. As Rex Reed conceded, "He's not an indelible Stanley, but at least he's created a character that is very much his own making." Lida appreciated Quinn's original approach by precisely targeting the actor's strategy: "Wisely, this small-framed actor does not try to embody Stanley's huge brutishness but focuses more on his cunning and sarcasm." Lida concluded that Quinn was "the best Stanley since Brando." Although Rich understood the merits of Quinn's performance – "he provides some ambiguous qualities appropriate to Stanley – his muscularity has its androgynous side, his boorishness its leavening humor" – he still found the actor unacceptable because he lacked enough "animal force."

Given Psacharopoulos's contemporary interpretation of the script, Quinn accurately portrayed another legitimate side of Stanley's temperament – his emotional tyranny. A jabbing, verbally caustic Stanley can just as piercingly wound a self-protecting Blanche. While in earlier productions, Stanley's physical violence overshadowed the performance, Quinn foregrounded Stanley's lethal verbal anger. But the critics persisted in valorizing stereotypes using Quinn's size to demean his portrayal. According to Barnes, Quinn was "oddly a subtle Stanley . . . more than simply a brute. He is mean, greedy, and totally self-centered." Stearns more pugnaciously claimed: "he's a wiry, obnoxious scrapper." And for Beaufort, Quinn was so "aggressively mean-spirited that one finds his moments of contrition and anguish difficult to accept." Ultimately, Quinn was not sexually menacing enough – there was "no aura of danger about him" (Rich). Yet Quinn at thirty, fifteen years younger than Danner's Blanche, nonetheless projected the bravado of cocky manhood endangering her magnolia pride. Interestingly enough, Christopher Walken's Stanley two years earlier was dismissed for being "thick-headed" even though his physical prowess was "imbued with the power of a battering ram" (Vineberg).

New York, 1992

On 12 April 1992, *Streetcar* was staged at the same theatre – the Barrymore – where the play had premiered forty-five years earlier.

This revival generated much enthusiastic anticipation. Running for 160 performances, it starred three famous film actors – Jessica Lange as Blanche; Alex Baldwin as Stanley; and Amy Madigan as Stella – and was directed by the former head of the Lincoln Center, Gregory Mosher, whose aim was to be faithful to Kazan's original production. Yet this revival ended up being an icon revisited but not recaptured. John Simon declared the production a "triumph of miscasting, misdirecting, wholesale butchery."[33] While extreme, Simon's sentiments were echoed by most critics, excluding Clive Barnes, who welcomed the revival with a "staging definitive for our time." Lange and Baldwin were clearly mismatched. As Alex Witchell quipped, "Ms. Lange got slammed by the critics. Mr. Baldwin got kissed." According to William A. Henry III, "the real fault lies with the director." Mosher's *Streetcar* was attacked for its "lack of poetry and passion" (Edwin Wilson). Linda Winer observed that Mosher was so "determined to avoid cheap emotional cliches that he let tension drain away altogether." A longtime director of David Mamet's plays, both at Chicago's Goodman Theatre and on Broadway, Mosher was adept at directing less poetic and more sparse scripts and he was "not at his best directing women" (Howard Kissel). Ultimately, Mosher's revival was reduced to a "museum piece" (Frank Rich). Even Ben Edwards's conventional set, attempting to evoke Kazan's triumph, looked more like the South Bronx than the French Quarter (Simon).

Sexy, blonde, and widely acclaimed for her films, Jessica Lange appeared highly appropriate for Blanche. But in this revival – her Broadway debut – she had difficulty making the transition from the world of film to that of the stage. She lacked "stage technique" (Rich) and "remain[ed] a cinematic creature" (Winer). Her performance ran counter to most revivals: she was a weak Blanche opposite a strong Stanley. Offering a minimalist, non-comunicative Blanche, Lange "moves . . . as if in a somnolent haze. There is no sense of the animation and improvisation of a woman who has . . . spun a web of charm and fantasy . . ." (Wilson). "Defeated from her first entrance" (Kissel), Lange began Blanche's journey already insane. She portrayed

Blanche as a "sacrificial victim" (David Richards), consistent with the screen roles (e.g., Frances Farmer) that made her famous, but she drained power from the role. Rich complained that Lange's Blanche was "weepy" and so "spaced out," she did not project Blanche as either tiger or moth. Lange's delivery was "too soft . . . which upsets the play's verbal balance" (Jack Kroll). She was no match for Baldwin's Stanley, verbally or physically. In fact, she "passes out before Stanley carries her to the bed . . . destroying any . . . complicity in the relationship and undermin[ing] any grander interpretation of Blanche" as "woman or society" (Winer). In underplaying the role, Lange traded Blanche's vitality and mystery for tepid pity.

After Shaw, Baldwin was one of the most successful post-Brando Stanleys. David Patrick Stearns conceded that he was "one of the few actors with the volatility and magnetism to rival Marlon Brando"; and according to Joel Siegel, Baldwin was "excellent . . . raw, tough, and real, his temper comes out of the character." Baldwin was a staunch Brando admirer – "we must have watched *On the Waterfront* 50 times; I loved Brando."[34] Like Brando, Baldwin exuded animal sexuality yet he made Stanley funnier, more ingenious. Baldwin had a Brando-esque violence and vulgarity, wiping his armpits with his shirt and nearly punching a stuck dresser drawer. But he also "side-step[ped]" Brando and the "Williams–Kazan magic" (Simon), which did not please the critics who enshrined Brando. Stearns lamented that Baldwin "clutter[ed] up an otherwise promising interpretation of Stanley Kowalski with tough-guy manners and an accent that sounds more like New Jersey than New Orleans." Fresh from playing in *Married to the Mob*, Baldwin may have carried over some gangster behavior into *Streetcar*. Or maybe he had seen *On the Waterfront* too often. His Bronx-sounding accent disturbed many, yet in retrospect Brando's own dialect echoed some New York pronunciations.

Baldwin was less menacing than earlier revival Stanleys. In Rich's view, he "comes across as an ingenious, almost-innocent working stiff," and Douglas Watt concluded that Baldwin's tantrums "seemed more like those of a streetkid than a hard-working . . . hard-drinking grown man." Labeling Baldwin's Stanley as "more unconventional," Barnes judged him as "almost sympathetic . . . [yet] as brutal, aggressive but quite low on sexual energy. This vulgarian Stanley is also a victim. . . ." Doubtless, Baldwin was limited by Lange's Blanche. Thirty-four at the time, Baldwin was ten years younger than Lange, just the right spread of years between the mighty opposites. Yet the sparks did not fly, the volcano of passion did not erupt. There were no "layers of [Blanche's] personality for Baldwin's Stanley to rip through" (Rich).

Amy Madigan's Stella turned in a "virtuoso" performance, upsetting and upstaging the traditional balance in the play. Of the three leading roles, Madigan's was "most on target" (Winer), clearly eclipsing Lange's Blanche. Not the naive younger DuBois sister escaping a decadent aristocratic past, Madigan played Blanche's sister "as if she were a cracker . . . poor white trash" (Kissel), a "comic female redneck" (Simon). Such an interpretation opens up new possibilities for a Stella successfully engaged in Kowalski enculturation. Timothy Carhart was "woefully miscast" (Henry) as Mitch. He did not look the part; he was "too slender" (Winer) and his "boyish appeal" (Stearns) did not fit the oafish character of Mitch. In fact, Carhart inappropriately played a "glamorous" Mitch, and "Glamour . . . is the last thing you want of Mitch" (Richards).

Dublin 1998

From 5 May through 27 June 1998 *Streetcar* was performed at Dublin's historic Gate Theatre, a small 370-seat house. This revival of *Streetcar*, divided into two acts lasting two hours and forty minutes, was directed by Robin Lefevre, costumed by Michael Kross, and designed by Allen Moyer. It starred Liam Cunningham as Stanley, Frances McDormand as Blanche, John Kavanagh as Mitch and Donna Dent as Stella. The cast in this revival featured an actor who had previously played a different role in *Streecar*: Frances McDormand had been Stella to Blythe Danner's Blanche in the

Circle in the Square production in 1988 (Interestingly, Marcello Mastroianni first played Mitch and then two years later was Stanley; Rudy Bond was the original Steve but became Mitch opposite Tallulah Bankhead in 1956.) Overall, the Dublin revival won mixed reviews. Matt Wolf claimed that "it might almost qualify as revisionist if it were not so off base" while David Nowlan argued that the production remained "emotionally precise and deeply telling." [35]

As in other revivals, Blanche makes or breaks the show. McDormand won much praise for her 1990s portrayal of Williams's southern belle. Susannah Clapp maintained that she brought "a modern sensibility to the play . . . she is statuesque, purposeful, deep voiced, and funny." But in her contemporaneity, McDormand revised the role to the consternation of critics wanting a moth-like, softer Blanche. McDormand's Blanche was bold, resolute, pragmatic, evoking sympathy for the character in ways substantially different from Tandy's, Leigh's, or even Lange's interpretation. In McDormand's representation Blanche "never unravels . . . she is too self aware" (Wolf). According to Luke Clancy, "She reins in the madness and offers instead a sharp, intelligent character who has . . . had the most appalling run of bad luck." Her "decline" was far less "inevitable" than that of earlier Blanches, since she was given not to "melting or wheedling" (Clapp) but to aggressiveness, onslaught. McDormand was all too convincing in her love of drink and sex, especially the latter. She touched Stanley's bare chest, planted a voluptuous kiss on the paperboy's mouth, sexualized aggressively before Mitch, and rubbed her knee against the doctor's as he takes her away. A Blanche far more in control than earlier Irish audiences had been accustomed to, McDormand, according to John Peter, showed that her "Every movement . . . every gesture, suggest[ed] power." Not only did director Lefevre emphasize Blanche's sexuality but his production, according to Nowlan, did "not flinch from the homosexual core of the central drama."

The other Irish actors in this revival also altered traditional representations of Williams's characters. Nowlan claimed Stanely was "more of an Irish farmer than the American son of Polish immi-grants." Cunningham's Stanley lacked "sexual swagger" for Clapp and his "sneering wiseacre" replaced Stanley's "brutish charisma with mere sarcasm" for Wolf: shades of Jon Voight and Aidan Quinn! This Irish Stanley was not the imminent threat that Brando or Baldwin posed for Blanche. Irish wit and verbal maneuvering were Cunningham's strengths. Kavanagh's portrayal of Mitch, on the other hand, was gruffer, more overbearing than earlier Mitches had been. According to Wolf, he "makes an unusually creepy gravelly Mitch," illustrating a performance phenomenon of Mitches growing stronger as Stanleys become weaker. Donna Dent's Stella drew support from the Dublin critics. Nowlan asserted that "The most effective perfor-mance . . . came from Dent . . . torn between the increasingly difficult balance between her love of Stanley and her love of Blanche." Clancy, however, dismissed her character as a "piece of emotional driftwood," since her Stella was unable to understand the tragedy unfolding before her, which perhaps may be Stella's new spine in a world of stronger Blanches, weaker Stanleys. Dent's Stella lacked Kim Hunter's amorous fervor, and her admonitions to Stanley carried little bite.

Moyer's set reflected Dublin architecture more than New Orleanian. Although the interior of the Kowalski apartment looked suitably crowded and despoiled, the "red brick" exterior resembled a "suburban (Irish) community" (Clapp).

The lesson of this Irish revival was that, as decades roll by, Williams's characters are evolving into radically different personalities than those witnessed by audiences and enshrined in the critical canons of the 1940s and 1950s. In this revival, as in others we have seen, Blanche is harder, blunter, and more aggressive while, corre-spondingly, Stanley flexes his brawn and sexual power less vigorously and often, the brute charisma of an Alec Baldwin or a Martin Shaw being the exception.

CHAPTER FOUR

RECASTING THE PLAYERS: EXPANDING AND RADICALIZING THE *STREETCAR* SCRIPT

Up to this point we have examined national premieres and revivals of *Streetcar* that have, for the most part, accepted the traditional ideologies of race – Eurocentric – and gender – heterosexual – upon which the Broadway premiere was based. But there is a vital counter production history of black and cross-gendered performances of Williams's play that foreground issues of race, ethnicity, and gender in provocative ways. The multivocal nature of Williams's text in terms of gender and ethnicity demonstrates how "canonical" theatre texts, on which a performance tradition has been built, can be reinterpreted and revitalized by new modes of performance. Since the mid-1950s, black and multi-racial productions of *Streetcar* have enlarged the boundaries of Williams's script, liberating it from the racially imposed constraints of a white theatre culture. Although these productions have too often been neglected or marginalized, they encode racial and political signs in the (sub)text of Williams's play that white productions ignored or were incapable of representing. In fact, these signs would never be privileged in a traditional (white) production because of the historical limits and possible preconceptions of the directors, actors, and audiences. White theatre history has been, a priori, the standard by which productions of *Streetcar* have been measured. Yet black productions free the play from so-called "prototypical" or "seminal" interpretations of roles played by white actors. Black and multi-racial productions reveal valid, alternative ways of representing humor, characterization, community, cultural anxieties, and even tragedy in *Streetcar*.

As black productions have expanded the *Streetcar* script racially, cross-gendered productions have liberated it from the stereotypes of heterogeneity. In rehearsals of the Broadway premiere, Williams himself played the Mexican woman for Kazan to see how new changes worked.[1] Playwright Megan Terry professed that *Streetcar* could easily be played by all-male or all-female casts.[2] There have been several attempts to perform *Streetcar* in cross-dressed productions. In 1997 an all-male *Streetcar* was performed in Holland. In a spoof, Williams's own brother Dakin took the role of Blanche in a 1993 production in Key West, Florida. Dressed in a "pink plaid dress, white long johns, two glistening strands of pearls and a curly wig," Williams's brother created a "one-person show" by performing a scene from *Streetcar* as Blanche at the Waterfront Playhouse Theatre Festival.[3] A fringe production of Streetcar by Seattle's General Company in July 1991 also demonstrated how elastic Williams's script was in terms of gender representation. As Calvin Bedient observed,

> Blanche was played by a male in drag (the evening began with the actor putting on his make-up and slip and dress at a table in front of the audience.) At moments he was brilliant, far and away the best thing in the show . . . The man and the woman [who] come from the mental home to take Blanche away were dressed . . . for Mardi Gras. Blanche, distraught, ran to the end of the stage/floor where a great sheet of milky plastic was hung from a balcony (her hallucinations had been acted out behind it), pulled it all down on top of her, somehow rolled under it, and disappeared entirely.[4]

But the most historically significant radicalizing of *Streetcar* through gender roles was in the 1991 play *Belle Reprieve*. Written and performed by gay and lesbian actors, *Belle Reprieve* realigned the traditional gendered roles of man and woman as they were represented in *Streetcar* and in the 1951 film version of Williams's play. In the process, *Belle Reprieve* interrogated the political and sexual implications of portraying woman as the object of male desire and man as the indomitable agent of that desire.

Both black and cross-gendered productions of *Streetcar* profitably problematize the issue of ownership of Williams's script. *Streetcar* is not the exclusive right or domain of any specific cultural repertoire.

BLACK AND MULTI-RACIAL PRODUCTIONS

On 14 July 1958 Arthur Gelb reported that a "desegregated 'Streetcar Named Desire' w[ould] begin an off-Broadway" run at the Carnegie Hall Playhouse on 17 September with black actress Hilda Simms as Blanche.[5] Simms was looking forward to playing Blanche, she said, since "most of the plays with roles for Negro actresses are inferior vehicles," and it is "altogether plausible to portray Blanche as a Creole, or of mixed French, Spanish and Negro ancestry." Williams gave his blessing to this "desegregated" *Streetcar* since, according to his agent Audrey Wood, "he has always been an avid admirer of Negro actors." Moreover, Williams permitted some of the dialogue to be changed "to fit the Negro characters." But a week after the projected 17 September premiere of the "desegregated" *Streetcar*, Louis Calta announced that, at Williams's request, this *Streetcar* was to be "shelved" until the following fall because of its "proximity in time to a new play," *Sweet Bird of Youth*, which opened on 10 March 1959. We may never unearth all the reasons why this multi-racial *Streetcar* never opened – financial, technical, Williams's possible apprehension. Speaking again for her client, Wood explained that Williams still considered *Streetcar* with black cast members in the central roles "an advance in relations and I look forward eagerly to it."[6]

Apparently unaware of these plans, Terry Carter of Pied Piper Productions on West 106th Street in New York wrote to Williams on 18 October 1958 "concerning the feasibility of reviving *Streetcar* with a predominantly Negro cast."[7] Carter emphasized that Eli Rill was eager to direct such a production and that Sidney Poitier "expressed a great interest in playing Stanley." Carter argued that "because of many parallels" *Streetcar* would be "easily adaptable to Negro life." For example, a light-skinned Blanche, from Louisiana quadroon society with its class consciousness and decadence, would believably look down on a darker Stanley. Carter further maintained that such a production would require few changes in the script and that it would endorse "Negro theatre." On 22 July Jane Roberts, Audrey Wood's assistant, sent a memo regarding a contract to Carter, and on 6 August Williams himself wrote to Rill, whom he had approved of as director on 26 July, to give his approval to a black *Streetcar*. Though this black production never materialized, Carter's mission was not in vain. Ironically, part of it had already been carried out or would soon be successfully accomplished by a number of black troupes.

Carter's case was well argued. A strong black presence has always inhabited *Streetcar*. Charles Gordone clearly sensed it: "In most of Williams's plays I have always detected the black existential lurking in between the lines."[8] The opening stage direction in *Streetcar* proleptically reads: "New Orleans is a cosmopolitan city where there is a relatively warm and easy intermingling of races in the old part of town." Emphasizing the cultural demographics of Williams's stage direction, a 1989 production of *Streetcar* directed by Ted Haley for the Los Angeles Art Theatre cast black actors Niva Rushcell and Lance Nichols as Eunice and Steve Hubbell, the Kowalskis' upstairs neighbors. *Streetcar* is saturated with a black synesthesia. Evoking the pleasures of sight, sound, and smell, Williams asks us to inhale "the warm breath of the brown river beyond the river warehouses" as if the Mississippi were transformed into a fragrant brown god of fertility. Moreover, "a corresponding air is evoked by the music of Negro entertainers at a room around the corner" where "a tinny piano [is] being played with the infatuated fluency of brown fingers." The honky-tonk music in *Streetcar* suggests the blues, jazz, and other black musical forms. As we saw, Jean Cocteau deeply felt the brown infatuation in his 1949 adaption of *Streetcar* by adding "Negro women dancers," whose pulsating, gyrating movements served as a conventional accompaniment – a racial cliché in fact – to *Streetcar's* intoxicating music of sexuality.

Staging *Streetcar* with an all-black or multi-racial cast offers directors, actors, and audiences advantages, both practical and theoretical. Affirming the universality of the play, a black or multi-racial production shows *Streetcar* to be an inclusive rather than an exclusive work. Moreover, black or multi-racial *Streetcars* have enlarged Williams's script, thus opening the play to racial and social messages not privileged in all-white productions. Of course, the text may have to be destabilized in the process. For example, actors of color doing *Streetcar* necessitate changes in the script, as Williams himself recognized by giving permission to Hilda Simms and others to produce the play in New York in 1958. Such changes reveal that the script can deconstruct racial and social views adhering to it through the traditions of stage history.

Additionally, productions of *Streetcar* with a black or multi-racial cast release Williams's characters from the stereotypes imposed by dominant white productions. On the most superficial level, a Blanche or Stanley of color challenges the received and restrictive notion that all Blanches should look and act like Jessica Tandy or Vivien Leigh and that all Stanleys must imitate Marlon Brando. On a deeper level, a black or multi-racial cast effectively disrupts what Sue-Ellen Case refers to as "cultural encoding":

> Casting blonde women in the roles of ingénues, and dark women in secondary and vamp roles is not based on the demands of the text, but betrays cultural attitudes about the relative innocence, purity[,] and desirability of certain racial features . . . For feminists, these discoveries help to illuminate how the image of a woman on stage participates directly in the dominant ideology of gender.[9]

Casting Blanche as a white Southern belle in the tradition of a debauched Scarlett O'Hara via Vivien Leigh or as a destitute aristocrat like Claire Bloom perpetuates cultural encoding, revealing the prejudices of the dominant white culture. Seeing Blanche as a Creole, for example, is entirely consistent with Williams's text and can easily be accommodated in production, as Terry Carter pointed out. Certainly Stanley does not have to be Polish to be Blanche's ravaging executioner and Stella's husband. Given the opportunity to portray Blanche, actors of color have interpreted the role from a black perspective, expanding both an acting tradition and the critical canons based upon that tradition.

Jefferson City, Missouri, 1953

Perhaps the first all-black *Streetcar* was done by the Summer Theatre Company at Lincoln University in Jefferson City, Missouri, on 3–4 August 1953, a historically black college. This *Streetcar* was directed by Thomas D. Pawley, a former classmate of Williams's at Iowa, and included professionals and students alike. Blanche was played by Carolyn Hill Stewart; Shauneille Perry, an acting instructor from North Carolina Agricultural and Technical College, was Stella, and another teacher, Bertram Martin, was Mitch. Students filled out the rest of the cast with Ray Parks as Stanley. Pawley made no attempt to adapt *Streetcar* for his predominantly black audience, but focused on Williams's presentation of human fallibilities. For Pawley, doing *Streetcar* with an all-black cast was no more daring than doing the play at all in conservative Central Missouri in 1953, where Williams was *persona non grata* because of his earthy subject matter, as Pawley elaborated:

> Staging *A Streetcar Named Desire* in the 1950s on a college campus was both a challenge and a risky venture. Colleagues at neighboring colleges wondered at my gall in doing the play since they dared not attempt it for fear of reprisals by their administrations. One told me that when it was rumored that he was considering a production of the play, a group of Southern ladies advised the president of the college that they would withdraw their daughters from the institution.[10]

Pawley did not need to politicize or change the script to establish its relevance for his audience.

Los Angeles, 1955, 1956

The first professional production of *Streetcar* with an all-black cast was done at Ebony Showcase Theatre in Los Angeles, which staged two productions, one from 19 February 1955 to 10 March 1955, and another in November and December of 1956, two and a half years before Carter wrote to Williams. Ebony was founded in 1949 by Edna and Nick Stewart to stage both Broadway and original plays with black casts. Nick Stewart worked in vaudeville, played at the Apollo and Cotton Club, and appeared (under the name of Nick O'Demus) as Lightnin' in the *Amos 'n Andy* television show. Edna Stewart, his wife, had an equally prominent career on the stage. The fact that Audrey Wood was also Stewart's agent helped make *Streetcar*'s performance at the Ebony possible. Wood sympathized with the Stewarts' desire to showcase black talent in important, serious theatre. In a 1990 interview, Nick Stewart recalled:

> Audrey Wood saw what I was doing at the Ebony to uplift the image in our community . . . and she helped me. I have been in several Broadway shows, and I saw how blacks were, in most cases, presented in the negative, and I thought that we would just do people plays, showing us as people, too. At that time there were no positive roles for black actors, who were cast as buffoons and clowns, images . . . damaging to the black community. Theatre can be used to change such attitudes.[11]

The Stewarts did more than change attitudes; they made theatre history. When they brought *Streetcar* to the Ebony, they did not make any changes for their actors or the audiences. In fact, Nick Stewart was strongly opposed to changing the script for racial reasons: "The play is not black; it is humanitarian. Some plays I have had to bring around, trying to correct attitudes and concepts, but not *Streetcar*. That was a good play." The Stewarts' pioneering *Streetcar*s did not escape notice by those who read them in light of contemporary racial issues. Writing of the 1956 production, Leo Guild observed that the Stewarts "have gathered a fine all-Negro cast to portray the dramatic story of a decadent white South, an ironic twist in these days of problems over segregation . . ."[12]

The Ebony *Streetcar* in February of 1955 was directed by Paul Rodgers and starred Camille Canady as Blanche, Vilmore Schexnayder as Stanley, Shirley Higgenbotham as Stella, and Sylvester Bell as Mitch. The production received strong reviews from both white and black critics. According to Harold Hildebrand, "This all-Negro troupe offer[ed] a vivid and moving portrayal . . . the story, of course, is old hat to most theatre and moviegoers. It [offered] . . . arresting performances necessary to carry it across the footlights."[13] Hazel L. Lamarre, Theatrical Editor for the *Los Angeles Sentinel*, the city's widely read black newspaper, enthusiastically urged readers: "If you like real, stark, heavy drama, be sure to see this one."[14]

Camille Canady stole the show. Katherine Von Blon applauded her "beautifully keyed performance which rose to moving heights in her last scene."[15] Lamarre remarked: "Canady's portrayal of the bewildered school-teacher will long be remembered . . . [her] voice, expression[,] and every gesture [are] in character with the psychopathetic heroine." Hildebrand was similarly effusive: "As Blanche, the talky, coquettish trollop, Camille Canady achieves an acting tour de force. . . . Canady delivers an exacting portrayal with proper shading and seasoned skill." The fair-skinned, fine-featured Canady played an elegant-looking Blanche, which no doubt contributed to the tragedy, for Blanche is notoriously proud about her aristocratic lineage. Canady was an excellent actress who, because of her race, was denied many parts in Hollywood.

Canady's co-star Vilmore Schexnayder did not receive the same unqualified praise. As Hildebrand warned, Canady "lets it be known that the role of Stanley Kowalski is not the most important." While Hildebrand did concede that Schexnayder's Stanley was "properly frank, loud, and carnal," others, including Lamarre, found him overbearing, perhaps imitating Brando too zealously: "Schexnayder's interpretation of the rough and rugged Stanley is, in our opinion, a little too rough and might be toned down" (3 March 1955). Readily deceived by Blanche's wiles and haughty airs, Sylvester Bell's Mitch was too easily her victim.

The second Ebony *Streetcar*, which opened on 28 November 1956, was staged because of the popular demand generated by the earlier production. It offered a new director, John Blankenship, and an all-new cast, except for Canady as Blanche. The critics raved about this repeat *Streetcar*. Wylie Williams asserted that the black cast could represent Williams's characters just as well as a white one could: "The play . . . is distinctive for its excruciating delineation of character – so much so that Stanley Kowalski is a household word for brute and Blanche DuBois is the epitome of a Southern aristocrat . . . James Edwards and Camille Canady do a highly creditable job of imperso-nating the hunter and his adversary."[16] The implication was that white actors did not have exclusive claim to Williams's characters. Kap similarly applauded the "valiant efforts of some of the cast," but found the new, larger Ebony at odds with the intimacy the play needed.[17] As in the earlier Ebony *Streetcar*, Canady stole the critics' praise. White critics were effusive. Leo Guild exclaimed that Canady's Blanche was "as good as you will ever see portrayed,"[18] and David Bongard praised her experience in the part: Her "successive playing of [Blanche] has brought into sharp focus the pathetic lights and shadows of the role."[19]

Hailed as "Hollywood's most popular Negro actor,"[20] Edwards brought a host of credits to the part of Stanley. Critics differed, though, in their opinions of his performance. Hazel Lamarre found him "thoroughly convincing as the bestial husband of Blanche's sister,"[21] and David Bongard claimed that Edwards was "ideally suited" to play the "brooding hulk" Stanley.[22] While acknowledging that what Edwards "lacks in physical requirements he is able to make up in acting prowess," Guild accused him of not being "quite tough or rough enough for the part of Stanley."[23] For Von Blon, Edwards's acting prowess was uneven, and the actor a bit reticent to get into the role. "The dynamic James Edwards did not come into his full stride until the last act when the full sweep of his power was felt."[24] Whatever his limitations, when Edwards and Canady faced each other "the pair really set sparks in their key scenes" for Bongard. Unquestionably, Edwards created a different, more subtle Stanley than that portrayed by Schexnayder, or Brando.

Also winning the critics' respect was Isabelle Cooley, who played Stella. A veteran actress who had recently done *Anna Lucasta*, Cooley was appreciated for her warmth, sincerity, and rich voice: "Cooley seems to be the only normal, well adjusted person on stage. She has good stage movements and is thoroughly believable as she tries to balance the personalities of the other two."[25]

Nick Stewart's dream of having his theatre change attitudes was surely realized when *Streetcar* was staged at the Ebony. *Streetcar* had crossed the color line.

West Berlin, 1974

A 1974 German production of *Streetcar* with a black Stanley (Günther Kaufmann) deserves more credit for what it showed as a failure than for what it contributed to the achievements of a black theatre aesthetic. Staged by the Free People's Theatre (Freie Volksbühne) in West Berlin in July 1974, and directed by Charles Lang, this production sparked a professional and legal controversy. The premiere, planned for 26 June, was prevented by the Supreme Court of Berlin, which slapped a restraining order on the Free People's Theatre, declaring that "performance was forbidden by request of the author." A story in the *Frankfurter Rundschau* reported that Williams as well as his German publisher – Kiepenheuer – objected to Kaufmann's playing Stanley and to Lang's cuts and changes to the ending of the play.[26] In Lang's version, the roles of the Mexican Woman, Eunice, and the Negro Woman were omitted and in Scene 10 Blanche supposedly took great pleasure in the rape (Ronald Holloway).

After considerable wrangling, Lang proposed a compromise with

Williams's publisher on 11 July 1974, by which Kaufmann would be allowed to play Stanley Kowalski provided he put on make-up that would give the impression he was white and wear a wig to make his dark, curly hair appear straight.[27] Lang's proposal deserves comparison with Bottom's view of theatrical illusion in *A Midsummer Night's Dream*. Although Maria Sommer, the representative for Williams's publisher, "rejected this Lang idea as a farce and a mockery of copyright,"[28] the court allowed the Free People's Theatre to stage *Streetcar*, provided Lang reinstate the omitted scenes and restore Williams's ending. Happily, Kaufmann never appeared in white face. Further, Lang had to pay a fine of 2,000 marks and a fee of 650 marks per performance.[29] The total sum turned out not to be terribly oppressive: Lang's *Streetcar* ran for only five closed performances for subscribers to the Free People's Theatre and then four public ones.

Lang strongly denied the charge that his production was based on racism. Yet "the cover of the playbill show[ing] a photo from . . . *King Kong* with the . . . gorilla . . . holding a white woman . . . obvious[ly] belies his denial."[30] On balance, German objections to a black Stanley Kowalski may have been motivated by considerations of race as well as concern over the sanctity of Williams's script. Kaufmann was an apt choice for his looks if not his speech, as Figure 7 shows. What may have troubled Germans, too, about Lang's casting Kaufmann as Stanley was that such a decision required fundamental changes in the *Streetcar* script, a play Germans knew extremely well. Ultimately, perhaps, German audiences may have regarded a black actor as another unjustifiable "experiment" by director Lang to draw attention to his work, which seems to be the reasoning behind Roland H. Wiegenstein's assessment that

> No one really understands why the Free People's Theatre picked *Streetcar*. Evidently Lang had intended a restructuring of a rather private conflict into a racial conflict. Even so it meant doing an injustice to the play. He might have given the piece some new and more timely focus. What the Free People's Theatre actually did was an indecisive performance which only approximates *Streetcar*.[31]

7. Scene from 1974 German production of *Streetcar* with a black Stanley (Günther Kaufmann) and white Blanche (Ute Uellner), directed by Charles Lang

In sum, German resistance to an interpretation of *Streetcar* based on racial conflict appears to have been rooted in a very traditional view of the play.

Berkeley, 1983

Race was more directly radicalized in director-playwright Charles Gordone's 1983 revival of *Streetcar* at the American Stage Company in Berkeley, California. The first black playwright to win the Pulitzer Prize (for his 1970 *No Place To Be Somebody*), Gordone had directed productions of *Night of the Iguana* and *Iceman Cometh*. His future wife, Susan Kouyomjian, was the artistic director of the American Stage Company. The first *Streetcar* to be produced in the Bay area in over twenty years, Gordone's production ran from 12 May through 12 June. Consistent with the American Stage Company's goal of developing "a uniquely American idiom for the classics that reflects today's changing social realities,"[32] Gordone cast black (Creole) actor Paul Santiago as Stanley but chose white actors for Blanche (Peggy Linz), Stella (Kate Black) and Mitch (Robert Pierson), as the Berlin production had done. While Gordone was firmly dedicated to an "American Theatre" in which there is "full participation for all of our performing artists," he did not want an all-black cast for his *Streetcar*, but contended that interracial casting with "a Stanley of color seemed more logical and historically correct to most audiences, not to mention the dramatic impact."[33]

Several reviews had incorrectly inferred that Tennessee Williams himself may have told Gordone that a Stanley of color was the best choice for the part. Gordone explained his reasoning for casting a Creole Stanley:

> I never heard Tennessee Williams say that he had originally intended Stanley to be black. Nor have I ever heard Elia Kazan mention it. But I did hear it rumored about in black theatre circles . . .The first time I heard it was by the late Frank Silvera, the well-known black actor in the 1940s and 1950s. Yet Blanche's warning to Stella "not to hang back with

the apes" and other derogatory remarks fit very well with the fact that
Stanley in her institutionally bigoted mind came from "a lower order."

There were those who thought casting Stanley as a black man reinforced the stereotype . . . a black Stanley raping Blanche, a white
woman, could be construed that way. However, the subtle use of a
socially and historically correct mixed-blooded Creole gives some
defense to the contrary. In most cases of rape it was "a power thing"
more than the sexual which gave the act a deeper meaning socially and
psychologically.[34]

To accommodate a Stanley of color, Gordone deleted references to
Stanley's being Polish and dropped the name of Kowalski. A Creole
Stanley, after all, would be a far more likely resident of New Orleans
in the 1940s (Williams's time frame) than a white Pole named
Kowalski.

Generally speaking, the critics approved of Gordone's decision.
Steve Jensen auspiciously noted, "Gordone's production . . . doesn't
suffer too badly by comparison to a legendary Broadway production
and a famous film version universally regarded as a four-star
classic."[35] Most reviews endorsed Santiago's Stanley, as did the
California Voice: "Santiago superbly portrays Stanley, creating a character filled with animal passion and human warmth . . . together
Santiago and Kate Black sizzle, creating an undercurrent of sexual
tension."[36] This is exactly the effect Gordone wanted. "Stanley is a
good-looking Creole with working class drive and brute sensuality,"
claimed Linda Aube.[37] Casting Santiago as Stanley was an encouraging sign to A. J. Está, who maintained that the actor allowed *Streetcar*
to "take on an even more tangled dimension and open up some unex-
plored aspects of this marvelous work." While Está found Santiago
"physically perfect for the role," he objected to the mumbling,
perhaps imitating Brando's speech.[38] The only strong objection to
Santiago came from Steven Winn: Stanley was "played by a type-
defying Creole, Paul Santiago, who suggests neither brutish silences
nor menacing sexual calculations that . . . precipitate Blanche's . . .
undoing."[39]

Santiago's Stanley and Peggy Linz's Blanche penetratingly enacted Gordone's racial/social/sexual message in *Streetcar* without distorting Williams's original intention. Under Gordone's direction, Linz performed Blanche as a Southern belle who was "at the same time, a charming bigot, an erudite patrician, a scholar, and a sexually starved individual treading a tightrope toward insanity."[40] The black Santiago significantly highlighted, and drew out, Blanche's multiple roles in ways no white actor could. Imagine the "absolute horror that Blanche (an aging Southern Belle who represents the passing of the Old South) feels when she discovers her brother-in-law" is a Creole, observed Está.[41] As Aube emphasized, "Stella's marriage to a non-white, lower-class, poor 'animal' is almost more than Blanche can bear, and Blanche's uppity attitude makes Stanley act even uglier and increases his desire to hurt her, which is inevitable."[42] In keeping with the "socio-economic framework" of this production, Blanche, as a representative of the Old South, carries with her "a value system grounded in oppression," as Gordone stressed.[43] Sympathy for this Blanche waned.

Blanche's sexual attraction to a Creole Stanley, the outsider, demonstrates how radically the subtext of *Streetcar* interrogates issues of gender and race. As Gordone pointed out, "Blanche's 'hang back with the apes' speech expresses a frighteningly literal prejudice."[44] Gordone's *Streetcar* thereby counteracted the hallowed critical view of this speech that places it next to Hamlet's "What is man" soliloquy as a paean to civilization. As Jensen insightfully concluded, "The discipline of the American Stage's careful production wipes away the encrustations of familiarity and allows Williams' great gifts for metaphor, humor, and strikingly original observation to shine anew."[45] Gordone's multi-racial cast empowered him to represent Williams's classic in profitably new and provocative ways.

New Orleans, 1984

A significant all-black *Streetcar* was done by the Dashiki Project Theatre at the Contemporary Arts Center in New Orleans from 1 through 18 November 1984. Celebrating its sixteenth anniversary, Dashiki assembled an excellent cast – the well-known Hollywood actor (and New Orleans native) Harold Sylvester as Stanley; Barbara Tasker, one of Dashiki's founding members, as Blanche; Gwendolyn Fox as Stella; Harold Evans as Mitch – which was directed by Theodore E. Gilliam, another of Dashiki's founding members. Gilliam did not stage *Streetcar* primarily to make a statement about race, though racial considerations played a tactical role in his production. "The conflict in *Streetcar* between Blanche and Stanley is universal," he stressed.[46] As Richard Dodds affirmed, "That Blanche could be black is reasonable; no race has a monopoly on shattered dreams."[47] Gilliam did not see *Streetcar* as "a white play. I see it more simply as an American work. We don't give enough attention to the fact that Americans, regardless of their backgrounds or complexions, are Americans with common experiences that cross all barriers."[48] In his note in the playbill, though, Gilliam observed that "In this *Streetcar* we have tried to remain faithful to the spirit of Williams's play. It is not intended to be *Streetcar* in blackface, but a rendering of the play from a black perspective."[49]

Staging *Streetcar* from a black perspective, however, necessitated changing the script. Dashiki altered a few phrases that seemed particularly white, especially of local place names, to make them consistent with the all-black cast. Stella and Blanche go to Mule's, not Galatoire's, for dinner; and Stanley talks about the Dryades YMCA, a traditionally black Y in New Orleans.[50] Moreover, "reference to the number of an army unit [was] changed to an actual black unit, and Stanley's bowling alley [was] given the name of an alley that catered to blacks during the 1940s."[51] Leaving Blanche as the owner of a plantation in Mississippi strained the critics' credulity, though. Gilliam maintained, however, that there were some slight changes in referring to the plantation, even though "there were several actual instances where a black person or family could inherit a plantation. Although a black plantation is rare, it is not implausible."[52] Recall Terry Carter's justification of a Creole Blanche from quadroon society. Fran Lawless found the plantation to be the only "flaw in this production," even though Blanche tried to "minimize the image" by explaining that it was just one house with columns and a few acres of land, the possibility is "highly unlikely." Lawless added: "The director could have expanded on the plausibility . . . had he added . . . such a predicament, that of a black female plantation owner, to Blanche's other problems."[53] Edward Real was more troubled by the plantation's being in Mississippi, a state which "hardly had the tradition of 'free people of color' that Louisiana did."[54] References to the plantation were as troublesome for critics as the allusions to Allen Grey's homosexuality were to the censors in the early 1950s.

A black *Streetcar* for many New Orleans reviewers seemed "radical" or "surprising," yet they thought it succeeded. The transition from an all-white to an all-black cast was not frustrated by Williams's script but actually aided by it, according to Richard Dodds: "most of the time, the Kowalski household at 632 Elysian Fields is right at home in a black environment . . . almost stereotypically so."[55] Edward Real similarly asserted that "there is much here that reflects the black experience, or at least popular notions of that experience," including "Stanley's self-consciously macho bearing, the domestic passions and violence of the Kowalski's [sic] and their neighbors, [and] the strong matriarchal influence in Mitch's family."[56] Although Gilliam conceded that Stanley and Stella's relationship may "resemble the stereotypical black family," he did not wholeheartedly endorse such a view.[57]

Harold Sylvester's reputation dominated the production, making the Dashiki *Streetcar* Stanley's play. A graduate of Tulane and a veteran of the Free Southern Theatre, Sylvester received garlands of publicity in the local press. Creating a Stanley far different from that portrayed by other actors, including Brando's, Sylvester acknowledged: "It's a real challenge to develop a character . . . a lot different from yourself . . . I'm not as mean and hateful as Kowalski is."[58] And in a profile on him in the New Orleans *Times-Picayune*, Sylvester explained: "Stanley is very raw, very different from my own personality. . . . I never [before] played a bad guy." In a *Times-Picayune* interview, Gilliam confessed: "I'm doing as much as possible to steer him away from that all-American image."[59] Yet Sylvester's Stanley was no mere brute, no ape to hang back with but more subtle, more sullen. As N. R. Davidson perceived, "You are aware of an animal cunning at work – alongside the spiteful child his character is."[60] Unlike Brando, Sylvester did not swagger or mumble; he injected considerable tenderness and wit in the role.[61] Sylvester was less muscular than Brando, as Marian Orr observed: he is "not the menacing, seductive, Marlon Brando type . . . just a straightforward guy who gets sweaty and likes his poker night . . ."[62] For Lawless, Sylvester's Stanley was a "blue collar Everyman." Although Sylvester was still a menacing presence, the rape seemed "less the brutal act that it is, and more an act of destiny."[63] Commenting on the warmer and darker sides of Sylvester's Stanley, Davidson warned, "there is a malevolence lurking behind his humor."[64]

Barbara Tasker's Blanche was less effective than Sylvester's Stanley, owing perhaps to Sylvester's experience. Though she may have begun as a wronged Southern lady, according to Orr, Tasker changed from that role "fairly abruptly" into a "real manipulator."[65] Correspondingly, Real found that, in Tasker's interpretation, "Blanche's airs are more the result of deliberate pretense and fantasy than of an actual declining aristocracy."[66] Lawless faulted Tasker's Blanche for not being amorous enough: "She carries off the image of the prima donna but fails to move the audience as the femme fatale."[67] Tasker's voice and gestures contributed significantly to a tougher Blanche. Davidson, for example, concluded that Tasker's "hoarse/husky voice seems to take her away from Blanche at times."[68] When asked how Tasker's Blanche compared with Tallulah Bankhead's, Gilliam laughed and said, "No, not that aggressive."[69] While Tasker may have been a more forceful Blanche than other actors, nothing in Williams's script forecloses such an interpretation. In fact, Tasker's Blanche was consistent with Gilliam's projection of the role. A black Blanche brought a different, albeit valid, response to the role, inviting audiences to rid themselves of expectations of a prototypical Blanche based on the mannerisms of leading white actors.

Chicago, 1987

A more racially aggressive production of *Streetcar* with an all-black cast was presented by the Black Ensemble at the Leo Lerner Theater in Chicago from 21 February through 29 March 1987. Directed by Marianne Zuccaro, it starred Jackie Taylor as Blanche, Darryl Manuel as Stanley, Bellary Darden as Stella, and David Barr III as Mitch. Taylor, who founded the Black Ensemble in 1976, was the driving force behind the Black Ensemble's *Streetcar*. Sid Smith summed up many critics' reactions: "The all-black casting proves no problems."[70] As Dashiki had done, the Black Ensemble perceptively interpreted Williams's *Streetcar* from an African American perspective. Before the play opens, audiences heard Billie Holiday music and during the production "occasional uses of a smoky blues score help[ed] set the right mood." Stanley and Stella "represent the real, seamy side of life, as well as the prototypes of the ordinary lower class household. As a black family melodrama, *Streetcar* falls right into place." The critics thought that more humor went into this production than in corresponding white ones. Manuel's Stanley was praised for being quite funny, and the neighbors' "indulging in a bit of funk br[ought] new life to their short atmospheric bits." As in other black productions, references to Stanley's Polish ancestry were dropped.

Jackie Taylor's extraordinary performance as Blanche represented the company's most formative statement about racial issues in *Streetcar*'s subtext. A Chicago native, Taylor grew up in the Cabrini Green housing projects on the near south side of the city, a heritage that lay behind her production:

> I've wanted to do this ever since I read *Streetcar* . . . I don't look at this in just black and white terms. But when I read the play I see a lot of it from the black perspective. It's a tragic story, but it's one that in some ways

we're still living today, especially from the viewpoint of the black woman.[71]

Taylor's feminist view of contemporary black history erased the kinds of (white) historical clashes that had dominated *Streetcar* since it premiered in 1947. Taylor played Blanche not as a faded, pretentious belle but as a "ghostly figure of fantasy and lost hope," the victim of a terrifying past and horrifying present. Concentrating on Blanche's mental deterioration, Taylor abandoned "the drippy belle mannerisms" that had undone many Blanches.[72] The "coquettishness, the sparkling flashes of wit, and the undiminished vanity [we]re kept quite low key," reported Hedy Weiss.[73] As if filtering Williams's play through the works of Adrienne Kennedy, Taylor created a Blanche who "c[a]me off fresh, her madness rooted in deeper psychological imbalance and horror." And drawing on a repertoire of nuances from her African American heritage, Taylor became a "kind of jazz actress who brings a truckload of styles and feelings to her many scenes."[74] Weiss, however, found Taylor too "severe" and "unyielding" – "This is a Blanche with a considerably tougher surface than one has come to expect: more brittle and belligerent than sexually provocative, more overtly bruised and angry."[75] Taylor's relationship with Stanley may have been less steamy but perhaps more realistic. While Tandy, Leigh, or Bloom may have modulated the aggressive side of Blanche's nature, Williams's script allows black actors such as Taylor and Tasker the freedom to emphasize the feistiness of the character as a woman much wronged. Such an interpretation certainly has sociological roots in poor black communities, such as Cabrini Green, where women have to be strong to survive and keep families alive. On aesthetic grounds, too, a more forceful Blanche deepens our appreciation of *Streetcar* as a feminist tragedy.

If Weiss was disappointed by Taylor's low levels of sexual energy, Manuel's Stanley was hardly perceived as a sex symbol. Weiss herself acknowledged that the "lack of sexual tension in this production [wa]s partly the result of Manuel's portrayal of Stanley." Though Manuel was cocky, had a "rich, vibrant voice," and was a good man for Stella, "he was no match for Blanche . . . too boyish and direct."[76] Manuel's Stanley lacked "the brutishness and sexual magnetism the part requires."[77] He more than met his match with Taylor's matriarchal Blanche.

Thanks to Taylor, the Black Ensemble *Streetcar* became a black feminist tragedy that did not need to oppose the traditionalism of Blanche's Southern aristocracy against Stanley's upstart Polish heritage to make the play work. The Black Ensemble's interpretation may have struck a rather strange historical chord for Weiss, making *Streetcar* "narrower and more personal in its focus – and somewhat difficult to place."[78] Yet this *Streetcar* situated the tragedy in the center of the black community that identified closely with its protagonist.

Washington, DC, 1988

A production of *Streetcar* done at Howard University in 1988 provided an overtly political performance of the script by a black theatre company. Presented from 10 March through 19 March in the university's small (sixty-seat) Experimental Theatre, this *Streetcar* featured an original rhythm-and-blues score by Thomas A. Korth. The production enjoyed a double cast of student actors. Blanche was alternately played by Andrea Hart and Robin McClamb, Stanley by Omar C. Coubourne and Mason Carmichael, and Mitch by Mason Carmichael and Ernest R. Mercer. Wendy D. Davis had the role of Stella all to herself. There were two student directors as well – Courtney Long and Danielle Peake. Vera Katz, the faculty director, was determined to stage a *Streetcar* with a highly charged set of conflicts for her predominantly black audience. Like Taylor, Katz departed from a conventional *Streetcar* polarizing the aristocratic Old South and the aggressive North and instead used Williams's play to declaim "intraracial racism." As Katz wrote in the playbill,

> We are attempting to bring you a new message . . . Our production
> focuses on the clash of class (education and background; French Creole

versus Gullah) and the clash of color (light-skinned versus dark). "People have to learn to tolerate each other's differences," says Stella . . . Traditions of Black people may vary; gradations of color may bring forth different hues, but the commonality of race is an ever binding factor that cannot be destroyed.[79]

Elaborating on the ways Katz's production developed color prejudice, Renée Simmons, the Howard acting coach for this *Streetcar*, supplied the following assessment in her "Notes on Creole & Gullah," also in the playbill:

> For this *Streetcar*, Blanche is not only a Southern belle but also a descendant of the "coloured" French Creoles . . . Many had large plantations, like Belle Reve, and some even owned slaves. They took pride in their ability to emulate the habits and social graces of their white counterparts. Many considered themselves "superior" to other Blacks because of their French heritage. Stanley, on the other hand, is no longer a Polish American, but is from the Sea Islands off the coast of South Carolina where they speak Gullah . . . a creolized form of English with survivals from many African languages spoken by slaves who were brought to South Carolina and Georgia during the 18th century . . . These independent slaves isolated themselves and were able to maintain much of their African heritage.[80]

To accommodate her interpretation attacking race polarization, Katz changed the characters' ethnic backgrounds and overall motivation. She daringly dislodged the traditional sympathy audiences acquire for Blanche and their animosity for Stanley. In her productions these two characters reversed symbolic places, but for reasons far different than in Kazan's directing of Brando in 1947. Blanche was no longer the weak victim whose refinement and tastes were seen as charming and whose mournful nostalgia was pitiable. Rather, she became the arrogant Creole, guilty of double racism, a negative rendition of what Carter saw as a strength in 1958. She acquired the prejudices of a bigoted white woman toward blacks while she herself was guilty of the prejudice of colorism. In white productions of *Streetcar*, Blanche's high-handed airs, flighty gestures, and self-consciously placed *bons mots* can be charming, comic, supercilious. But in the *Streetcar* Blanche's airs became subversive, as Katz pointed out again in the program note:

> The audience found Blanche to represent racism within the African-American culture which favors those of lighter color than the darker. This is a sensitive topic within the Black community as witnessed in Spike Lee's film *School Daze*, which opened six months after my production of *Streetcar*. Blanche's airs and her visual hostility to Stanley made the audience respond with jeers and titters of awareness of the problem.

In the political subtext of Katz's *Streetcar*, Stanley became Blanche's victim, the sympathetic underdog for the audience. No longer Polish, he's now Stanley Williams with a Jamaican accent approximating the Gullah, a ready target for Blanche's racist snubs. Prejudice against him extended to his lack of formal education which clearly "represented the gap that exists between educated and uneducated blacks" in a city such as Washington, DC, with its large black population.[81] Educational advantages signal economic and political ones as well. Blanche was arrogant because of her educational background (she is an English teacher – a role more playfully interpreted by Leigh). These advantages in the Katz production were grounds for Blanche's exploitation of and alienation from the black community, represented by Stanley. Regrettably, the commonality of race binding the DuBois sisters was destroyed in this *Streetcar*. "We must not follow their paths," asserted Katz.

BELLE REPRIEVE (1991)

Unquestionably, the most radical response to the *Streetcar* script is *Belle Reprieve*, a queer/camp production, the result of collaboration among Peggy Shaw and Lois Weaver from the lesbian Split Britches and Bette Bourne and Paul Shaw (a.k.a. Precious Pearl) from the London drag troupe Bloolips, "the dowager empress of ideologically

8. Cast of *Belle Reprieve* (1991), a queer/camp adaptation of *Streetcar* with Bette Bourne (Blanche), Precious Pearl (Mitch), Peggy Shaw (Stanley), and Lois Weaver (Stella)

correct high camp" (John Lyttle).[82] Premiering at London's Drill Hall from 1 to 14 January 1991, *Belle Reprieve* moved to La MaMa, an experimental theatre on New York's East 40th Street, for a two-week run during March 1991. Afterwards, the play went to One Dream in TriBeCa in New York. *Belle Reprieve* – a mélange of cross-dressing, tap dancing, risqué songs, farce, bathhouse humor, gay cabaret scenes, vaudeville, and British music hall skits – investigates and challenges the way gender is (re)presented in *Streetcar*. The title puns on Blanche's ancestral home – Belle Reve – to stress the liberation of characters from conventional gender roles. Transgressive role playing was at the heart of *Belle Reprieve*. For example, Mitch (Precious Pearl) is "a fairy disguised as a man"; Stella (Weaver) is "a woman disguised as a woman"; Stanley (Peggy Shaw) is cast as a "butch lesbian"; and Blanche (Bourne) is a "a man in a dress," a drag queen.[83] Through its irreverent approach to sexual roles in *Streetcar*, *Belle Reprieve* used the techniques of camp and butch/femme role playing to "deconstruct the gender relationships in *Streetcar* from a gay perspective" (Rowena Chapman). As Alissa Solomon noted, "*Belle Reprieve* messed with a masterpiece, multiplied combinations of sexual couplings, wrought endless gender [jokes], and rendered hetero licentiousness strange."[84] In radicalizing Williams's script to transform the way audiences think about gendered roles and power in society, *Belle Reprieve* demands comparison with the cross-dressed performers of Kabuki and the Elizabethan boy actors. The audiences that jeered at Bankhead's *Streetcar* in 1956 would have bravely applauded *Belle Reprieve*.

Opinion about this provocative performance piece was, not surprisingly, divided. Wilbourne Hampton in the *New York Times* dismissed *Belle Reprieve* as "a campy drag show," a "musical sendup of" Williams's play, "more sophomoric than sophisticated." John Bell at *Theatre Week*, however, honored *Belle Reprieve* as "a stunning mediation on men and women's social and sexual roles grounded on that fascinating icon of American theatre . . . *Streetcar* . . . [It] ranks . . . with 'new historicist' theories of Foucault." Erika Milvey found the performance "fun – but ultimately irrelevant." Overall, the gay press endorsed the production. John Hammond at the *N.Y. Native*, for example, praised *Belle Reprieve* as "one of the best essays in sexual politics to come along in a decade."

The relationship of *Belle Reprieve* to Williams's play and the 1951 film version is provocative. Hampton asserted that *Belle Reprieve* "uses Williams's play as a point of departure" but that there is "little to connect the two works." Milvey similarly affirmed that *Reprieve* "uses *Streetcar* as a starting point but strays from the source." Yet for Lyttle *Belle Reprieve* makes "many points about Williams's blend of theatre and sexual fantasy." Undeniably, *Reprieve* was not just a gay performance of Williams's play; it was a distinct script under and through which lie many of *Streetcar*'s symbols, sets, and characters, transgressively rendered, of course. Half the length of *Streetcar*, *Reprieve* played for ninety minutes and offered some familiar *Streetcar* scenes – Stanley going through Blanche's trunk; Blanche's suspicion of Stanley and her warning to Stella; Stanley and Stella's steamy sexuality and Mitch and Blanche's (homoerotic) trysts. It also transformed some of Williams's famous dialogue for comic purposes, e.g. drag queen Bourne's Blanche says: "I have always depended on the strangeness of strangers."

Yet *Reprieve* was far more political than parody. It did not so much attempt to play *Streetcar*, even comically, as to invert the sexual stereotypes that the play, and particularly the film, promulgated. The achievement of *Reprieve* was to show "gender's fluidity, its unreliability" and "instability" (Alissa Solomon) that were subtextually present in Williams's script. In the filmed *Streetcar*, for example, Malden's Mitch, the mama's boy, displayed a doubtful masculine identity working in the "spare parts" department; Brando combined macho brutality with feminine qualities; Kim Hunter projected a narcotized sexuality; and Leigh's Blanche was both insistent and volatile. Claire Armitsteed perceptively noted that the time had come not to play *Streetcar* straight, since "Blanche was just waiting for a drag queen to have his wicked way with her" – clothes, pretension, hysteria, and all. Perhaps, too, as Solomon argued, *Belle Reprieve* exteriorized the self-reflexive Williams hidden in *Streetcar*.

Belle Reprieve was true to the tradition of camp where gender is unstable, performative. According to David Savran, "gender is masquerade and all costume is a form of drag." Williams himself took such a view by challenging traditional codes of sexuality in the 1950s with plays that "disrupt orthodox modes of genderization by cutting diagonally across the binary oppositions between masculinity and femininity, heterosexuality and homosexuality."[85] *Reprieve* became the 1990s ultimate radicalization of Williams's disruptions by breaking down and apart any identity based on costume/gender equations. Mitch wears a fairy outfit; Blanche steps out of a tub wearing a bubble dress. The stereotypes of stud and cheerleader, both comically performed in *Reprieve*, are undependable. As Weaver's Stella says to the lesbian Stanley: "Did you figure it out yet? who's who, what's what, who gets what, where the toaster is plugged in?" (*Reprieve*, p. 998).

Shaw's Stanley beautifully illustrated the topsy-turvy world of camp sexuality filtered through *Belle Reprieve*'s encounter with *Streetcar*. Striving to play Stanley as the quintessential stud, this butch lesbian wore a black hat, white T-shirt, and swaggered across the stage, boasting of manhood. In a highly erotic song, "Sweet Little Angel," Shaw's Stanley wooed Weaver's Stella. Parodying the Muddy Waters song, Shaw belted out "I'm a Man" and sang "All you pretty women, standing in a line / I can make love to you in an hour's time." Stanley's speech was filled with bawdy references – "When it comes to big hands I got no competition." Shaw comically tried to outbrave the fairy Mitch with expressions of manhood – Mitch: "I'm gonna eat a tree"; Stanley: "I'm gonna eat the sun and then I'll sweat." Shaw openly compared herself favourably to Brando – "Marlon was not there for me" – yet imitated his patois by adopting a Brooklyn dialect. Her performance mocked Brando's machismo as much as it sought to incorporate it.

But *Reprieve* aggressively sought to redline the fissures in the role, in the genderization of Stanley Kowalski. Radically and comically transforming Blanche's admonition to Stella – "Don't hang back with the apes" – Bourne's Blanche mocks Stanley's manhood. In an outrageous parody of Blanche's impassioned attack on Stanley's brutality, Bourne tells Stella: "The noises he makes, the way he walks like Mae West, the sensual way he wears his clothes, this is no garage mechanic . . . perhaps he was a man in some former life . . . I think he is a fag." There is no hiding behind stereotype here – a drag queen calls a butch lesbian dressed as the macho Kowalski a fag. Gender identity becomes a joke, as do hallowed theatrical conventions which *Belle Reprieve* deconstructs. Intentionally undermining the illusions of her own performative manhood, Shaw self-reflexively confessed as Stanley: "I feel I'm never safe . . . I was born this way. I didn't learn it at theatre school. I was born butch. I'm so queer I don't even have to talk about it." Her Stanley is "afraid of the dark." Rather than raping Blanche, Shaw's Stanley sings a song with Stella at the end of *Reprieve*. Stanley's masculinity in *Reprieve* was patently a disguise.

Like Williams's Blanche, Bourne's drag queen version is a consummate role player. "Only someone as skilled as I am at being a woman can pick up these subtle signs," he tells Stella (999). Using the resources for which Bloolips is famous, Bourne offered a "clownish, almost ethereal drag (and male privilege) to dismiss" the traditional gender system.[86] In key ways, Bourne's Blanche tested and taunted the serious critical pronouncements about Blanche's sexuality – she does exhibit a masculine as well as a feminine side, sometimes both simultaneously. Bourne comically rendered many of Blanche's traits that have most alarmed critics – her pretensions, exaggerations, duplicities, and even aggressions. Mocking such critical strictures, Bourne freed Blanche from narrow gender categories. He transformed Blanche's fictions into drag queen bravura, literalizing pretense by having audiences see the man underneath the frills, the woman masquerading over the male. Blanche may have been "in many ways the quintessential gay character in American closet drama,"[87] yet Bourne exploded the closet walls in comic hyperbole and mocking pathos.

Bourne artfully called attention both to the character and to the actor in "romping about in the avant-garde" (1001), fusing drag performance and film/stage history. "My namesake is a role played by that incandescent star Vivien Leigh, and although the resemblance is not immediately striking I have been told we have the same shoulders" (993). If Bourne's Blanche could have met Brando at the filming of *Streetcar*, "I'd want to lick his armpits" (999). Transvestite bonds with movie star. Borrowing Blanche's famed haunts and props, Bourne exclaims leaving the bathroom: "Thank heavens for bathrooms, they always make me feel new." Blanche's most famous symbol – the Chinese lantern – is radically physicalized in *Reprieve*. As Bourne sings "The Man I Love," three "tap-dancing Chinese lanterns" accompany him. Bourne's sexual encounters with Mitch (Precious Pearl) are scandalously hilarious. She blows smoke in his face and flirts shamelessly with Mitch, who aptly projects his own psycho-biography onto Williams's character – "It all started to go wrong when I wasn't allowed to be a boy scout." Dressed in his fairy costume, Mitch is "behind a scrim . . . perched on a ladder and looking down on Blanche in the tub" as he plays a ukelele and sings "The Fairy Song" promising to be Blanche's "sweetie-pie." Precious Pearl intensified Mitch's reputation among critics for his "unmanly sensitivity, arrested adolescence, even sexual confusion."[88] But the audience's beliefs in conventional gender identities are bombarded with comic confusions here – Blanche the drag queen is both man and woman being wooed by an actor who is both man and fairy. What may have been latent and opaque in *Streetcar*, *Reprieve* disclosed through seething revelations.

At the end of *Reprieve*, Stella and Stanley tell Blanche that she can star in a real play – *Streetcar* – and they begin performing Scene 10. "You want realism, you can have it," Stella assures Blanche. Stanley "squirts" beer all over the stage and, mocking *Streetcar*, calls Blanche a queen who wears "that worn-out party dress from a third-rate thrift store." Instead of a broken beer bottle, though, Blanche lunges at Stanley with "one of her stiletto-heeled shoes" (1002). Ultimately she backs down: "I don't want to get raped and go crazy. I just wanted to wear a nice frock . . ." (1002). *Reprieve* cannot enter the world of *Streetcar* tragedy. It can resist, as well as parody and deconstruct, stereotypical sexual roles that *Streetcar* promulgated, but it must stop there. As Solomon wisely concludes, *Reprieve* says a great deal about how Williams's play has been performed, but in "casting an actual drag queen as Blanche reveals how impossible, flattening it would be to read Blanche as such in a production; it just makes no sense." But it is through senselessness that *Belle Reprieve* succeeded in radicalizing Williams's play.[89]

CHAPTER FIVE

STREETCAR IN OTHER MEDIA

Except for a Shakespearean play, perhaps no other drama has inspired such frequent and widely differing adaptations in other media as *Streetcar* has. Within five years of the Broadway premiere Williams's play became a film and a ballet. In the 1980s *Streetcar* was adapted for television and very close to its fiftieth anniversary, it made history as André Previn's first opera. In each medium, *Streetcar*'s resilient power and appeal were reinterpreted through performance. Film, ballet, teleplay, and opera each uncovered further texts in and contexts for Williams's play

STREETCAR AS FILM

It is not surprising that Williams's award-winning play became a film classic in 1951. *Streetcar* had Hollywood success written all through it. Shot from 14 August through mid November 1950 on location in New Orleans, *Streetcar* was released by Warner Brothers in New York in September 1951, and the following March in London. Williams's sensational subject matter, vivid characterization, and cinematic techniques made *Streetcar* a coveted property for Hollywood producers. Further whetting Hollywood attention, *Streetcar* had already achieved world-wide publicity by premiering in seventeen countries, not to mention productions all across America. Producer Charles K. Feldman acquired the film rights for what the studio billed as "the most exciting Warner screen offering"[1] and persuaded Kazan to direct the film, with an astonishing offer of $175,000.[2] Williams himself went to Hollywood to help with the screenplay, which was adapted for film by

9. Scene from the Warner Bros. film version of *Streetcar* (1951) with Vivien Leigh as Blanche and Marlon Brando as Stanley

Oscar Saul. Warners was fortunate in having most of the original Broadway cast appear in the film, too – Brando (who commanded a salary of $75,000), Malden, and Hunter. Vivien Leigh replaced Jessica Tandy at the studio's insistence. As with Williams's play, the filmed *Streetcar* was costumed by Lucinda Ballard and scored by Alex North.

Streetcar ran for 122 minutes, though in 1993 three "lost" minutes were added in the "Director's Cut" release to include "previously excised tension between Blanche and Stanley and Stella's passion for her husband Stanley,"[3] material deemed too sensational for 1951. Roger Ebert explained that "In 1951, you had to guess at a lot of things that are now made clear,"[4] specifically, Stella's slower, more suggestive descent from Eunice's to Stanley's arms at the end of Scene 3. As the "teaser" (promotional material) for Warner Brothers said in 1951 of Stella: She "took a lot because she loved a lot."

Streetcar was one of the most significant films ever made. The reviewer in *Look* proclaimed: "*Streetcar* now seizes a place among Hollywood's rare great movies." [5] The film won an unprecedented number of Academy Awards – to Leigh for Best Actress, Malden for Best Supporting Actor, and Hunter for Best Supporting Actress. Surprisingly, though, Brando lost to Humphrey Bogart (in *African Queen*) for Best Actor. Set director George James Hopkins and art director Richard Day won Oscars as well. Bosley Crowther declared that the film "becomes as fine if not finer than the play."[6] Even Williams admitted: "This is the first time I have seen a stage play actually increase with stature when transferred to the screen" (Warner publicity). Like the play, the filmed *Streetcar* received immense praise for its innovations. Maurice Yacowar listed some of its "firsts": "It is an invaluable record of a legendary production. It is also something of a landmark in American cinema. It introduced Method Acting to the mass audience and it had the first major film score based on jazz."[7] According to R. Barton Palmer, *Streetcar* was "the first adult film" and "inaugurate[d] a commercial American art cinema."[8] Williams's play readily came to the movies.

Yet censorship hounded *Streetcar* in its film version. Warner Brothers wanted it to receive approval as a family film to ensure a lucrative box office, and in order to do that, it had to be passed by the motion picture Production Code Administration. The PCA, the official censor of the film industry, was headed by the arch-conservative Roman Catholic Joseph Breen, whose charge was to safeguard morality. Because of his immense power the PCA was called the Breen Office. After seeing Saul's adaptation, Breen insisted on "sixty-eight major and minor changes from the Broadway version."[9] Among the most significant were eliminating any reference to homosexuality, getting rid of, or considerably weakening, the rape, outlawing any erotic behavior in either Blanche's conduct (nymphomania) or Stanley's lovemaking with his wife, and punishing Stanley for raping Blanche by having Stella leave him. Interestingly, before Warner Brothers ever acquired the rights to *Streetcar*, Irene Selznick, sensing that *Streetcar*'s explicit subject matter would run into trouble with the censors, commissioned playwright Lillian Hellman to prepare a more acceptable "shooting script" for the film version, but precisely because Hellman's solution to the censorship problems anticipated Breen's – dispensing with homosexuality entirely; making Blanche's marriage problems indefinite; and casting doubt on the rape itself – her script was not used.[10]

As both Kazan and Williams feared, the changes Breen wanted would cripple, even destroy, the artistic integrity of the film. Confronted with the censor's powerful veto, Kazan and Williams "turned the tables and made potentially destructive constraints work constructively in the movie."[11] For example, Allan Grey's homosexuality – directly mentioned in the play when Blanche tells Mitch in Scene 6 that she discovered her young husband in a room with "an older man" – became ingeniously indefinite in Kazan's version. All Blanche says is that the boy "was tender," with the cautiously expressed inference that he was gay. Forbidden to show, or even suggest, a rape, Kazan employed a series of symbols laden with sexual overtones. When Stanley threatens Blanche the camera moves to her throwing a whiskey bottle at him, but missing Stanley, it smashes into a highly decorative mirror. Everything we see from this point is reflected in the broken mirror as Blanche passes out and is picked up into Stanley's arms. Immediately thereafter, in a successive frame we see gushing water from a street cleaner washing away the debris in the gutter in front of the Kowalski house. The blast of water then turns into a drizzle. Kazan commented on this censor-safe adaptation: "Some of the symbolic cutting in the film . . . from the rape to the street cleaner's hose, seems, in retrospect, to be a little too obvious . . .

though I thought it was good at the time. In any event, it was certainly a forceful cut and enabled me to underline the rape implicitly using the phallic symbolism of the hose . . ."[12]

Again obeying the letter but not the spirit of the Breen Office, Williams rewrote the ending to show Stanley's punishment. Rather than have Stanley and Stella embrace, as in the play, Stella runs up to Eunice's after Blanche's departure to the madhouse, whispering to the Kowalski infant in her arms: "We're not going back in there. Not this time. We're never going back." Stella's resolve was considerably weakened, though, when audiences recalled that she escaped one other time from Stanley's to Eunice's – in Scene 3, the night of the poker game – but came down soon after a penitent Stanley shouted her name. No doubt Stanley, the film implied, would be repentant and persuasive again. Williams, however, deplored the censor-imposed ending, claiming: "*A Streetcar Named Desire* was a brilliant film until the very end, when the distortions of the censorial influences made it appear that Stella would no longer live with Stanley because of what had happened to Blanche at his hands . . ."[13]

Kazan ingeniously employed all the resources of the cinema, unavailable in a stage production. Initially intending to open up Williams's play, he decided instead to stick closely to the script but did expand the number of locations to accommodate a cinematic medium and audience. He began the film in a New Orleans train depot where Blanche emerges from a cloud of steam (a proleptic symbol of her ethereal pretensions, softness, and desire for concealment) while a wedding party rushes by her, an ominous sign of what she desires but is denied. She then speaks to a young sailor dressed in white, a fellow sexualized traveler as well as a stranger upon whom Blanche depends for kindness. Instead of using the Kowalski apartment in Scene 1 for the reunion of the DuBois sisters, Kazan transferred the action to a local bowling alley where, amid the wrangle of quarreling men and falling bowling pins, Blanche first sees Stanley, the loud and brutish game player. Kazan moved Scene 6 away from the Quarter to an amusement park on Lake Pontchartrain, as in the play, as Blanche tells Mitch about Allan Grey. The watery setting and the dark ambience of the park conveyed Blanche's tragic nostalgia and Mitch's doomed romanticism. All these places Kazan found mentioned in the script, but at the end of Scene 7 he shifted to a location not even suggested in the play, the factory where Mitch and Stanley work, with its clamorous, almost deafening din of turbines suggesting the impending clash between the two men over Blanche. Kazan interpolated this action to supply relevant background information for a film audience about Stanley's investigating Blanche's past in Laurel.

The way *Streetcar* was shot also displayed Kazan's genius for adapting Williams's play for the screen. Filmed in black and white, *Streetcar* projected a shadowy, even spectral quality emphasizing Blanche's "discomfort in light."[14] Afraid to reveal her age, Blanche is rarely seen in daylight, preferring to stay inside or wait until dark. Kazan surrounded her with soft lights, such as those in Scene 3, contrasting with the lurid light above the poker players in the next room. When Mitch confronts her in Scene 9, Blanche is in a darkened room, "violated by the flickering neon light outside."[15] In one of the most horrific moments in the film, Mitch strips the Chinese paper lantern off the light bulb and holds Vivien Leigh's wrinkle-worn face under the electrifying glare of the naked bulb. As the camera came in for a close-up, Leigh's face showed a level of painful intimacy denied to a stage audience. As Linda Cahir observed, "we sense the sting of the light as Blanche does and we feel the violence against her . . . [the] paper lantern [is] . . . her dual symbol of ruptured purity and the ruptured illusions of purity . . . [while] the plain, hard lightbulb inside of it [is] . . . his symbol . . . "[16] The lantern was Kazan's signature symbol.

Given the wide, continuing audience for Kazan's film, no other actor has been more closely identified with Blanche in the popular imagination than has Vivien Leigh. She received rave reviews. The reviewer for the *New York Mirror*, for example, claimed that she gave "one of the finest performances ever seen on screen."[17] She was the first to attempt the role for a non-theatre audience. Feldman and Jack

Warner themselves selected her for the role because she was uniquely qualified: she had played Blanche in the British stage premiere in 1949. Moreover, having starred in *Gone with the Wind* in 1939, Leigh had the box office appeal that was essential to Warner Bros. Significantly, Leigh played the two most publicized women in Southern culture – Scarlett O'Hara and Blanche DuBois. In fact, her role as Scarlett coalesced with her Blanche.

Leigh got the role over the objection of Kazan, who believed that she would obstreperously introduce Olivier's interpretation in a script Kazan had worked on for four years. His fears proved wrong. Under Kazan's direction, Leigh played a spirited Blanche, though far different from Tandy's or Hagen's. While Olivier brought out a "soft and gentle creature," Kazan wanted a more forceful Blanche "whose tongue was the weapon of a frustrated woman." [18] She successfully combined the two roles, aided by her stylized, classical acting, a "tradition . . . Method Actors rejected." Using this more "full toned acting," Leigh was "pitted against Brando's Method Acting," representing Blanche as "the skilled purveyor of illusion." She did a masterful job of conveying Blanche's theatricality, her many roles. "Thus, in paradox, Leigh's classical acting, thought to be inappropriate, speaks to the essence of Blanche DuBois, and . . . constitute[s] a form of Method Acting."[19] She portrayed Blanche as a sophisticated lady played out – fighting wrinkles and loneliness. Displaying the many sides of Blanche, Leigh was condescending to Stanley, censorious with Stella, arrogant, even dismissive with Mitch. Yet her Blanche could be bitterly realistic, even accusatory with Mitch in Scene 10 and feisty with Stanley in Scene 3 and at the fated birthday party.

Despite Blanche's reputation among the critics – and the merchant Kiefaber – for being a nymphomaniac, Leigh's Blanche was more coy and restrained in her flirting with Stanley, preferring verbal encounters to physical ones, and even guarded in her seduction of Mitch. With the newspaper boy, Leigh was more the poet than the Circean temptress, dripping with magnolia not salivating with desire. Leigh's desire was prophylactically poetic. As Palmer perceptively concluded:

"Significantly Vivien Leigh's body is never eroticized or glamorized in the film."[20] As the Warner publicity claimed, "Blanche did all she could to remain a lady," which was more tease than truth since Leigh never portrayed Blanche as anything but a lady down on her proprieties.

In her representation of Blanche's madness Leigh was haunting. She showed early signs of falling apart when the "Varsouviana" played in Scene 1 and then more agitatedly at the amusement park in Scene 6. When Mitch returned to Stanley's in Scene 9, Blanche's descent into madness became swift, inexorable. Malden's Mitch rightly asks "Are you boxed out of your mind?" When Mitch attempts to rape her, Blanche flies through the house and then outside as if she were pursued by the Furies. Leigh's gestures, the eerie alarm of North's music, and the maddening sweep of the camera were all part of the orchestrated frenzy. In the last scene, Leigh's mad Blanche is fearful, even ashamed, hiding in the bathroom as Eunice and Stella try to coax her out. But then the crescendo of her madness increases. Seeing the doctor and nurse, Leigh again rushes through the house, this time pursued by Stanley, whose words "Do you want to take these bottles with you, Blanche?" are filtered through an echo chamber, taking the audience directly into Blanche's madness. Yet even in defeat, Leigh's Blanche retained her carriage, her aplomb, her innate aristocracy.

If Leigh's desire was poetically cooled, Brando's sizzled red hot, even more so than in the stage production. His film version of Stanley became the palimpsest for many subsequent interpretations (read: imitations). Transferring the techniques of Method acting to the screen, Brando's Stanley was "mean, coarse, violent, and magnificent" (Warner Bros. promotional material). He unleashed all of his passion in ways even more animalistic than on stage. It seemed as though Brando were in a constant rage, a fomenting dynamo, shoving food in his mouth or his hands or fists in people's faces. Most memorable, of course, was Brando in his torn T-shirt, his muscles and strong back even more prominent, and available to audiences, on camera than at the Barrymore. Through Kazan's film Williams made the male anatomy the object of desire, "assuming what is conventionally a female position."[21] Brando's sexuality electrified audiences.

STREETCAR AS BALLET

The first ballet based on *Streetcar* was choreographed by Valerie Bettis and premiered in Montreal at Her Majesty's Theatre on 9 October 1952, with subsequent performances in Boston, Chicago, Cleveland, and St. Louis ("'Streetcar' en Pointe").[22] The Broadway premiere was at the Century Theatre from 8 December 1952 through 3 January 1953. The *Streetcar* ballet was danced by the Slavenska–Franklin troupe, with classic ballerina Mia Slavenska performing Blanche, Frederic Franklin as Stanley, Lois Ellyn as Stella, and Marvin Krauter as Mitch. Bettis received Williams's approval to choreograph his play, and Alex North allowed her to use, with cuts and a smaller orchestra, his score from the Kazan film of a year earlier. The reviewer for *Time* declared this "steamy ballet" to be both "gripping and disturbing." Bettis's work was bold, even radical for the time, hard to define generically yet challenging to see in relationship to Williams's script. John Martin hailed it "a distinguished experiment." Douglas Watt described it as " a lurid piece, its style resembling that of those rambling ballets that keep working themselves into musical films . . ." Blending classic ballet, modern dance, and jazz, Bettis's dance translation projected a frenzied and frenetic mood. "It is directed at your bare nerves. In movement it rarely boasts a completed phrase but twitches its way through – a wilderness of bits and pieces, some of them realistic, some of them symbolic, and all of them afflicted with a technical tic" (Martin). Walter Terry concluded that "violence and desperation are everywhere and haunting sadness, too, in this stunning, explosive creation."

Translating *Streetcar* into ballet provided yet another way to explore and expand Williams's script. A dialogue-less ballet did not necessarily deprive an audience of *Streetcar's* power, poetry, and sexual tension, as Bettis provocatively visualized the way Williams's script could be danced. Louis Biancolli affirmed that "the inner world of Blanche DuBois's twisted fancy is visualized and given life in a way that the spoken word could never duplicate and the tragic division of her mind is carried out in a sustained splendor of symbolism." Although much shorter (only forty minutes) than the play, Bettis's ballet preserved much of its action. According to Watt, "It hits all of the high spots of the original." In Bettis's choreography Blanche's seduction of Stanley and his arousal by her, conveyed in the play through her flirtatious language, became a whirlwind dance in which Stanley and Blanche alternately drew each other closer and then pushed each other farther apart. Stanley's poker game in Scene 3, "accompanied by jaunty, free-style jazz" (Watt), showed pantomime players drawing and throwing cards. Expressing their love at the end of Scene 3, Stanley and Stella danced a sensual *pas de deux* and pirouetted with expansive gestures as an amazed Blanche jealously gyrated alone. In the rape scene, Stanley furiously chased Blanche through a number of shuttered doors, resembling those of New Orleans houses. Peter Larkin's set – a flange of open archways with slatted doors all against a black curtain – emblematically synchron-ized with the *danse macabre* performed by the mad Blanche. These archways were moved on stage throughout the ballet to signal different moods and places.

Bettis's ballet added to an understanding of Williams's script by confronting, translating, and altering it. Most significantly, Bettis told "the story [of *Streetcar*] through the neurotic personality of Blanche, the faded Southern belle, and her shadowy existence between the real and the not real" (*St. Louis Post-Dispatch*, 26 October 1952). Yet Franklin's Stanley, according to many critics, "dominated the ballet throughout" (Terry). As Blanche tells the story of Allan Grey, she escapes into a spirited dance, electrified nervous energy. Bettis added a "dream sequence" in which Blanche danced with two boyfriends, shades of former romantic conquests. When Blanche left at the end of *Streetcar*, it was not with the doctor but with the figure of Death, hauntingly enacted by Karel Williams. And

Bettis choreographed Blanche's famous exit line – "I have always depended on the kindness of strangers" – as a curtsy, an apt signifier of her gentility and grace in triumphant defeat. Bettis's ballet proved that kinesis can be mimetic.

An African American ballet adaptation of *Streetcar* was performed by the Dance Theatre of Harlem (DTH), first in Montreal in October 1981 and then at the City Center in New York in January 1982. Shortly before her death, Valerie Bettis reset her 1952 ballet for the DTH. Dedicated to Williams in honor of his seventieth birthday, the DTH *Streetcar* freely adapted the play by introducing symbolic characters, including Blanche's young husband Allan Grey, and by including flashbacks. Virginia Johnson was Blanche; Lowell Smith was Stanley; Carol Crawford played Stella; and Ronald Perry was Mitch. The DTH redid their *Streetcar* for PBS in February in 1986 in a co-production sponsored by WNET-TV in New York and Dansmark Radio. Filmed in Denmark, this *Streetcar* ballet also ran for forty minutes, as did Bettis's, and again starred Johnson and Smith, with Julie Felix as Stella and Donald Williams as Mitch. A number of reviewers in 1986 asked why the Harlem troupe decided to do *Streetcar* when so many of its works came from African American composers. Arthur Mitchell, DTH's artistic director, responded that "DTH is not a black ballet company. It is a ballet company that just happens to be black" and thus reinforced that "universality" claimed by Williams's play (quoted by Allan Ultich).[23]

Undeniably, the DTH troupe brought a renewed vitality, a true grit, to the ballet – and hence the play. Lewis Segal summed up the reaction of many critics: "Johnson and Smith dance the roles to blazes." In place of Vivien Leigh's impetuously frightened Blanche, Johnson offered a "less ravaged, more willful Blanche" (Segal), whom Nancy Goldner described as "provocative . . . a troublemaker who's out to get Stanley." Unlike Brando's interpretation of the role, Lowell Smith's Stanley was, in Goldner's estimation, in a state of "befuddlement and horror with himself"; he was the "victim" in the DTH's *Streetcar*. Segal concurred: Smith played "an unusually confused

Stanley who is partly victimized by events." On the other hand, while the wordless ballet obviously did not allow Smith to yell Stella's name or shout anything, it would be misleading to dismiss Smith's Stanley as passive or submissive. Reviewing the 1982 production, Anna Kisselgoff emphasized that Stanley grabs Blanche's hanky and wipes the sweat from his body. Like Brando, Smith first wore an undershirt, but it was yellow, and later put on a "bright red windbreaker with a yellow lining." In a jazzy chase sequence, a feverish Stanley, dressed in his red pajamas, pursued Blanche again "through all the portals" of a set of "movable shutters," to suggest different rooms of the Kowalski household (Kisselgoff).

The DTH's *Streetcar* was effective because of the strength of its prima ballerina, jazzy choreography, and innovative interpretation of Williams's characters by African American dancers who challenged traditional expectations associated with those roles.

Streetcar *as teleplay*

Two widely seen teleplays of *Streetcar* have been done, one in 1984 and the other in 1995. The first adaptation of *Streetcar* was broadcast on ABC TV on 4 March 1984.[24] Directed by John Erman and produced by Keith Barish, this *Streetcar* was prepared for television by Oscar Saul (who also adapted *Streetcar* for the Kazan film) and ran for two and a half hours, considerably shorter than a stage production. Ann-Margret starred as Blanche, Treat Williams as Stanley, Randy Quaid as Mitch, and Beverly D'Angelo as Stella. Williams himself wanted Ann-Margret for the role; ironically enough, he gave his approval for the teleplay only a few days before his death in 1983. Popular composer Marvin Hamlisch wrote the score, a blend of jazz and Hollywood mood music.

Comparisons with the Kazan film were inevitable and illustrative. Though far shorter than Williams's play, Erman's teleplay was closer to Williams's original script than Kazan's film had been, in large measure because Erman did not have to worry about the censorship

10. Teleplay of *Streetcar* (ABC Television, 1984) with Treat Williams (Stanley) and Ann-Margret (Blanche)

issues that plagued Kazan. For example, Erman was able to restore lines stricken in the film (e.g., Blanche's "Voulez vous coucher" to Mitch; Stanley's riposte to Blanche about "getting ideas"), to disclose Allen Grey's homosexuality, and, most significantly, to show Stella's reconciliation with Stanley. Jack Curry claimed that Erman's *Streetcar* "was far more than a token remake. It is a redefinition of a classic . . . the season's most powerfully moving psychodrama." Not everyone agreed. Some reviewers claimed it was vulgar and trashy.

But, undeniably, the *Streetcar* teleplay subjected Williams's script to a challenging reinterpretation appropriate for the times – the 1980s – and the medium – television. In fact, Erman's production compelled audiences to reinterpret the *Streetcar* script in light of the violence of TV culture during that decade. Erman gravely foregrounded contemporary issues – wife-beating, violence, and pervasive eroticism. Harry F. Waters quipped that the "television treatment . . .[of *Streetcar*] oozed raw sexuality." A few critics, however, complained that Erman "defanged" *Streetcar*, pulling it down to the level of commercialism by omitting such cultural points as Blanche's "Della Robbia blue" dress or her allusions to Poe, Hawthorne, and Whitman (John Simon).

Ann-Margret's Blanche was nothing like Vivien Leigh's willowy portrayal, or any other actor's for that matter. Taller and far more aggressive than Leigh as Blanche, Ann-Margret (age forty-two) arrived on a trolley briskly rolling down St. Charles Avenue, a sign of her independence, not on a train engulfed in a cloud of ethereal smoke. According to Simon, "Ann-Margret's face did not look patrician and worn, merely common and hard; this Blanche is not so much beat up as toughened. No aristocrat at the end of her tether . . .," very unlike Leigh's or Bloom's representation. During her struggle with Mitch in Scene 9 and with Stanley in the rape scene, Ann-Margret was a scraper who hits, pounds, attacks. Her arms were covered with bruises from the raw realism (Nancy Griffin).

Ann-Margret deserved the honor of being the most voluptuous Blanche up to that time, a characteristic she had ample credentials to portray. Appearing in over forty films, she received an Oscar nomination for *Carnal Knowledge*, a subject in which her Blanche excelled, and also had a track record playing tinsel shows in Las Vegas. Earthy and sensual, she also cultivated a Southern dialect (she had a coach and interviewed twenty women in Montgomery [Kenneth Turan]) that was far more raspy and seductive than Leigh's and without any of her timorousness. As June Schlueter wisely observed, Ann-Margret "converts Leigh's coyness into shameless flirtation."[25] In her first encounter with Stanley, her Blanche was overtly seductive – touching Stanley's arm as he lights her cigarette, running her hands over her legs, and casting bedroom eyes at Stanley's torso. Similarly with Mitch, Ann-Margret's Blanche behaved more like a seasoned pro than a genteel lady down on her luck. While she electrified audiences with her perfumed magic and erotic gestures, she risked alienating them from Blanche. Schlueter again raises a troubling point about the teleplay: "The more Ann-Margret's performance – coupled with her inescapably sensuous appearance – insists upon her sexuality, the more Blanche invites not sympathy but scorn."[26]

Unlike Leigh – and Tandy as well – Ann-Margret showed few signs of encroaching madness until the end of the play. Far more in control of Blanche's psyche and her lies than was Leigh, Ann-Margret was not as agitated or nervous. John Leonard remarked: "She'll tough it out before she cracks, putting on her dreams like war paint. She will stalk where [Leigh] cringed." Doing meticulous homework, Ann-Margret consulted a psychiatrist to learn about (and incorporate) "three different stages of psychosis . . ." into the role (Turan), yet even in Blanche's neurasthenic guises, Ann-Margret made her languor sensual, focused. Though Erman analogized Blanche as "the female Hamlet" (Turan), Ann-Margret was less introspective and more calculating than such a comparison promised. Even in madness, her Blanche was ritualized but not subdued or devastated. Ironically, though, Ann-Margret, like Leigh, was pushed to the brink by playing the role. "Blanche broke me," she exclaimed (Griffin).

Despite Ann-Margret's voluptuousness, no other director more powerfully elevated Williams's character into sanctification. Departing radically from both the stage history of *Streetcar* and Kazan's film, Erman introduced a novel ending by having Blanche leave in a black sedan which headed directly toward the spires of St. Louis Cathedral, its bells ringing, in the heart of the French Quarter. Not only did Erman defy New Orleanian geography (to do this Blanche would have had to drive up from the Mississippi River) but he left a lasting image of her as a saint purified in madness, an effective ending, though not possible on the stage.

Treat Williams's Stanley was not well received; he "had to do battle with a celluloid ghost" – Brando (Waters). In his T-shirt Williams looked suitably muscular; he had just starred in the film on prizefighter Jack Dempsey. Dark, handsome, and having perfected a simian gait, he was more crude than Brando with little of his sensitivity, charm, or intuitive cunning for some critics. Perhaps the most oral Stanley on record, Williams ate all through *Streetcar*. "The food in the Erman film establishes a crudity quite apart from Stanley's sensuality and more akin to the animal brutality he will later display in the rape."[27] Critics found very little of Stanley's magic and fantasy of colored lights in Williams's performance. He was a "Fascist wet dream" for Leonard. Seven years older than Brando was when he starred in *Streetcar* in 1947, Williams, according to Simon, "has deflated Stanley into a nervy lower-class but rather cleaned-up fellow whose plebeian taste . . . will not halt his upward mobility into middle-class age."

Consistent with the television violence that Erman pounded into the script, Treat Williams was one of the most brutal Stanleys, more menacing than Brando, Quinn, or even Rip Torn. The rape established this performance of Scene 11 beyond doubt as the most graphic and explicit in the history of *Streetcar*. No stage production had ever been so brutal; Erman spared his television audience of millions little agony and none of the cruelty. After struggling with Ann-Margret's hell-cat Blanche, Williams hurled her onto a large bed (more elegant than the Kowalskis should have owned), jumped on top of her, and tore off her tawdry Mardi Gras ball gown. Then, when the camera angle shifted, the audience watched the actual rape from the top of the bed looking down on Williams orgiastically pulsating, punishing his sister-in-law for daring to seduce and then to act superior to him. Erman did not have to resort to Kazanian symbols of mandatory indirection – broken mirrors and bottles, streetsweepers, phallic signifiers.

As Mitch, Randy Quaid was compared with Karl Malden. According to Leonard, Quaid "plays splendidly, the same mother-afflicted lummox that won Malden his Academy Award." Yet while Quaid was the right size (perhaps even larger than Malden) and temperament as a mama's boy, his interpretation of Mitch differed in several ways. Initially, he was more timid, hesitant, and softer-spoken, projecting a greater degree of vulnerability than Malden did. Perhaps because of Ann-Margret's overbearing sexual charisma, Quaid also fell even more deeply in love with Blanche than Malden's Mitch had. Although Simon complained that Quaid was "miscast" because he was "a funny-faced simpleton . . . bereft of pathos," Quaid's powerful representation of Mitch's disappointments in the teleplay challenged such an interpretation.

Beverly D'Angelo's Stella did not measure up to Kim Hunter, according to some critics. Simon, for example, found her Stella to be "a simpering goody-goody nonentity." Unlike other Stellas, D'Angelo justified the incredulity of critics over the cultural kinship of the DuBois sisters. She did not resemble Ann-Margret's Blanche in looks or in speech, despite having studiously worked on a Southern dialect which subsequently interfered with her making a record album. D'Angelo nonetheless earned high marks for her love of Stanley. Ultimately for Waters, though, she assimilated Stella too closely to "the unabashed lustiness of Debra Winger," again showing the bond between Erman's teleplay and the Hollywood culture of the 1980s.

A second teleplay of *Streetcar* was broadcast on 29 October 1995 on the CBS "Playhouse 90" series. Jessica Lange and Alec Baldwin repeated their 1992 Broadway *Streetcar*, now directed by Glenn Jordan, who also produced the teleplay, but with two major cast changes, John Goodman as Mitch and Diane Lane as Stella. "This *Streetcar* is the first on-screen adaptation faithful to Williams's text (it runs three hours), including the ending that the 1951 production code deemed shocking for Kazan's film" (Rick Schultz).[28] Referring to the Kazan film, John O'Connor praised the Lange–Baldwin teleplay because the "production does not . . . get trapped in the memorable Kazan interpretation of the play." Overall, Lange received much better reviews for her televised *Streetcar* than for the stage production three years earlier. Ward Howard Rosenberg affirmed, "whatever her flaws, if any, they are not evident here." Lange's Blanche was far less fragile than Leigh's, and Baldwin's Stanley was seen as Lange's match at last. Reviewers emphasized that Baldwin brought credibility to the role, portraying a Stanley more complex than brutish, a major performance.

STREETCAR AS OPERA

The San Francisco Opera Company (SFO), the second largest opera house in North America, performed the world premiere of the opera based on Williams's play at the War Memorial Opera House eight times from 19 September to 11 October 1998. The idea for translating *Streetcar* into opera was the brainchild of Lotfi Mansouri, the General Director of the SFO, who had tried unsuccessfully to recruit Stephen Sondheim and Leonard Bernstein to compose it. But in 1994 Mansouri quickly convinced André Previn to write the score: his first opera. Philip Littell wrote the libretto, Colin Graham was the stage director, and, for the first four performances, Previn himself conducted. Tickets went for as high as $1,500, with an audience crowded with celebrities and dignitaries, including Mark Morial, the Mayor of New Orleans, as guest of the Mayor of San Francisco, and more than 130 music critics, too. Previn's *Streetcar,* divided into three acts, took three and a half hours to perform. Deutsche Grammophon recorded the opening night's performance, and subsequent performances were scheduled for the San Diego Opera, Opera Pacific, the National Opera of Wales, and Australian National Opera. PBS, American public television, broadcast Previn's opera on 30 December 1998.

Previn brought distinguished credentials to transforming Williams's play into opera. Having composed music for over sixty films, he had won Oscars for *Gigi* (1958), *Porgy and Bess* (1959), *My Fair Lady* (1964), and *CoCo* (1969). A widely respected pianist, Sir André had also been principal conductor of the London Symphony Orchestra. But Previn offered "neither the movie music some feared nor the jazz score others had hoped for" (Barry Paris).[29] Instead, he assiduously avoided the jazzy score that infused Alex North's compositions so his music displayed the "undercurrents of Central European Modernism" (Alex Ross) as well as the influence of such composers as Benjamin Britten, Samuel Barber, and Ralph Vaughan Williams. Theodore P. Mahane claimed: "[t]hroughout 'Streetcar' Previn's cinematic origins are evident. The music conveys the drama well, both complementing it and commenting on it. At times it is almost Straussian in its emotional orchestral richness." More specifically, Michael Kennedy observed, Previn's "orchestral writing is colourful with special attention to woodwind and brass solos, and sparing use of percussion." Criticism of Previn's score centered on "a paucity of animal spirits"(Tim Page) and "a lack of a distinct musical picture of each character" (Ross), while for Bernard Holland it did not capture the Southernness of Williams's play, in music or in gesture.

These objections of course raise central questions about composing an opera based on an illustrious play. Previn contended that "I always thought that *Streetcar* was an opera that was just missing the music" (Paris, 226). Yet not everyone shared his belief. Alan Rich rejoined that "There is so much music implicit in the melancholy prose of . . . *Streetcar* that the notion of adding more, by turning the play into an actual opera, becomes an exercise in redundancy." Admittedly, *Streetcar* as opera required a different scope, delivery, and sense of casting from *Streetcar* as play. Singing Williams's words was far different from speaking them. Moreover, Kennedy astutely reminded readers, "Characters become more sympathetic, less rough-edged, in their operatic guises; if we view them with more understanding, that is the result of the power of music." Previn's powerful score successfully overcame many objections about turning *Streetcar* into opera.

Not only did Previn transform Williams's play into opera but he also recovered and advanced a significant interpretation of character and script. He challenged Kazan's valorization of Stanley at Blanche's expense: "I looked at the [1951 Elia Kazan] film before I wrote note one and not since, because it's dangerous. The emphasis got switched when everybody's consciousness became suffused with Brando's performance. The play is really about her, and she has an absolutely enormous part in the opera" (Paris). As Paul Hertelendy remarked, "This is no longer Stanley vs. Blanche, with Stella the wife trying vainly to play peacemaker. This is Blanche's show, keeping the soprano on stage for all nine scenes." Although the 69-year-old Previn did not see the Broadway *Streetcar*, he endorsed Claire Bloom's and Ann-Margret's interpretation of Blanche as a doomed woman. Previn thought Bloom "was simply transcendent" (Jesse Hamlin).

Previn clearly explained his reasoning for building the opera around Blanche: "Some people think very critically about Blanche, but I don't . . . I find her a heartbreaking character . . . There's no way for that girl to redeem her life . . . In the movie, when she's led off by the doctor, Alex North's score . . . goes into really triumphant music, and I never understood that . . . it's a genuine tragedy, and I did my best to make it so" (Hamlin). Mark Swed remarked that Previn "might well have titled the opera 'Blanche.'" Given the dominant role of the diva in opera, Previn's emphasis on Blanche was not unjustified. It is worth recalling that Previn wrote the score of the film *Valley of the Dolls*, with its Blanche-like drugged, wounded women.

11. Scene from the San Francisco Opera's *Streetcar* (San Francisco, September 1998) score by André Previn and starring Renee Fleming as Blanche and Rodney Gilfry as Stanley

Unquestionably, Previn's music harmonized with his view of Blanche. According to David Patrick Stearns, Previn's score "establishes the mental instability behind Blanche's pretensions."

While no musical restrictions were placed upon Previn, librettist Philip Littell had strict rules to follow from the Williams estate which prohibited his rewriting or extensively tampering with Williams's script. What Littell did, though, was masterful. While creating a libretto "where every word comes from the play," he cut the 17,000-word *Streetcar* back to 7,500 words (Richard Dyer), significantly reducing but not minimizing the script. "He trimmed and telescoped the play without sacrificing any major scenes" (Ross). Such reduction was necessary to make Williams's play "singable." As Littell affirmed, "Williams's thought goes very poetical and lyrical. But he won't go straight into selling. You'd scream with laughter" (quoted in Jan

Breslauer). Littell had a formidable task, as he pointed out in an interview for *Opera News*:

> With a play like [*Streetcar*], people know it, and then they think they know it, so I've got to rediscover what they've forgotten about the play, as well as making sure they feel they're seeing the original . . . I found myself an advocate for certain things that people don't pay attention to. Everybody is very aware of the magic Blanche makes, but . . . Blanche's achievement is that she makes magic out of dross. I tried to make sure the dross was still there. I'm a great advocate of the sleazy side of the play.   ("Notes for *Streetcar*").

Of course, the demands of opera necessitated that Littell cut some parts and expand others in Williams's play. Basically, he rearranged Williams's prose to make it singable: "Without hurting the play, I had to make room for the music – I had to trim a bit of fat" (quoted by J. A. van Sant). As Stearns observed, "Concise dramatic points spoken in the theatre need more room in opera. Lines that give offhanded, conversational insights into their characters wilt when enshrined in music." According to Littell: "It's sort of like doing a believable skin graft. It had to sound like Tennessee could have done it" (quoted in Breslauer). He expanded the roles of the Mexican flower seller to accommodate an aria but omitted the business of Shep Huntleigh calling Blanche. Littell also responded to the demands of an operatic score with several arias for Blanche, including one on the loss of Belle Reve in Act I, another on "Soft People" in Act II, and two in the last act – "I Want Magic" ("the opera's strongest showpiece," according to Theodore P. Mahane), and "I Can Smell the Sea Air." With Previn, Littell decided that Stanley should shout, not sing, "Stella," to avoid inappropriate laughter from the audience and that Blanche address her famous words "I have always depended on the kindness of strangers" directly to the audience as her exit line. Dennis Harvey found that Littell's "finale fills this work's frank erotic tension." Most important of all, when Stanley rapes Blanche not a word is uttered. Five minutes of Previn's uninterrupted orchestral music played on a darkened stage. Though Page complained there was "nothing primal about the interlude,"audiences found it powerful.

Michael Yeargan's $400,000 set was indebted to, but provocatively departed from, Jo Mielziner's for the Broadway premiere. Yeargan's design consisted of "two revolving units – for the Kowalski apartment" (Rich) – alternatively revealing interior and exterior scenes, and showing the iron railings of a New Orleans balustrade. The set offered "transparent walls allowing lighting to convey . . . psychological landscape but not its atmosphere" (Stearns). According to Daniel Webster, "In paring down the work for opera, the creators have subtly shifted the focus even more closely to Blanche. The [set] makes it all a reflection of her distorted vision, her dementia. The transparent house tilts a little; nothing is quite vertical, nothing surely horizontal" ("André Previn Scores"). Perhaps the most haunting effect of the setting was that during the rape the stage suddenly "shifts in two, a spectacularly surrealistic expression of Blanche's fractured state" (Page).

Also costuming the production, Yeargan clad Blanche "in things [that]are in faded tones – mauve, lilac, chiffon over satiny material, very moss-like and fragile-looking. The others [characters] are in much bolder colors – they're alive, happy" (Paris). Thomas Munn's expressionistic lighting greatly contributed to Previn's – and Yeargan's – representation of Blanche's psyche: "In her first appearance Blanche came in with just soft white light with blue mist. Only gradually does she step forward as the overdressed woman with a shabby suitcase" (Webster). Emphasizing Stanley's animalism, Munn flooded the stage "in jungle foliage" (Rich) when he struts with masculine pride.

"As for the singing, only superlatives will do," exclaimed Kennedy of the *Sunday Telegraph.* John Allison of *The Times* similarly declared that there were "no weak links in the San Francisco Opera's cast." Soprano Renee Fleming magnificently filled the lead role of Blanche wearing a large blonde wig. At age thirty-nine, Fleming was a distinguished veteran of the New York Metropolitan and La Scala, and voted the 1997 Vocalist of the Year by *Musical America*. With Previn's approval, she recorded all of Blanche's arias, independent of the opera, for Decca Records. Mansouri hailed Fleming as "my dream Blanche" because of "her stunning vulnerability . . . Blanche must make me cry, but at the same time, must have a strength" (quoted in Paris). Fleming blended pathos and power. Allan Ulrich concluded, however, that her "Old South accent has to go." Although Page did not find Fleming consistently convincing, he nonetheless applauded her virtues: "The lyricism, oral luster, and patrician style she brought to Previn's quieter, more reflective passages were impeccable and sometimes deeply wrenching."

Other critics disagreed. Ross conceded that Fleming had "a luminous, aristocratic soprano voice . . . not everyone would have expected her to wallow in madness, lust, and despair. She did not"; and Paris complained that "there is little evidence of inner frailty or mental dissolution" in Fleming's portrayal. But such criticism may be more attuned to the stage Blanches of Leigh or Tandy and less focused on an operatic Blanche. A "thoroughly modern diva" (Terry Teachout, 17), Fleming may have been "soft-centered" at times but she was hardly as vulnerable as those Blanches venerated in the earlier stage tradition of *Streetcar*. Underpinning Previn's view of Williams's character, an operatic Blanche had to be more assertive, more "strong," as Mansouri emphasized. Frailty is hardly a coveted asset when singing an aria marked *fortissimo*.

Coloratura soprano Elizabeth Furtel stole the show with her Stella. For Swed, Furtel "delivered the most interesting performance." With her "youthful freshness" (Paris), Furtel looked like Fleming's sister. Webster found Furtel to be "an ideal partner" for Fleming: "Her singing always contrasts with Fleming's creating emotional distinctions that crystallize an arresting character." For Ross she "turned in a brilliant scene-stealing performance [yet]. . . her clarion voice cut through the bustling orchestra more easily than Fleming's . . ." Like Kim Hunter or Beverly D'Angelo, Furtel's Stella exuded a healthy wedded love – "The sexual chemistry between her and Stanley is almost tangible," affirmed Kennedy. Her ensemble with Stanley – "It's Going to Be All Right" – expressed their mutual commitment.

Rodney Gilfry's Stanley sang and looked the part. "I just hear Stanley as a baritone," announced Previn (*San Francisco Examiner*, 6 September). Gilfry "has a lock on opera's greatest studs," quipped Robert Holfer. Six foot 3 inches tall, and weighing 200 pounds, Gilfry performed such roles as Guglielmo in *Così fan tutte*, the title role in *Don Giovanni*, and the Count in *Le nozze di Figaro*. His Stanley was filled with "lust, sadism, and vocal power" according to William Aguier, Jr., and when Gilfry removed his T-shirt on stage, American opera entered the record books for a revelation more common in theatre. Stephanie von Buchau graphically commented that Gilfry was "smoldering with just the sort of testosterone poisoning that makes a girl like Blanche itch all over." Yet Stearns found Gilfry's "Mozartian baritone too hard too often." Even so, Previn's score for Stanley did not valorize the part as Kazan had done thanks to Brando. Demonstrating again Blanche's centrality to Previn's *Streetcar*, Gilfry remarked: "Stanley speaks in utterances like an animal, so my part doesn't have long lyrical passages . . . Blanche gets all the arias." Gilfry was "not given interesting music and [so] Stanley lacks Blanche's magnetism in the role," according to Swed. Yet Paris singled out Gilfry's "skill at chewing gum while singing," besting Brando in orality if not in acting.

Musically and physically contrasting with Gilfry's Stanley was tenor Anthony Dean Griffey's Mitch. A newcomer compared to the rest of the cast, Griffey had made his Metropolitan Opera debut only three years before *Streetcar*. Portly and timid-looking, Griffey was a vulnerable Mitch easily trapped by Blanche and yet the catalyst for his rage against her. With Previn's music, Griffey made Mitch both "a sweet hopeful suitor and a harsh realist" (Webster). Previn's ensemble for Mitch and Blanche at the end of Scene 6, when Blanche reveals the tragedy of Allan Grey, was touching and sensitive.

With the Previn opera, Williams's play has come full circle since its Broadway premiere. Although performed half a century and a full continent away from that premiere, *Streetcar* as opera demonstrates again the sustaining power and protean magic of Williams's script, one of the three or four most influential dramas in the twentieth century. It is fitting that such a powerful play should have been transformed into an opera. Unquestionably, *Streetcar Named Desire* is Williams's most musical, most lyrical play, and basing an opera on it is further proof that Williams's characters, narrative techniques, poetic nuances, visual poetry, and haunting sets energize an audience, regardless of the medium in which they see them performed. The opera affirms – as do the national premieres, revivals, and radicalizations – that *Streetcar* will continue to be successfully staged, adapted, and assimilated through the twenty-first century, saying as much about the times and places in which it was performed as it does about the creative genius of the man who, like his most memorable character, Blanche, bids world theatre "En avant!"

SELECT PRODUCTION CHRONOLOGY

1947

3 Dec., Barrymore Theatre, New York, 855 perf.
Dir. Elia Kazan, Des. Jo Mielziner, Prod. Irene Selznick, Music Alex
North, Costumes Lucinda Ballard

BLANCHE Jessica Tandy   STANLEY Marlon Brando
STELLA Kim Hunter   MITCH Karl Malden
EUNICE Peg Hilias   PABLO Nick Dennis
STEVE Rudy Bond

1948

9 July, Salia Talia, Pronato del Teatro, Havana
Dir. Modesto Centeno, Des. Luis Marquez, Lighting Armado Soler

BLANCHE Marisabel Sáenz   STANLEY Sergio Doré
STELLA Viloetta Casal   MITCH Luis Baralt

4 Dec.–12 Dec., Palacio de Bellas Artes, Mexico City
Dir. Seki Sano, Patron Diego Rivera

BLANCHE María Douglas   STANLEY Wolf Ruvinskis
STELLA Lillian Oppenheim   MITCH Reynaldo Rivera

1949

21 Jan., Eliseo Theatre, Rome
Dir. Luchino Visconti, Des. Franco Zeffirelli

BLANCHE Rina Morelli   STANLEY Vittorio Gassman
STELLA Vivi Gioi   MITCH Marcello Mastroianni

1 Mar., Gothenburg City Theatre
Dir. Ingmar Bergman, Des. Carl Johan Ström

BLANCHE Karin Kavli   STANLEY Anders Ek

27 Sept.–7 Oct., Aldwych Theatre, London, 326 perf.
Dir. Laurence Olivier, Des. Jo Mielziner, Prod. Hugh Beaumont,
Costumes Beatrice Dawson

BLANCHE Vivien Leigh   STANLEY Bonar Colleano
STELLA Renee Asherson   MITCH Bernard Braden
STEVE Lyn Evans   PABLO Theodore Bickel

19 Oct., Théâtre Edouard VII, Paris
Dir. Raymond Rouleau, Des. Lila de Nobili

BLANCHE Arletty   STANLEY Yves Vincent
STELLA Helena Bossis   MITCH Daniel Inverne

1949–50 Road Companies (Rochester, Chicago, St. Louis, Kansas City, Pittsburgh, Dallas, etc.)

BLANCHE Uta Hagen   STANLEY Anthony Quinn
STELLA Jorja Cartright   MITCH George Mathews

BLANCHE Judith Evelyn   STANLEY Ralph Meeker
STELLA Jorja Cartright   MITCH Jim Nolan

1950

23 Jan.–30 Jan., Royal Alexandra Theatre, Toronto

BLANCHE Uta Hagen   STANLEY Anthony Quinn
STELLA Mary Welch   MITCH George Matthews

Mar. Stadtheater, Pforzheim, Germany
Dir. Hans Karl Zeiser

BLANCHE Gisela Hagenau   STANLEY Heinz Kiefer
STELLA Gisela Leininger   MITCH A. M. Rüffer

14 Apr., Thalia Theatre, Hamburg
Dir. Willi Maertens

BLANCHE Gisela Von Collande   STANLEY Heinz Klevenow
STELLA Margrit Ensinger   MITCH Josef Dahmenals

24 May, City Center Theatre, New York, 14 perf.
Dir. Harold Clurman, Des. Jo Mielziner, Prod. Irene Selznick

BLANCHE Uta Hagen   STANLEY Anthony Quinn
STELLA Jorja Cartright   MITCH George Mathews

18–24 Dec., Royal Alexandra Theatre, Toronto

BLANCHE Louise Platt   STANLEY Philip Kenneally
STELLA Ellen Davey   MITCH Harry Kersey

1951

20 Apr., Burgtheater, Vienna
Dir. Berthold Viertel, Des. Ita Maximowa, Music Alexander
Steinbrecher

BLANCHE Kathe Gold   STANLEY Curt Jürgens
STELLA Maria Kramer   MITCH Franz Nicklisch

Sept., Warner Bros. Film
Dir. Elia Kazan, Screenplay Oscar Saul, Des. George James Hopkins,

Prod. Charles K. Feldman, Music Alex North, Costumes Lucinda Ballard, Art Des. Richard Day

BLANCHE Vivien Leigh	STANLEY Marlon Brando
STELLA Kim Hunter	MITCH Karl Malden
EUNICE Peg Hilias	PABLO Nick Dennis

Basel, Switzerland
Dir. Werner Kraut

BLANCHE Blanche Aubry	STANLEY Rudolf Bechmann
STELLA Hilde Harvan	MITCH Kurt Nachmann

1952

8 Dec.–3 Jan. 1953, Slavenska–Franklin Ballet Company, New York, Century Theatre, Ballet choreographed Valerie Bettis, Music Alex North

BLANCHE Mia Slavenska	STANLEY Frederic Franklin
STELLA Lois Ellyn	MITCH Marvin Krauter

1953

19 Mar.–30 May, Bungakuza, Toyko and Road Company, 54 perf.
Dir. Ichiro Kawaguchi, Des. Kiska Ito

BLANCHE Haruko Sugimura	STANLEY Kazuo Kitamura
STELLA Tomoko Fumino	

1955

19 Feb.–10 Mar., Ebony Showcase Theatre, Los Angeles
Dir. Paul Rodgers, Prod. Nick Stewart

BLANCHE Camille Canady	STANLEY Vilmore Schexnayder
STELLA Shirley Higgenbotham	MITCH Sylvester Bell

1956

16 Feb., City Center Theatre, New York
Dir. Herbert Machiz

BLANCHE Tallulah Bankhead   STANLEY Gerald O'Laughlin
STELLA Frances Heflin   MITCH Rudy Bond

1957

21 Dec., Teatr Ziemi Pomorskiej, Torun
Dir. Maria d'Alphonse, Des. Antoni Muszynski

BLANCHE Celina Bartyzel   STANLEY Tadeusz Tusiacki
STELLA Tatiana Pawlowska   MITCH Marian Szul

21 Dec., Rozmaitosci Teatr, Wrocław
Dir. Zygmunt Hübner, Des. Zbigniew Klimczyk

BLANCHE Daniela Makulska   STANLEY Tadeusz Tusiacki
STELLA Jadwiga Kukulska   MITCH Marian Skorupa

1958

June, Union Theatre Repertory Company, Melbourne
Dir. Wal Cherry, Des. Wendy Dickson

BLANCHE Patricia Conolly   STANLEY Edward Webster
STELLA Audine Leith   MITCH Tony Hulme

1960

24 Nov., Theatre of Peter Bezruče, Ostrava
First public performance in Czechoslovakia
Dir. Jana Kačera, Des. Lubos Hrůza

BLANCHE Nina Divišková   STANLEY Bohus Vaclav
STELLA Jirina Třebická   MITCH Josef Kriz

1973

21 Mar.–28 Apr., Ahmanson Theatre, Los Angeles
Dir. James Bridges, Des. Robert Tyler Lee

BLANCHE Faye Dunaway   STANLEY Jon Voight
STELLA Lee McCain   MITCH. Earl Hollliman

26 Apr.–29 July, Vivian Beaumont Theatre, New York, 110 perf.
Dir. Ellis Rabb, Des. Douglas Schmidt, John Gleason, Nancy Potts

BLANCHE Rosemary Harris   STANLEY James Farentino
STELLA Patricia Conolly   MITCH Philip Bosco

11 July, Freie Volksbühne, West Berlin, 5 perf.
Dir. Charles Lang

BLANCHE Margit Carstensen STANLEY Günther Kaufmann
STELLA Ute Uellner   MITCH Franz Gery

1971

Mayakovsky Theatre, Moscow
Dir. A Goncharov

BLANCHE Svetlana Nemolyaeva STANLEY Armen Dzhigarkanyan

1974

14 Mar., Piccadilly Theatre, London, 90 perf.
Dir. Edwin Sherin, Des. Patrick Robertson

BLANCHE Claire Bloom   STANLEY Martin Shaw
STELLA Morag Hood   MITCH Joss Ackland

1975

July–Aug., Intimate and Nico Malan Theatres, Johannesburg
Dir. James Roose-Evans

BLANCHE Anne Rogers   STANLEY Michael McGovern
STELLA Gillian Garlick

1976

8 June, Academy Festival Theatre, Lake Forest, Illinois, 20 perf.
Dir. Jack Gelber

BLANCHE Geraldine Page   STANLEY Rip Torn
STELLA Flora Elkins   MITCH Jack Hollander

1983

12 May–12 June, American Stage Company, Berkeley, CA
Dir. Charles Gordone

BLANCHE Peggy Linz   STANLEY Paul Santiago
STELLA Kate Black   MITCH Robert Pierson

1984

1–18 Nov., Dashiki Project Theatre, New Orleans
Dir. Theodore E. Gilliam

BLANCHE Barbara Tasker   STANLEY Harold Sylvester
STELLA Gwendolyn Fox   MITCH Harold Evans

4 Mar., ABC TV
Dir. John Erman, Music Marvin Hamlisch

BLANCHE Ann-Margret   STANLEY Treat Williams
STELLA Beverly D'Angelo   MITCH Randy Quaid

1986

Williamstown Theatre Festival, Massachusetts
Dir. Nikos Psacharopoulos

BLANCHE Blythe Danner   STANLEY Christopher Walken
STELLA Sigourney Weaver   MITCH James Naughton

1987

21 Feb.–29 Mar., Leo Lerner Theatre, Chicago
Dir. Marianne Zucarro

BLANCHE Jackie Taylor   STANLEY Darryl Manuel
STELLA Bellary Darden   MITCH David Barr III

1988

10 Mar.–22 May, Circle in the Square, New York
Dir. Nikos Psacharopoulos

BLANCHE Blythe Danner   STANLEY Aidan Quinn
STELLA Frances McDormand   MITCH Frank Converse

21 Oct.–15 Nov.; 9 Dec., Tianjin People's Art Theatre, Tianjin, 15
perf; Beijing First Chinese Drama Festival
Dir. Mike Alfreds

BLANCHE Zhang Lu Yen   STANLEY Lu Yi
STELLA Chu An Li   MITCH Wang Shi Wen
YOUTH Li Zhong   FLOWER WOMAN Mei Ai Hua

1991

Belle Reprieve
Radical gay-lesbian adaptation

1–14 Jan., Drill Hall, London; Mar., La MaMa, New York
Dir. Peggy Shaw.

BLANCHE Bette Bourne   STANLEY Peggy Shaw
STELLA Lois Weaver   MITCH Precious Pearl

28 Aug.–21 Sept., Intiman Theatre Co., Seattle
Dir. Eliz Huddle

BLANCHE Julia Fletcher   STANLEY Scott MacDonald
STELLA Suzanne Boachard   MITCH Ken Strange

1992

12 Apr., Barrymore Theatre, New York, 160 perf.
Dir. Gregory Mosher, Des. Ben Edwards

BLANCHE Jessica Lange   STANLEY Alex Baldwin
STELLA Amy Madigan   MITCH Timothy Carhart

1995

29 Oct., CBS "Playhouse 90," CBS TV
Dir. Glenn Jackson

BLANCHE Jessica Lange   STANLEY Alex Baldwin
STELLA Diane Lane   MITCH John Goodman

1998

5 May–27 June, Gate Theatre, Dublin
Dir. Robin Lefevre, Des. Allen Moyer, Costumes Michael Krass

BLANCHE Frances McDormand STANLEY Liam Cunningham
STELLA Donna Dent   MITCH John Kavanagh
EUNICE Susan Slott   STEVE Alan Archbold

NOTES

1 *A Streetcar Named Desire* – the Broadway premiere and beyond

1 Thomas P. Adler, *American Drama, 1940–1960: A Critical History* (New York: Twayne, 1994), 141.

2 Howard Barnes, *New York Herald Tribune* 4 Dec. 1947. For the sake of economy and convenience I list here alphabetically all the Broadway and tryout reviews that I cite parenthetically in this chapter: Brooks Atkinson, *New York Times* 4 Dec. 1947: 42, rpt. *New York Theatre Critics' Reviews* 8: 252; *New York Times* 14 Dec. 1947, sec. 2: 3, rpt. *New York Times Theatre Reviews; New York Times* 12 June 1949, sec. 2: 1, rpt. *New York Times Theatre Reviews;* Howard Barnes, *New York Herald Tribune* 4 Dec. 1947: 25, rpt. *New York Theatre Critics' Reviews* 8: 252; Eric Bentley, *Theatre Arts* Nov. 1949: 14, rpt. *In Search of Theatre* (New York: Knopf, 1953), 31–34; William Beyer, *School and Society* 67 (27 Mar. 1948): 241–43; John Mason Brown, *Saturday Review* 27 (Dec. 1947): 22–24; John Chapman, *New York Daily News* 4 Dec. 1947: 8, rpt. *New York Theatre Critics' Reviews* 8: 249; Robert Coleman, *New York Daily Mirror* 4 Dec. 1947: 38, rpt. *New York Theatre Critics' Reviews* 8: 252; Richard P. Cook, "New Williams Drama," *Wall Street Journal* 5 Dec. 1947: 10; George Currie, *Brooklyn Daily Eagle* 4 Dec. 1947: 8; Robert Garland, *New York Journal American* 4 Dec. 1947, rpt. *New York Theatre Critics' Reviews* 8: 251; John Gassner, *Forum* 109 (Feb. 1948): 86–88; Wolcott Gibbs, *New Yorker* 13 Dec. 1947: 50–54; Rosamond Gilder, *Theatre Arts* Jan. 1948: 10–13; William Hawkins, *New York World-Telegram* 4 Dec. 1947: 36, rpt. *New York Theatre Critics' Reviews* 8: 251; Elinor Hughes, *Boston Herald* 4 Nov. 1947: 10; Ibee, "Plays on Broadway – *A Streetcar Named Desire,*" *Variety* 10 Nov. 1947: 68; Louis Kronenberger, *PM* [New York] 5 Dec. 1947, rpt. *New York Theatre Critics' Reviews* 8: 250; Linton

Martin, "The Call Boy's Chat: 'Streetcar Named Desire' Is Strong Dramatic Meat!" *Philadelphia Inquirer* 23 Nov. 1947: 23; Mary McCarthy, *Partisan Review* 25 (Mar. 1948): 357–60, rpt. *Sights and Spectacles 1937–1956* (New York: Farrar, 1956), 131–35; Ward Morehouse, *New York Sun* 4 Dec. 1947: 44, rpt. *New York Theatre Critics' Reviews* 8: 250; George Jean Nathan, *New York Journal American* 15 Dec. 1947: 14; Nathan, "Williams's Drama A Theatrical Shocker," *New York Journal American* 20 Dec. 1947: 20; *New York World Telegram* 16 Oct. 1947; Elliot Norton, "Plot But No Pity in 'A Streetcar Named Desire': Second Thoughts of A First-Nighter," *Boston Sunday Post* 9 Nov. 1947: A9; Jack O'Brian, "New Williams Drama Is Best of the Year," *St Louis Globe-Democrat* 14 Dec 1947: 2F; T.H.P. [Theodore H. Parker], "'Streetcar' Williams's Finest Play," *Hartford Courant* 1 Nov. 1947: 15; Kappo Phelan, *Commonweal* 47 (19 Dec. 1947): 254–55; Edwin H. Schloss, "'*A Streetcar Named Desire*' Opens on Walnut Theater Stage," *Philadelphia Inquirer* 18 Nov. 1947: 42; R. E. P. Sensenderfer, "Streetcar Named Desire," *Philadelphia Evening Bulletin* 18 Nov. 1947; Irwin Shaw, *New Republic* 22 Dec. 1947: 34–35; "Theater: 'A Streetcar on Broadway,'" *Newsweek* 15 Dec. 1947: 82–83; Richard Watts, Jr., *New York Post* 4 Dec. 1947: 43, rpt. *New York Theatre Critics' Reviews* 8: 249; and Euphemia Van Rensselaer Wyatt, *Catholic World* 166 (Jan. 1948): 558.

3   "The News Hour with Jim Lehrer," 11 Nov. 1997, Show no. 5996. Transcript available from "Strictly Business," Overland Park, Kansas 66212.

4   Philip C. Kolin, "*A Streetcar Named Desire*: A Playwrights' Forum," *Michigan Quarterly Review* 29 (Spring 1990): 188.

5   *Ibid.*, 184.

6   *New York Evening Post* (2 May 1958).

7   C. W. E. Bigsby, *Modern American Drama, 1945–1990* (Cambridge: Cambridge University Press, 1992), 51.

8   Kolin, "*Streetcar*: A Playwrights' Forum," 199.

9   John Clum, *Acting Gay: Male Homosexuality in Modern American Drama* (New York: Columbia University Press, 1992); David Savran, *Communists, Cowboys and Queers: The Politics of Masculinity in the Work of Arthur Miller and Tennessee Williams* (Minneapolis: University of Minnesota Press, 1992).

10   "Streetcar," *Tomorrow* Feb. 1948: 52; rpt. in *The Collected Works of Harold Clurman* (New York: Applause Theatre Books, 1994), 131.

11   Kolin, "*Streetcar*: A Playwrights' Forum," 191.

12   Quoted in *Confronting Tennessee Williams's A Streetcar Named Desire: Essays in Critical Pluralism*, ed. Philip C. Kolin (Westport, CT: Greenwood, 1993), 4.

13   Nancy M. Tischler, *Tennessee Williams: Rebellious Puritan* (New York: Citadel, 1961), 140.

14   Dan Isaac, "No Past to Think In: Who Wins in '*A Streetcar Named Desire*?'" *Louisiana Literature* 14 (Fall 1997): 26.

15   Walter Davis, *Get the Guests: Psychoanalysis, Modern American Drama, and the Audience* (Madison: University of Wisconsin Press, 1994).

16   Joseph Wood Krutch, *Modernisn in Modern Drama* (Ithaca: Cornell University Press, 1953).

17   Thomas P. Adler, "*A Streetcar Named Desire*": *The Moth and the Lantern* (Boston: Twayne, 1990), 54.

18   Joseph N. Riddell, "*A Streetcar Named Desire* – Nietzsche Descending," *Modern Drama* 5 (Feb. 1963): 423.

19   Robert C. Jennings, "Interview with Tennessee Williams," *Playboy* Apr. 1973: 72.

20   Quoted in Nancy M. Tischler, "Sanitizing the *Streetcar*," *Louisiana Literature* 14 (Fall 1997): 55.

21   Georges-Michel Sarotte, *Like a Brother, Like a Lover*, trans. Richard Miller (Garden City: Anchor, 1978).

22   Brenda Murphy, *Tennessee Williams and Elia Kazan: A Collaboration in the Theatre* (Cambridge: Cambridge University Press, 1992), 25.

23   Ronald Hayman, *Tennessee Williams: Everyone Else Is an Audience* (New Haven: Yale University Press, 1993), 112.

24   Anne Fleche, *Mimetic Disillusion: Eugene O'Neill, Tennessee Williams, and U.S. Dramatic Realism* (Tuscaloosa: University of Alabama Press, 1997), 99.

25   "Irene Mayer Selznick: Her Streetcar Rang the Bell," *Look* 20 July 1948: 31.

26   Dakin Williams and Shepherd Mead, *Tennessee Williams: An Intimate Biography* (New York: Arbor, 1983), 149.

27   "Irene Mayer Selznick."

28 Billy Rose, "Pitching Horseshoes with Billy Rose," *New York Evening Post* 2 Dec. 1947.

29 AP Staff Writer, "Housewife's Dream Rides 'Streetcar.'"

30 Ward Morehouse, *Pic Magazine* [New York] Nov. 1947.

31 Audrey Wood, with Max Wilk, *Represented by Audrey Wood* (Garden City: Doubleday, 1981), 154.

32 "Tennessee Tells All," *Cue* 20 Dec. 1947: 15.

33 Elia Kazan, *A Life* (New York: Knopf, 1988), 342.

34 "Tennessee Tells All."

35 Murphy, *Tennessee Williams and Elia Kazan*, 13.

36 *Ibid.*, 93.

37 Quoted in *Ibid.*, 17.

38 Kazan, *A Life*, 329–30.

39 Murphy, *Tennessee Williams and Elia Kazan*, 40.

40 Thomas H. Pauly, *An American Odyssey: Elia Kazan and American Culture* (Philadelphia: Temple University Press, 1983), 86.

41 Elia Kazan, "Notebook for *A Streetcar Named Desire*," *Directors on Directing: A Source Book of the Modern Theatre*, ed. Toby Cole and Helen Krich Chinoy, 2nd (rev.) edn. (Indianapolis: Bobbs-Merrill, 1976).

42 Tennessee Williams, *Where I Live* (New York: New Directions, 1978), 116, 172.

43 Susan Spector, "Alternative Visions of Blanche DuBois: Uta Hagen and Jessica Tandy in *A Streetcar Named Desire*," *Modern Drama* 32 (1989): 558.

44 Clurman, "Streetcar."

45 Arthur Miller's phrase; quoted in Brenda Murphy, *Congressional Theatre* (Cambridge: Cambridge University Press, 1999), 2.

46 Harry W. Smith, "Tennessee Williams and Jo Mielziner: The Memory Plays," *Theatre Survey* 23 (Nov. 1982): 227.

47 Jo Mielziner, *Designing for the Theatre: A Memoir and A Portfolio* (New York: Atheneum, 1965), 141.

48 Thomas P. Adler, "Tennessee Williams: 'Personal Lyricism': Toward an Androgynous Form," in *Realism and the American Dramatic Tradition*, ed. William Demastes (Tuscaloosa: University of Alabama Press, 1996), 179.

49 Murphy, *Tennessee Williams and Elia Kazan*, 28.

50 Felica Londré, "A Streetcar Running Fifty Years," in *The Cambridge Companion to Tennessee Williams*, ed. Matthew C. Roudané (Cambridge: Cambridge University Press, 1997), 48.

51 Mielziner, *Designing for the Theatre*, 141.

52 Robert Downing, "Streetcar Conductor: Some Notes from Backstage," *Theatre Annual* 8 (1950): 29, 30.

53 Mielziner, *Designing for the Theatre*, 141.

54 Downing, "Streetcar Conductor," 31.

55 *Ibid.*, 30.

56 Murphy, *Tennessee Williams and Elia Kazan*, 27.

57 Mielziner, *Designing for the Theatre*, 142.

58 Quoted in Mike Steen, *A Look at Tennessee Williams* (New York: Hawthorn, 1968), 179.

59 All references in this paragraph are from Downing, "Streetcar Conductor," p. 28.

60 Harry W. McCraw, "Tennessee Williams, Film Music, Alex North: An Interview with Luigi Zaninelli," *Mississippi Quarterly* 48 (Fall 1995): 770.

61 Mark Evans, *The Music of the Movies* (New York: Hopkinson and Blake, 1975), 254.

62 John S. Bak, "Wagnerian Architectonics: The Plastic Language of Tennessee Williams's *A Streetcar Named Desire*," *Tennessee Williams Literary Journal* 4 (Fall 1997): 45.

63 Quoted in Steen, *A Look at Tennessee Williams*, 119.

64 Quoted in *ibid.*, 120; see also Tischler, *Rebellious Puritan*, p. 141.

65 Quoted in Spector, "Alternative Versions."

66 Quoted in Steen, *A Look at Tennessee Williams*, 179.

67 Harry Rasky, *Tennessee Williams: A Portrait in Laughter and Lamentation* (New York: Dodd, Mead, 1986), 24.

68 Murphy, *Tennessee Williams and Elia Kazan*, 44.

69 Adler, "Tennessee Williams: 'Personal Lyricism,'" 179.

70 Quoted in Deborah G. Burks, "'Treatment is Everything': The Creation and Casting of Blanche and Stanley in Tennessee Williams' 'Streetcar,'" *Library Chronicle of the University of Texas at Austin* 41 (1987): 27.

71 Murphy, *Tennessee Williams and Elia Kazan*, 43–44.

72 Spector, "Alternative Versions," 558.

73 Letter appears in Steen, *A Look at Tennessee Williams*, 180.

74 Quoted in *ibid.*, 174.

75 Murphy, *Tennessee Williams and Elia Kazan*, 40.

76 Kazan, *A Life*, 345.

77 Marlon Brando, *Brando: Songs My Mother Taught Me* (New York: Random House, 1994), 122–24.

78 Anca Vlasopolos, "Authorizing History: Victimization in *A Streetcar Named Desire*," *Theatre Journal* 38 (Oct. 1986): 322–38.

79 Harold Clurman, *The Divine Pastime: Theatre Essays* (New York: Macmillan, 1974), 16–17.

80 Wallace Card, "Is This Trap Necessary: Ann-Margret and Treat Williams Hop Aboard a TV Remake of *Streetcar*," *People Weekly* 20 (15 Aug. 1983): 98.

81 Pauly, *An American Odyssey*, 84.

82 Burks, "'Treatment is Everything,'" 31.

83 *Life*, 341.

84 Quoted in Murphy, 19.

85 Quoted in Burks, "'Treatment is Everything,'" 32.

86 Kazan, *A Life*, 344.

87 Brando, *Brando: Songs My Mother Taught Me*, 121–22.

88 Roger Boxill, *Tennessee Williams* (New York: Macmillan, 1987), 88.

89 Kazan, *A Life*, 343–44.

90 Charles Higham, *Brando* (New York: New American Library, 1987), 81.

91 John Gronbeck-Tedesco, "Ambiguity and Performance in the Plays of Tennessee Williams," *Mississippi Quarterly* 48 (Fall 1995): 739.

92 Higham, *Brando*, 84.

93 Carla McDonough, *Staging Masculinity: Male Identity in Contemporary American Drama* (Jefferson, NC: McFarland, 1997), 25.

94 Quoted in Higham, *Brando*, 82.

95 Quoted in *ibid.*, 79.

96 Burks, "'Treatment is Everything,'" 30.

97 Clurman, "Streetcar."

98 McDonough, *Staging Masculinity*, 25.

99 Pauly, *An American Odyssey*, 82.

[100] Murphy, *Tennessee Williams and Elia Kazan*, 58.

[101] Quoted in *ibid.*, 48.

[102] Reviews of the Hagen and Quinn *Streetcar* cited parenthetically include:
Brooks Atkinson, "'Streetcar' Passenger: Uta Hagen Takes Over the Leading Part," *New York Times* 12 June 1949, sec. 2: 1; Sue Bentley, "Back to Broadway," *Theatre Arts* Nov. 1949: 14; Claudia Cassidy, "On the Aisle," *Chicago Daily Tribune* 23 Sept. 1948, sec. 3: 1; Richard S. Davis, "Glowing Star Is Uta Hagen: 'Streetcar' at Davidson," *Milwaukee Journal* 2 June 1949; George Eells, "The Third Saint Joan," *Theatre Arts* Nov. 1951: 88–89; Robert Garland, "Streetcar," *New York Journal American* 6 July 1948: 12; William Hawkins, "'Streetcar' Clangs into City Center," *New York World-Telegram* 24 May 1950: 4D; Kahn, "Legit Follow Up: Streetcar Named Desire," *Variety* 14 July 1948: 52; Myles Standish "Streetcar," *St. Louis Post-Dispatch* 6 Apr. 1949; Clarissa Start, "She Caught 'A Streetcar Named Desire,'" *St Louis Post-Dispatch* 8 Apr. 1949; and Richard Watts, Jr., "Two on the Aisle," *New York Post* 24 May 1950: 71.

[103] *New York Star* 8 Aug. 1948: 21.

[104] Clurman, *Divine Pastime*, 115.

[105] Uta Hagen, with Haskel Frank, *Respect for Acting* (New York: Macmillan, 1973), 37.

[106] All of Quinn's quotations come from his and Daniel Paisner's *One Man Tango* (New York: Harper Collins, 1995), 93, 96.

[107] James Schevill, "Playwrights' Forum," 195.

2 *Streetcar* on the world stage: the national premieres, 1948–1953

[1] Included in the Wood Papers at Harry Ransom Humanities Research Center (hereafter HRHRC) at the University of Texas at Austin.

[2] See Philip C. Kolin, "Tennessee Williams's *A Streetcar Named Desire* in Havana: Modesto Centeno's Cuban *Streetcars*, 1948–1965," *South Atlanta Review* 60 (Nov. 1995): 89–110.

[3] See Philip C. Kolin, "The Mexican Premiere of Tennessee Williams's *A Streetcar Named Desire*," *Mexican Studies/Estudios Mexicanos* 10 (Summer 1994): 315–40.

4 Jürgen Wolter, "The Cultural Context of *A Streetcar Named Desire* in Germany," in *Confronting Tennessee Williams's A Streetcar Named Desire: Essays in Critical Pluralism*, ed. Philip C. Kolin (Westport, CT: Greenwood, 1993) 199–222.

5 Christian Gilles, *Arletty ou La Liberté D'Etre* (Paris: Librairie Séguer, 1988): p. 75.

6 See Philip C. Kolin, "'Cruelty and Sweaty Intimacy': The Reception of the Spanish Premiere of *A Streetcar Named Desire*," *Theatre Survey* 35 (Nov. 1995): 45–56.

7 See Philip C. Kolin, "The First Polish Productions of *A Streetcar Named Desire*," *Theatre History Studies* 12 (1992): 67–88.

8 Irene Shaland, *Tennessee Williams on the Soviet Stage* (Lanham, MD: University Press of America, 1987), 11–21.

9 See Philip C. Kolin and Sherry Shao, "The First Production of *A Streetcar Named Desire* in Mainland China," *Tennessee Williams Literary Journal* 2 (Winter 1990–91): 19–31.

10 Housed in the Wood Papers, HRHRC.

11 The Mexican reviews cited in this section include: "Radar Filmico," *El Nacional* 8 Dec. 1948, sec. 2A: 1; "El teatro: Lo que ha essenito hasta ahora Tennessee Williams, por que abordo *Un Tranvía Llamado Deseo*," *Novedades* 7 Dec. 1948: 3; "El teatro: Quien es Tennessee Williams, a quien se considera como 'el nuevo O'Neill,'" *Novedades* 4 Dec. 1948: 3; "El teatro moderno marcha hacia una de las más estujantes realidades, jamás vista," *Ultimas Noticias* 14 June 1949: 3; "*Un Tranvía Llamado Deseo*," *Excelsior* Part 2 (8 Dec. 1948): 2; "Trotamundos de espectaculos," *Novedades* 14 Dec. 1948: 3; Manuel Altolaguirre, "*Un Tranvía Llamado Deseo*," *Excelsior* 22 May 1949; Armando de María y Campos, "El teatro: A propósito de la interpretación por aficionados de *Un Tranvía Llamado Deseo*," *Novedades* 11 Dec. 1948: 3; Luis de Cervantes, "Foros y artistas," *Ultima Hora* 5 May 1949: 9; Antonio Magaña Esquivel, "Un estreno, una actriz, y un actor," *Revista Mexicana de Cultura*, Sunday Supplement of *El Nacional* 12 Dec. 1948: 14; Rafael Estrada, "Entre bambalinas," *Novedades* 16 Dec. 1948: 4; Efrain Huerta, "Radar filmico," *El Nacional* 11 Dec. 1948, sec. 2A: 3; Francisco Monteverde, "Obras e interpretaciones," *El Universal* 6 Dec. 1948, sec. 2: 26; and Arturo Mori, "Foro y melodía," *Cinema Reporter* 18 Dec. 1948: 2.

12 Roni Unger, *Posia en voz alta in the Theater of Mexico* (Columbia: University of Missouri Press, 1981), 4.

13 Playbill, Teatro Esperanza, May 1949.

14 Dolores Carbonell and Luis Javier Mier Vega, "Una crónica de *Un Tranvía*... Sano, Sarrás, y Luna," in *3 crónicas del Teatro en México* (Mexico City: Instituto de Bellas Artes, 1988), p. 50.

15 *Ibid.*, 145.

16 *Ibid.*, 49–50.

17 William Kleb, "Marginalia: *Streetcar*, Williams, Foucault," in *Confronting Tennessee Williams's A Streetcar Named Desire: Essays in Critical Pluralism*, ed. Philip C. Kolin (Westport, CT: Greenwood, 1993), pp. 27–44.

18 Philip C. Kolin and Auxiliadora Arana, "An Interview with Wolf Ruvinskis: The First Mexican Stanley Kowalski," *Latin American Theatre Review* 26 (Spring 1993): 163.

19 The reviews quoted from in this section include: "*Un tram che si chiama desiderio* all'Eliseo," *Il Momento Sera* 22 Jan. 1949; M.C., "*Un tram che si chiama desiderio* all'Eliseo," *Il Paese* 23 Jan. 1949; Giovanni Calendoli, "*Un tram che si chiama desiderio* all'Eliseo," *La Repubblica* 22 Jan. 1949; Ermanno Contini, "*Un tram che si chiama desiderio* all'Eliseo," *Il Messaggero di Roma* 23 Jan. 1949; Silvio D'Amico, "Tennessee Williams all 'Eliseo," *Il Tempo* 23 Jan. 1949; Achille Fiocco, "Visconti all'Eliseo," *La Fiera Letteraria* 30 Jan. 1949; A. Fratelli and Rosso di San Secundo, "*Un tram che si chiama desiderio* all'Eliseo," *Il Giornale Della Sera* 22 Jan. 1949; Gian Domenico Giagni, "5 Bottles, 100 Cigarettes: The Needs of *Streetcar* are Unbelievable," *BIS* 22 Jan. 1949; Vito Pandolfi, "*Un tram che si chiama desiderio* all'Eliseo," *Il Dramma* 1 Feb. 1949; A. Possenti, in *Teatri Del Primo Novocento*; Raul Radice, "During Rehearsals Morelli Lost Five Kilos," *L'Europeo* 30 Jan. 1949; and Carlo Trabucco, "*Un tram che si chiama desiderio* all'Eliseo," *Il Popolo* 23 Jan. 1949.

20 Franco Zeffirelli, *The Autobiography of Franco Zeffirelli* (London: Weidenfeld and Nicolson, 1986), p. 80.

21 Quoted in Stephen Faber, "'Vita Vittorio': Explores the Actor's Condition," *New York Times* 18 Sept. 1984: C17.

22 Tennessee Williams, "Anna Magnani: Tigress of the Tiber," *New York Herald Tribune*, 11 Dec. 1955: D1.

23 Zeffirelli, *Autobiography*, 80.

24 Monica Sterling, *A Screen of Time: A Study of Luchino Visconti* (New York: Harcourt, 1979), 82.

25 Gaia Servadio, *Luchino Visconti: A Biography* (New York: Franklin, 1983), 121.

26 Zeffirelli, *Autobiography*, 93.

27 Quirino Galli, "From Vito Pandolfi's Psychological Realism to Luchino Visconti's Historic Realism," in *Teatro Contemporaneo*, 2 vols. (Rome: Lucarini Editore, 1984), I: 248.

28 Zeffirelli, *Autobiography*, 94.

29 Quoted in Michael Church, "A Director Looms into Shot Again," *The Observer* 4 Apr. 1993: 53.

30 "Vittorio Gassman," *Encyclopedia of World Theatre* (New York: Scribner's, 1977).

31 Gideon Bachman, "Marcello Mastroianni: Yesterday, Today, and Tomorrow," *Scanorama* Sept. 1990: 46.

32 "Marcello Mastroianni," Filplex, 1995 <http://www.gigaplex.com/celebs/mastro.html/

33 *Ibid.*

34 *Stage and Society in Sweden – Aspects of Swedish Theatre Since 1945*, trans. Paul Britten Austin (Stockholm: The Swedish Institute, 1972), 30.

35 The reviews cited in this section include:
Elis Andersson, "Den fulländade succé," *Göteborg-Posten* 2 Mar. 1949; A. Gunn Bergman, "Teaterspårvagn i Göteborg och i Malmö," *Aftonbladet* [Malmö] 2 Mar. 1949: 3; Herbert Grevenius, "Göteborgs Stadsteater: Spårvagn till Lustgården," *Stockholms-Tidningen* 1 Mar. 1949; Kjell Hjern, "Spårvagn till Lustgården," *Handelstidningen* 2 Mar. 1949; Erwin Leiser, "Teaterspårvagn i Göteborg och i Malmö," *Aftonbladet* [Gothenburg] 2 Mar. 1949: 3; and J. Thin, "Stor kväll på Stadsteatern," *Göteborg Tidningen* 2 Mar. 1949.

36 "Ingmar Bergman," *McGraw-Hill Encyclopedia of World Drama* (1984), 328–29.

37 Lise-Lone Marker and Frederick J. Marker, "Ingmar Bergman as Theater Director: A Retrospective," *Yale Theatre* 11 (1979): 15.

38 Quoted in Henrik Sjögren, *Ingmar Bergman på teatern* (Stockholm: Almqvist and Wiksell, 1968), 293.

39 Quoted by Parliamentary Correspondent, *Daily Mail* 9 Dec. 1949: 5.

40 "Royalty Rejects American Play," *New York Times* 5 Nov. 1949: 10.

41 The reviews included in this section on the British premiere are: "Streetcar," *Daily Mail* 13 Oct. 1949, sec. 2: 3; Brooks Atkinson, *New York Times* 11 Dec. 1949: 3; George Bishop, "Vivien Leigh in Exacting Part," *Daily Telegraph and Morning Post* 13 Oct. 1949: 6; Lionel Collier, "Theatre," *Time & Tide* 22 Oct. 1949: 1052; Peter Fleming, *Spectator* 21 Oct. 1949: 533; Walter Hays, "*Streetcar*: A Triumph for the Oliviers," *Daily Graphic* 13 Oct. 1949: 2; Harold Hobson, "Miss Vivien Leigh," *Sunday Times* 13 Nov. 1949: 2; David Levin, "Spotlight," *Daily Express* 12 Oct. 1949: 3; F.S., "*Streetcar*," *Theatre World* Nov. 1949: 8; N.S., "Manchester Opera House: *A Streetcar Named Desire*," *Manchester Evening News* 28 Sept. 1949: 3; R. D. Smith, *New Statesman and Nation* 22 Oct. 1949: 451; J. C. Trewin, *Illustrated London News* 5 Nov. 1949: 712; Trewin, "Plays in Performance," *Drama* 3, no. 15 (Winter 1949): 7; and Kenneth Tynan, *He That Plays the King: A View of the Theatre* (London: Longman, Green, 1950), 170.

42 Felix Barker, *The Oliviers: A Biography* (Philadelphia: Lippincott, 1953), 340–41. I am indebted to Barker for most of the information in this paragraph.

43 "Lord Chamberlain's Cuts," 12 July 1948, Wood Papers, HRHRC.

44 Telegram from Selznick to Hugh Beaumont, 21 July 1948, Wood papers, HRHRC.

45 For a text of Olivier's letter, see Philip C. Kolin, "'Affectionate and mighty regards from Vivien and me': Sir Laurence Olivier's Letter to Tennessee Williams on the London Premiere of *A Streetcar Named Desire*," *Missouri Review* 13 no. 3 (1992): 143–57.

46 Quoted in Philip Oakes, "Return Ticket," *Sunday Times* 17 Mar. 1974: 35.

47 Personal interview, Mar. 1991.

48 Quoted in T. Kiernan, *Olivier: The Life of Sir Laurence Olivier* (London: Sedgwick and Jackson, 1980), 239.

49 *Ibid.*

50 See Philip C. Kolin, "*A Streetcar Named Desire*: A Playwrights' Forum," *Michigan Quarterly Review* 39 (Spring 1990): 197.

51 Quoted in Anthony Holden, *Laurence Olivier* (New York: Atheneum, 1988), 256.

52 Quoted in *ibid.*, 257.
53 Barker, *The Oliviers*, 341.
54 Holden, *Olivier*, 257.
55 Laurence Olivier, *Confessions of an Actor* (New York: Simon and Schuster, 1982), 165.
56 See Kolin, "'Affectionate and mighty,'" 155.
57 "Mostly About People," *New York Herald Tribune*, Paris Edition, 14 Oct. 1949: 5.
58 Lewis W. Falb, *American Drama in Paris, 1945–1970* (Chapel Hill: University of North Carolina Press, 1973), 25.
59 The reviews of the French production cited in this section include: "Un Tramway," *Paris Match* 29 Oct. 1949; "*Un Tramway Nommé Désir*," *Figaro* 1 Feb. 1957; *Les Nouvelles Littéraires* 27 Oct. 1949; M.A., *La Critique de France Soir* 20 Oct. 1949; André Alter, "Au Théâtre Edouard VII . . .," *L'Aube* 20 Oct. 1949; P.C., *Le Soir* 28 Dec. 1950; Frank Dorsey, "'Un Tramway Nommé Désir' New Hit of the Paris Season," *New York Herald Tribune* 6 Nov. 1949 5: 3; Max Favelelli, "Le Théâtre," *Paris Presse* 19 Oct. 1949; Jean Jacques Gautier, "'Un Tramway Nommé Désir,'" *Figaro* 19 Oct. 1949; Jean Grandrey-Réty, "Le Théâtre," *Ce Soir* 19 Oct. 1949; Claude Jamet, *Parôles Françaises* 28 Oct. 1949; G. Jolly, *L'Aurore* 20 Oct. 1949; Jean Louiguy, *France Dimanche* 23 Oct. 1949; André Ransan, "*Un Tramway Nommé Désir*," *Ce Matin* 19 Oct. 1949; and André Singer, *Figaro* 20 Oct. 1949.
60 "Tale of 3 Cities," *Theatre Arts* Jan. 1950: 35.
61 Falb, *American Drama*, 28.
62 "Mostly About People."
63 Philip C. Kolin, "Williams in Ebony: Black and Multi-Racial Productions of *A Streetcar Named Desire*," *Black American Literature Forum* 25 (Spring 1991): 148.
64 George W. Crandell, "Misrepresentation and Miscegenation: Reading the Radicalized Discourse of Tennessee Williams's *A Streetcar Named Desire*," *Modern Drama* 40 (1997): 337–46.
65 Gilles, *Arletty ou La Liberté D'Etre* 75.
66 *Streetcar* was first staged at the Mainichi Hall in Osaka City from 19 March through 27 March 1953 for twelve performances. Then on 28 and 29 March it was performed three times in Kyoto. From there

Bungakuza brought the play to Tokyo's Daiichi-Semei Hall from 4 April through 19 April 1953, with two additional performances on the 20th, totaling thiry-four performances in Japan's capital. On 27 and 28 May *Streetcar* played three times in Nagoya; and on 30 May Bungakuza ended their history-making debut of *Streetcar* in Shizuoka with two performances.

67 Benito Ortolani, *The Japanese Theatre: From Shamanistic Ritual to Contemporary Pluralism* (Leiden: E. J. Brill, 1990), 300.

68 *Ibid.*, 238.

69 *Ibid.,*. 239.

70 Shiro Narumi, personal letter to Philip C. Kolin, 15 Dec. 1994.

71 *The History of the Bungakuza Dramatic Company* (Tokyo: Bungakuza, [n.d.]), 6.

72 The reviews from the Japanese premiere I cite include: "The Success of the Powerful Staging in the Last Half of *A Streetcar Named Desire*," *Yomiuri* [Osaka] 23 Mar. 1953; K. Kakitani, "Bungakuza's *Streetcar* Offers Carefully Engraved Characters," *Shin-Kansai*, 28 Mar. 1958; Ko, "Bungakuza's *Streetcar* is Their Highest Accomplishment," *Yomiuri* [Tokyo edn.] 19 Apr. 1953; K.M.O., "Haruko Sugimura Brilliant in *Street Car* [sic] *Named Desire*," *Mainichi* [Tokyo edn.] 10 Apr. 1953; Ohoka, "Bungakuza's Hit Production is Worth Attending," *Kokusai* [Tokyo] 21 Mar. 1953; Yamaguchi, "Bungakuza's Show a Masterpiece: *A Streetcar Named Desire*," *Mainichi* [Osaka edn.] 23 Mar. 1953; K. Yamawaki, "Bungakuza's *Streetcar* More Interesting Than Film Version," *Asahi* [Tokyo] 6 Apr. 1953.

3 *Streetcar* revivals on the English-language stage

1 "Happy Birthday," *New Yorker* 5 May 1973: 81.

2 "Blanche Wins the Battle," *New York Times* 1 Apr. 1973, sec. 2: 1.

3 *New York Observer* 21 Mar. 1988.

4 "Sanitizing the *Streetcar*," *Louisiana Literature* 14 (Fall 1997): 48.

5 Reviews of the Center Coconut Grove/Center Theatre 1956 revival include:
Brooks Atkinson, "The Theatre: 'Streetcar' Is Revived," *New York Times* 16 Feb. 1956: 24, rpt. *New York Theatre Critics' Reviews* 17: 362 (responses: *New York Times* 11 Mar. 1956, sec. 2: 3; and "Theatre:

'Streetcar,'" *New York Times* 4 Mar. 1956: 18); George Bourke,
"Tallulah Lights Up 'Streetcar,'" *Miami Herald* 17 Jan. 1956: 17–A;
Arthur Bronson, "Shows on Broadway, *Streetcar Named Desire*," *Variety*
22 Feb. 1956: 56; John Chapman, "Miss Bankhead Makes a Novelty
Out of 'Streetcar,'" *New York Daily News* 16 Feb. 1956: 46, rpt. *New
York Theatre Critics' Reviews* 17: 365; Robert Coleman, "'Streetcar'
Rolls Again With Talu at Helm,'" *New York Daily Mirror* 17 Feb. 1956:
30, rpt. *New York Theatre Critics' Reviews* 17: 364; Thomas R. Dash, "'A
Streetcar Named Desire,'" *Women's Wear Daily* 16 Feb. 1956: 78;
Wolcott Gibbs, *New Yorker* 25 Feb. 1956: 90–93; William Hawkins,
"Tallulah Brilliant in 'Streetcar' Role," *New York World-Telegram and
Sun* 16 Feb. 1956: 20, rpt. *New York Theatre Critics' Reviews* 17: 362;
Hawkins, "Theater: Tallulah Hits 'Streetcar' – Head On," *New York
World-Telegram and Sun* 11 Feb. 1956: 9; John Keating, "The Theatre:
Danger! Streetcar Off Its Track," *Cue* 25 Feb. 1956: 10; Walter F. Kerr,
New York Herald Tribune 16 Feb. 1956: 14, rpt. *New York Theatre
Critics' Reviews* 17: 364; John McClain, "Talu Gives a Sunday Try," *New
York Journal American* 16 Feb. 1956: 18, rpt. *New York Theatre Critics'
Reviews* 17: 363; Herb Rau, "A Streetcar Named Tallulah," *Miami
Daily News* 17 Jan. 1956: 413; Stanley Richards, "On and Off
Broadway: Commercial Theatre," *Players Magazine* 32 (May 1956):
180; *Theatre Arts* Apr. 1956: 24; "*A Streetcar Named Desire*," *Time* 13
Feb. 1956: 32; *Time* 27 Feb. 1956: 61; and Euphemia Van Rensselaer
Wyatt, "'A Streetcar Named Desire,'" *Catholic World* 183 (Apr. 1956):
67.

6   "T. Williams's View of T. Bankhcad," *New York Times* 29 Dec. 1963:
3.

7   Lee Israel, *Miss Tallulah Bankhead* (New York: Putnam's, 1972): 301.

8   "Drama Mailbag": "A Tribute From Tennessee Williams to 'Heroic
Tallulah Bankhead,'" *New York Times* 4 Mar. 1956, sec. 2: 3, 7.

9   "Drama Mailbag," *New York Times* 11 Mar. 1956, sec. 2: 3.

10 "Tennessee Williams Turns Sixty," *Esquire* Sept. 1971: 107.

11 *Something Cloudy, Something Clear* (New York: New Directions, 1995),
58.

12 Israel, *Miss Tallulah Bankhead*, 303.

13 *Ibid.*, 302.

14 *Ibid.*, p. 300.

15 Brooks Atkinson, "Theatre: 'Streetcar,'" *New York Times* 4 Mar. 1955: 18.

16 "Where My Head Is Now and Other Questions," *Performing Arts* [L.A.] 7 (Apr. 1973): 26.

17 Reviews of the Los Angeles 1973 revival include: Edwa, "'A Streetcar Named Desire,'" *Variety* 4 Apr. 1973: 124; Stephen Farber, "Blanche Wins the Battle," *New York Times* 1 Apr. 1973, sec. 2: 1, 15; Jody Jacobs, *Los Angeles Times* 22 Mar. 1973, sec. 4: 15; Ray Loynd, "Voight, Dunaway Star in 'Streetcar Named Desire,'" *Los Angeles Herald-Examiner* 21 Mar. 1973, sec. D: 2; J. Moriarity, "25 Passing Years Have Dimmed *Streetcar*'s Impact," *The Advocate* [L.A.] 9 May 1973: 29; "News Makers," *Newsweek* 2 Apr. 1973: 44; Ron Pennington, "*Streetcar Named Desire*," *Hollywood Reporter* 21 Mar. 1973: 10; and Dan Sullivan, "'Streetcar' On, Off Track," *Los Angeles Times* 21 March 1973, sec. 4: 1, 10.

18 Quoted in *Newsweek* 2 Apr. 1973.

19 Reviews from the New York Lincoln Center 1973 revival include: Lillian Africano, "Theatre: Effort Falls Short," *Villager* 17 May 1973: 10; Clive Barnes, "Stage: A Rare *Streetcar*," *New York Times* 27 Apr. 1973: 31; John Beaufort, "*Streetcar*," *Christian Science Monitor* 30 Apr. 1973; Martin Bookspan, "*Streetcar*," WPIX-TV (2 May 1973); Harold Clurman, "Theatre," *Nation* 216 (14 May 1973): 635–36; Brendan Gill, "Happy Birthday," *New Yorker* 5 May 1973: 81; Martin Gottfried, "The Theatre: *Streetcar* Is Running Again," *Women's Wear Daily* 30 Apr. 1973: 18; Catherine Hughes, *America* 128 (26 May 1973): 495; T. E. Kalem, "Beast v. Beauty: *A Streetcar Named Desire*," *Time* 7 May 1973: 88–90, rpt. *New York Theatre Critics' Reviews* 34: 283; Walter Kerr, "Of Blanche the Victim," *New York Times* 6 May 1973, sec. D: 1, 10; Judy Klemesrud, *New York Times* 10 June 1973, sec. 2: 1, 3 [interview with Farentino]; Jack Kroll, "Battle of New Orleans," *Newsweek* 7 May 1973: 109–10, rpt. *New York Theatre Critics' Reviews* 34: 283; Julius Novick, *Village Voice* 3 May 1973, sec. 3: 5; George Oppenheimer, "Williams's 'Streetcar' Rolls On," *Newsday* [Garden City, NY] 27 May 1973, sec. 2: 9, 25; Rex Reed, "An Unhappy Birthday to 'Streetcar,'" *New York Daily News* 13 May 1973, sec. 3: 5, Kevin Sanders, ABC-TV, 26 Apr. 1973, rpt. *New York Theatre Critics' Reviews* 34: 284; Marilyn

Stasio, "Theatre," *Cue* 5 May 1973: 7; Douglas Watt, "Rep Ends Era with 'Streetcar,'" *New York Daily News* 27 Apr. 1973: 66, rpt. *New York Theatre Critics' Reviews* 34: 281; Douglas Watt, *New York Daily News* 6 May 1973, sec. 3: 3; and Edwin Wilson, "Two Revivals That Succeed," *Wall Street Journal* 14 May 1973: 12, rpt. *New York Theatre Critics' Reviews* 34: 282–83.

20 Quoted in Reed, "An Unhappy Birthday to 'Streetcar,'" *New York Daily News* 13 May 1973, sec. 3: 5.

21 Reviews of the London 1974 revival include:
Clive Barnes, "London Theatre: Classics and Sexism," *New York Times* 17 Aug. 1974: 16; Ian Christie, "*Streetcar*," *Daily Express* 15 Mar. 1974: 12; Robert Cushman, "More Cheers for Chekhov: Theatre," *The Observer* 17 Mar. 1974: 35; Helen Dawson, "'A Streetcar Named Desire,'" *Plays and Players* 21 (1974): 28–31; "Eye" [*sic*], "*Streetcar* in London," *Women's Wear Daily* 18 Mar. 1974: 8; Robert F. Hawk[ins] "Shows Abroad: 'A Streetcar Named Desire,'" *Variety* 27 Mar. 1974: 72; Harold Hobson, "'Streetcar' Bolsters Broadway's British Name," *Christian Science Monitor* 27 Mar. 1974: F6; Kenneth Hurren, "Down Yonder," *Spectator* 16 March 1974; Eric Johns, "No Ghost Will Haunt Claire Bloom's Blanche," *Stage and Television Today* [London] 14 Mar. 1974: 10; Jeremy Kingston, "Theatre: *Streetcar* Blooms," *Punch* 27 Mar. 1974: 519; J. W. Lambert, "*Streetcar*," *Drama* (Summer 1974): 45–46; R.B.M[arriott], "Return of Blanche DuBois," *Stage and Television Today* [London] 21 Mar. 1974: 9; Sheridan Morley, "Claire Bloom: Always in the Limelight," *London Times* 14 Mar. 1974: 15; Benedict Nightingale, "Theatre: Death and Decay," *New Statesman* [London] 22 Mar. 1974: 420–21; Milton Shulman, "Miss Bloom and the Marriage Trap," *Evening Standard* 15 Mar. 1974: 23; Arthur Thirkell, "*Streetcar*," *Daily Mirror* 15 Mar. 1973: 18; Jack Tinker, "*Streetcar*," *Daily Mail* 21 Mar. 1973; John Walker, "London Theatre: Splendid Revival of 'Streetcar' Stars Claire Bloom," *International Herald Tribune* 23–24 Mar. 1974: 7; and Irving Wardle, "New Trip on Old Streetcar," *London Times* 15 Mar. 1974: 15.

22 Quoted in Philip Oakes, "Return Ticket," *Sunday Times* 17 Mar. 1974: 35.

23 Claire Bloom, *Leaving A Doll's House* (Boston: Little, Brown, 1996): 132.

24   Quoted in Gore Vidal, *Palimpsest* (New York: Random House, 1995), 155–56.

25   N.A.F., *Natal Witness* 8 Jan. 1951.

26   Reviews of the Johannesburg 1975 revival include: David Coleman, "Drama," *Natal Witness* 29 July 1975; Bill Edgson, "*Streetcar,*" *Star* 15 Aug. 1975; Lynne Kelly, "'Streetcar' Is Still Moving," *Mercury* 4 July 1975; "A Mind Out of Control," *Pretoria News* 7 Aug. 1975; "'Streetcar' is Still Exciting," *Johannesburg Sunday Times* 17 Aug. 1975; and Garth Verdal, "Theatre," *Argus* 7 July 1975.

27   Personal letter to Philp C. Kolin, 16 Nov. 1988.

28   Reviews of the Gelber Lake Forest 1976 revival include: Edward Andrew, " *Streetcar,*" *Chicago* 12 June 1976; Dorothy Andries, "Page: Poignant, Powerful," *Lake Forester* [Illinois] 16 June 1976; Claudia Cassidy, "*Streetcar,* " WFMT [Chicago] 13 June 1976; David Elliott, "'Streetcar' Moves with Express Power," *Chicago Daily News* 12 June 1976; Bury St. Edmund, "Drama," *Chicago Reader* 18 June 1976; Glenna Syse, "A Strange, Long 'Streetcar' Production," *Chicago Sun-Times* 11 June 1976; Linda Winer, "'Streetcar' Rides a Rough Road," *Chicago Tribune* 11 June 1976; and Dan Zeff, "Tennessee Would Like Page's Blanche," *Waukegan* [Illinois] *News-Sun* 17 June 1976.

29   Quoted in Sandra Hochman, *New York Times Biographical Service* 3 Aug. 1994.

30   *Ibid.*

31   Reviews of the New York Circle in the Square 1988 revival include: Clive Barnes, "Revisionist 'Streetcar,'" *New York Post* 11 Mar. 1988: 28, 30; John Beaufort, "This 'Streetcar' Offers Bumpy Ride to Familiar Theatrical Territory," *Christian Science Monitor* 14 Mar. 1988, rpt. *New York Theatre Critics' Reviews* 49: 343; Mel Gussow, "Has Stanley Kowalski Become an Unactable Role?" *New York Times* 14 Mar. 1988, sec. 3: 13; Sandra Hochman, "Williams's Broken Women and Macho Men Endure," *New York Times* 26 June 1988; Caryn James, *New York Times* 6 Mar. 1988, sec. 2: 1, 24; Howard Kissel, "A So-So 'Streetcar,'" *New York Daily News* 11 Mar. 1988, rpt. *New York Theatre Critics' Reviews* 49: 339–40; Mimi Kramer, *New Yorker* 28 Mar. 1988: 81–82; David Lida, "'Streetcar' – A Review," *Women's Wear Daily* 11 Mar. 1988, rpt. *New York Theatre Critics' Reviews* 49: 340; William A. Raidy, "This 'Streetcar' Derailed," *Staten Island* [New York] *Advance* 12 Mar.

1988; Rex Reed, "On the Town With Rex Reed," *New York Observer* 21 Mar. 1988; Frank Rich, "Danner and Quinn in a New Streetcar," *New York Times* 11 Mar. 1988, sec. 3: 3; Joel Siegel, WABC-TV, 10 Mar. 1988, rpt. *New York Theatre Critics' Reviews* 49: 342–43; David Patrick Stearns, *USA Today* 18 Mar. 1988, rpt. *New York Theatre Critics' Reviews* 49: 344; Steven Vineberg, "*A Streetcar Named Desire*," *Theatre Journal* 39 (May 1987): 235–36; Douglas Watt, "'Streetcar' on a Cool Track," *New York Daily News* 18 Mar. 1988, rpt. *New York Theatre Critics' Reviews* 49: 341; Linda Winer, "A Slow 'Streetcar,'" *New York Newsday* 11 Mar. 1988, rpt. *New York Theatre Critics' Reviews* 49: 344.

32 Georgia Dullea, "Not Entirely Out of Character," *New York Times Biographical Service* 3 Aug. 1994.

33 Reviews of the New York 1992 revival include:
Clive Barnes, "Hop on 'Streetcar,'" *New York Post* 13 Apr. 1992; William A. Henry III, "More Heat Than Desire," *Time* 20 April 1992; Howard Kissel, "'Streetcar' Named Disaster," *New York Daily News* 13 Apr. 1992; Jack Kroll, "What Becomes a Legend," *Newsweek* 27 Apr. 1992; Frank Rich, "Alec Baldwin Does Battle With the Ghosts," *New York Times* 13 Apr. 1992: C11, C17; David Richards, "This *Streetcar* Doesn't Travel Far Enough," *New York Times* 19 Apr. 1992: sec. 2: 5; Joel Siegel, "A Streetcar Named Desire," WABC-TV, rpt. *New York Theatre Critics' Reviews* 1992: 129; John Simon, "A Streetcar Named Desire," *New York* 27 Apr. 1992; David Patrick Stearns, "Star-Powered 'Streetcar' Crawls Along," *USA Today* 13 Apr. 1992; Douglas Watt, "A Streetcar Named Desire," *New York Daily News* 17 Apr. 1992; Edwin Wilson, "A Streetcar Named Desire," *Wall Street Journal* 20 Apr. 1992; Linda Winer, "'A Streetcar' Without Desire," *New York Newsday* 13 Apr. 1992; Alex Witchell, "A Cup of Cappuccino Named Desire," *New York Times* 20 May 1992: C1.

34 Quoted in Patrick Pacheo, "Alex Baldwin's Career Rides a 'Streetcar,'" *New York Times* 5 Apr. 1992.

35 Reviews of the Dublin revival I cite include:
Luke Clancy, "Theatre: Crazy for Blanche," *The Times* 12 May 1998, sec. 2: 37; Susannah Clapp, "Theatre," *The Observer* 10 May 1998: 12; John Peter, "*A Streetcar Named Desire*," *The Times* 17 May 1998: 11: 16; Matt Wolf, "*A Streetcar Named Desire*," *Variety* 18–24 May 1998: 82.

4 Recasting the players: expanding and radicalizing the *Streetcar* script

1 Brenda Murphy, *Tennessee Williams and Elia Kazan: A Collaboration in the Theatre* (Cambridge: Cambridge University Press, 1992), carefully documents the close working relationship between Kazan and Williams and Williams's involvement in the production process (16–23).

2 Philip C. Kolin, "*Streetcar Named Desire*: A Playwrights' Forum," *Michigan Quarterly Review* 19 (Spring 1990): 199.

3 "This is Show Business," *Key West* [Florida] *Citizen* 29 Sept. 1993.

4 Quoted in *Confronting Tennessee Williams's A Streetcar Named Desire: Essays in Critical Pluralism*, ed. Philip C. Kolin (Westport, CT: Greenwood, 1993), 3.

5 Arthur Gelb, "Negroes Stated for 'Streetcar,'" *New York Times* 14 July 1958: L16.

6 Louis Calta, "Opening of Play," *New York Times* 25 Sept. 1958: 30.

7 Unpublished letter included in Wood Papers, Harry Ransom Humanities Research Center, University of Texas at Austin.

8 Quoted in Kolin, "*Streetcar*: Playwrights' Forum," 182.

9 Sue-Ellen Case, *Feminism and Theatre* (New York: Methuen, 1988), 117.

10 Unpublished letter to Philip C. Kolin, 16 August 1990.

11 Telephone interview conducted by Philip C. Kolin, 24 August 1990.

12 Leo Guild, "Play Review: 'A Streetcar Named Desire' (Ebony Showcase Theatre)," *Hollywood Reporter* 3 Dec. 1956: 3.

13 Harold Hildebrand, "Vivid Acting in 'Streetcar,'" *Los Angeles Examiner* 19 Feb. 1955.

14 Hazel L. Lamarre, "Applause! In the Theatre," *Los Angeles Sentinel* 3 Mar. 1955: A10.

15 Katherine Von Blon, "'Streetcar' Offered at Ebony Showcase," *Los Angeles Times* 25 Feb. 1955, sec. 1: 22.

16 Wylie Williams, "All-Negro Cast Scores with 'Streetcar Named Desire,'" *Citizen News* [Hollywood, CA] 29 Nov. 1956: 21.

17 Kap, "Legit Review: *Streetcar Named Desire* (Ebony Showcase)," *Variety* 30 Nov. 1956.

18 Guild, "Play Review."

19 David Bongard, "'Streetcar' Revived at Ebony Showcase Theatre," *Los Angeles Herald & Express* 1 Dec. 1956: B7.

20 "James Edwards Stars in Ebony's 'Streetcar,'" *Los Angeles Sentinel* 22 Nov. 1956: 4.

21 Lamarre, "Applause! In the Theatre."

22 Bongard, "'Streetcar' Revived at Ebony Showcase Theatre."

23 Guild, "Play Review."

24 Katherine Von Blon, "'A Streetcar Named Desire' Begins Run at Ebony Showcase," *Los Angeles Times* 1 Dec. 1956, sec. 3: 2.

25 Harold Hildebrand, "'Streetcar' on Stage at Ebony," *Los Angeles Examiner* 30 Nov. 1956.

26 "Williams-Aufführung verboten," *Frankfurter Rundschau* 28 June 1974.

27 Roland H. Wiegenstein, "Hubners beste Talente Liegen brach . . . Nach dem Williams-Skandal," *Frankfurter Rundschau* 16 July 1974: 9.

28 Ronald Holloway, "Stop that 'Streetcar' Named Lang: Berlin Failed to Tell Dramatist of Slight Switch, A Black Lead," *Variety* 17 July 1974: 103.

29 "Freie Volksbühne darf nun doch . . . 'Endstation Sehnsucht' spielen," *Frankfurter Rundschau* 11 July 1974: 6.

30 Jürgen C. Wolter, "The Cultural Context of *A Streetcar Named Desire* in Germany," in *Confronting Tennessee Williams's A Streetcar Named Desire: Essays in Critical Pluralism*, ed. Philip C. Kolin (Westport, CT: Greenwood, 1993), 211.

31 Wiegenstein, "Hubners beste Talente."

32 Quoted in A. J. Está, "Gordone Directs New 'Streetcar,'" *Drama-Logue* 23 June 1983: 22.

33 Unpublished letter to Philip C. Kolin, 29 May 1990.

34 Unpublished letter to Philip C. Kolin, 12 June 1990.

35 Steve Jensen, "Impressive Revival of 'Streetcar,'" *Berkeley Gazette: Berkeley's Weekly Entertainment Magazine* 20 May 1983: P1.

36 "A Hot Streetcar," *California Voice* 3 June 1983: 20.

37 Linda Aube, "'Streetcar' on the Right Track," *Argus* 18 May 1983: 25.

38 Está, "Gordone Directs New 'Streetcar.'"

39 Steven Winn, "A Vivid Blanche DuBois in a Murky 'Streetcar,'" *San Francisco Chronicle* 26 May 1983: 70.

40 Aube, "'Streetcar' on the Right Track."

41 Está, "Gordone Directs New 'Streetcar.'"

42 Aube, "'Streetcar' on the Right Track."

43 Unpublished letter to Philip C. Kolin, 29 May 1990.

44 Unpublished letter to Philip C. Kolin, 12 June 1990.

45 Steve Jensen, "Impressive Revivial."

46 Telephone interview with Theodore Gilliam, 29 June 1990.

47 Richard Dodds, "Black 'Streetcar' Travels Well," *Times-Picayune* [New Orleans] 8 Nov. 1984: E3.

48 Theodore Gilliam, "Dashiki Theatre Producing Tennessee Williams Classic," *Louisiana Weekly* [New Orleans] 3 Nov. 1984, sec. 1: 4.

49 Dashiki playbill, 1 Nov. 1984.

50 Marian Orr, "A Line of Streetcars," *Gambit* [New Orleans] 10 Nov. 1984: 3.

51 Richard Dodds, "Minimal Rewriting Needed to Create a Black 'Streetcar,'" *Times-Picayune* [New Orleans] 1 Nov. 1983: E3.

52 Telephone interview with Philip C. Kolin, 29 June 1989.

53 Fran Lawless, "Critique 'Streetcar': A Triumph," *Spectator News Journal* [New Orleans] 14 Nov. 1984.

54 Edward Real, "Life Upon the Wicked Stage," *Impact* [New Orleans] 9 (16 Nov. 1984): 17.

55 Dodds, "Black 'Streetcar' Travels Well."

56 Real, "Life Upon the Wicked Stage."

57 Telephone interview conducted by Philip C. Kolin, 29 June 1989.

58 "Visitations: New Orleans Actor Wants to Build Film Industry Here," *Data Newsweekly* [New Orleans] 20 Nov. 1984: 6.

59 "Lagniappe," *Times-Picayune* [New Orleans] 2 Nov. 1984: 3.

60 N. R. Davidson, "This *Streetcar*'s Flawed But Not Easily Forgotten," *Louisiana Weekly* [New Orleans] 10 Nov. 1984, sec. 1: 6.

61 Lawless, "Critique 'Streetcar.'"

62 Orr, "A Line of Streetcars."

63 Lawless, "Critque 'Streetcar.'"

64 Davidson, "This *Streetcar*'s Flawed."

65 Orr, "A Line of Streetcars."

66 Real, "Life Upon the Wicked Stage."

67 Lawless, "Critique 'Streetcar.'"

68 Davidson, "This *Streetcar*'s Flawed."

69 Telephone interview conducted by Philip C. Kolin, 29 June 1989.

70 All the quotations in this paragraph are from Sid Smith, "'Streetcar' Risky But Refreshing," *Chicago Tribune*, "Tempo," 23 Feb. 1987: 4.

71 Quoted in Sid Smith, "Black Ensemble Boards 'Streetcar,'" *Chicago Tribune* 29 Jan. 1987, sec. 5: 9.

72 Smith, "'Streetcar Risky.'"

73 Hedy Weiss, "Ensemble Takes 'Streetcar' for Bumpy, Interesting Ride," *Chicago Sun-Times* 3 Mar. 1987: 46.

74 Smith, "'Streetcar' Risky."

75 Weiss, "Ensemble Takes 'Streetcar' for Ride."

76 *Ibid.*

77 Fred Nuccio, "Taylor a Standout in 'Streetcar' Role," *Skyline* [Chicago] 10–11 Mar. 1987, sec. 2: 1.

78 Weiss, "Ensemble Takes 'Streetcar' for Ride."

79 Playbill, *A Streetcar Named Desire*, Howard University, 10 Mar. 1988.

80 *Ibid.*

81 Alison Bethal, "Drama Department Performs *Streetcar* Derivation," *Hilltop* [Howard University] 8 Mar. 1988.

82 Reviews of *Belle Reprieve* cited in this section include: Claire Armisteed, "Belle Reprieve," *Financial Times*, 14 Jan. 1991, rpt. in *London Theatre Record* 11 (1991): 23; John Bell, "Bloolips and Split Britches," *Theatre Week* 4 Mar. 1991: 38; Rowena Chapman, "Belle Reprieve," *What's On* 16 Jan. 1991, rpt. in *London Theatre Record* 11 (1991): 23; Debra Griboff, "Belle Reprieve," *Show Business* 27 Feb. 1991: 23; John Hammond, "Beauty and the Beast," *N.Y. Native* 4 Mar. 1991: 26; Wilbourne Hampton, "A Sendup of 'Streetcar,'" *New York Times* 11 Mar. 1991: C14; John Lyttle, "Belle Reprieve," *Independent* 18 Jan. 1991, rpt. in *London Theatre Record* 11 (1991): 23; and Erika Milvey, "Southern Discombobulation," *The West Side Spirit* [New York] 12 Mar. 1991: 25–26.

83 All quotations from *Belle Reprieve* come from W. B. Worthen, ed., *The Harcourt Brace Anthology of Drama* (Fort Worth: Harcourt Brace College Publishers, 1995). Numbers in parentheses refer to page numbers of this volume.

84 Alissa Solomon, *Re-Dressing the Canon: Essays on Theatre and Gender* (London: Routledge, 1997), 157.

85 David Savran, *Communists, Cowboys and Queers: The Politics of Masculinity in the Work of Arthur Miller and Tennessee Williams* (Minneapolis: University of Minnesota Press, 1992), 116.

86 Solomon, *Re-Dressing the Canon*, 157.

87 John Clum, *Acting Gay: Male Homosexuality in American Drama* (New York: Columbia University Press, 1992), 150.

88 William Kleb, "Marginalia: *Streetcar*, Williams, and Foucault," in *Confronting Tennessee Williams's A Streetcar Named Desire: Essays in Critical Pluralism*, ed. Philip C. Kolin (Westport, CT: Greenwood, 1993), 33.

89 Solomon, *Re-Dressing the Canon*, 163.

5 *Streetcar* in other media

1 Promotional materials from Warner Bros. are available at the Harry Ransom Humanities Research Center, University of Texas at Austin.

2 R. Burton Palmer, "Hollywood in Crisis: Tennessee Williams and the Evolution of the Adult Film," in *The Cambridge Companion to Tennessee Williams*, ed. Matthew C. Roudané (Cambridge: Cambridge University Press, 1997), 217.

3 Sleeve of "Director's Cut" release, 1993.

4 Roger Ebert, "A Streetcar Named Desire," *Chicago Sun-Times* Nov. 12 1993.

5 "Streetcar," *Look* Sept. 1951.

6 Bosley Crowther, *New York Times* 20 Sept. 1951: 37.

7 *Tennessee Williams and Film* (New York: Ungar, 1977), 24.

8 Palmer, "Hollywood in Crisis," 212.

9 Thomas Pauly, *An American Odyssey: Elia Kazan and American Culture* (Philadelphia: Temple University Press, 1983), 131.

10 Nancy M. Tischler, "Sanitizing the *Streetcar*," *Louisiana Literature* 14 (Fall 1997): 48–55.

11 Linda Constanzo Cahir, "The Artful Rerouting of *A Streetcar Named Desire*," *Literature/Film Quarterly* 22 (1974): 72.

12 Gene D. Phillips, S.J., "*A Streetcar Named Desire*: Play and Film," in *Confronting Tennessee Williams's A Streetcar Named Desire: Essays in Critical Pluralism*, ed. Philip C. Kolin (Westport, CT: Greenwood, 1994), 231.

13 *Ibid.*, 232.

14 Maurice Yacowar, *Tennessee Williams and Film* (New York: Ungar, 1977), 18.

15 *Ibid.*, 17.

16 Cahir, "Artful Rerouting," 72.

17 *New York Mirror*, 20 Sept. 1951.

18 Rudolph Goodman, ed., *Drama on the Stage* (New York: Rinehart, 1961), quoted in Phillips, "*A Streetcar Named Desire*: Play and Film," 229.

19 Cahir, "Artful Rerouting," 73.

20 Palmer, "Hollywood in Crisis," 221.

21 *Ibid.*, 220.

22 Reviews of the 1952 ballet cited parenthetically include: Louis Biancolli, "Streetcar," *New York World Telegram and Sun* 9 Dec. 1952: 23; John Martin, "Ballet Company Stages 'Streetcar,'" *New York Times* 9 Dec. 1952: 42; Walter Terry, "Slavenska, Franklin Ballet," *New York Herald* 9 Dec. 1952: 34; Douglas Watt, "Back to New Orleans," *New Yorker* 20 Dec. 1952: 103–04; "'Streetcar' en Pointe," *Newsweek* Dec 1952: 71; and "Streetcar," *St. Louis Post-Dispatch* 26 Oct. 1952.

23 Reviews of the ballets done by the Dance Theatre of Harlem include: Nancy Goldner, "Cameras Enhance Performance of Dance Theatre of Harlem," *Youngstown* [Ohio] *Vindicator* 21 Feb. 1986: 23; Anna Kisselgoff, "Dance: Harlem Troupe Performs 'Streetcar,'" *New York Times* 16 Jan. 1982: L11; Lewis Segal, "PBS on the Right Track with 'Streetcar' Ballet," *Los Angeles Times* 21 Feb. 1986, se.c 6: 26; and Allan Ulrich, "Harlem Dance Returns to TV," *San Francisco Examiner* 21 Feb. 1986: E1.

24 Reviews of the Ann-Margret – Treat Williams *Streetcar* teleplay include: Jack Curry, "Tough Times Only Made Her Tougher," *USA Today* 2 Mar. 1984: 1; Nancy Griffin, " A Fine Madness," *Life* Mar. 1984: 73–76; John Leonard, "A Liberated Streetcar," *New York* 5 Mar. 1984: 98,100; John Simon, "The New Streetcar: Doing Battle with Brando," *Vogue* 174 (Feb. 1984): 71; Kenneth Turan, "It Was Very Frightening," *TV Guide* 3 Mar. 1984: 28–35; and Harry F. Waters, *Newsweek* 5 Mar. 1984: 91.

25 June Schlueter, "Imitating an Icon: John Erman's Remake of Tennessee Williams's *A Streetcar Named Desire*," *Modern Drama* 28 (1985): 141.

26 *Ibid.*

27 *Ibid.*, 142.

28 Reviews of the 1995 Lange/Baldwin teleplay include: John O'Connor, "Williams's 'Streetcar,' Not Kazan's," *New York Times* 27 Oct. 1995: D 22; Ward Howard Rosenberg, "Streetcar Rides on

Lange's Performance," *Los Angeles Times* 27 Oct. 1995: F1, F2; Rick Schultz, "A Streetcar to be Desired," *Mr. Showbiz Reviews*, Internet, http://www.abcnews.com 27 June 1997.

29 Reviews of the *Streetcar* opera cited parenthetically include: William Aguier, Jr., "Previn Turns 'Streetcar' Into a Fine Opera," *Hokubei* (Mainichi) 3 Oct. 1998: 14; John Allison, "Opera: A Previn Premiere: Fruitless Pursuit of Streetcar," *The Times* 23 Sept. 1998: 37; Jan Breslauer, "Just the Right Words," *Los Angeles Times* "Calendar" 20 Sept. 1998: 7, 55; Richard Dyer, "An Opera Named 'Desire,'" *Boston Globe* 23 Aug. 1998: N1, N2; Jesse Hamlin, "Taking *Streetcar* to the Opera," *San Francisco Chronicle*, "Datebook," 6 Sept. 1998; Dennis Harvey, sidewalk.com/Link "A Streetcar Named Desire"; Paul Hertelendy, "Triumphant Debut for 'Streetcar,'" *San Jose Mercury News* "Entertainment" 21 Sept. 1998: 4C; Robert Holfer, *Talk of LA Buzz* Sept. 1998; Bernard Holland, "To a Southerner, a Belle and a Butterfly Are Different," *New York Times* 24 Sept. 1998: 79; Michael Kennedy, "Full-blooded Kindness of Strangers," *Sunday Telegraph* 27 Sept. 1998; Theodore P. Mahane, "'Streetcar' The Opera Stays Right on Track and Give the Audience a Wonderful Ride," *Times-Picayune* [New Orleans] 4 Oct. 1998: E1; and "Notes for *Streetcar*. Librettist Philip Littell," *Opera News* 63 (Sept. 1998): 40; Tim Page, "Opera: 'Streetcar' Derailed by High Ideals," *Washington Post* 21 Sept. 1988: D5; Barry Paris, "A Knight at the Opera," *Vanity Fair* Sept. 1998: 222–34; Alan Rich, "Opera: 'Streetcar Named Desire," *Variety* 28 Sept. – 4 Oct. 1998: 191; Alex Ross, "Off the Tracks," *New Yorker* 5 October 1998; David Patrick Stearns, "'Streetcar' Desirable, If Slightly Off Track: Opera Review," *USA Today* 21 Sept. 1998, D30; Mark Swed, "Theater Review: A Strained 'Streetcar' Rolls Into San Francisco," *Los Angeles Times* 21 Sept. 1998, sec. F ("Calendar"): 1, 6; Terry Teachout, "Short Takes: Opera: A Streetcar Named Desire," *Time* 5 Oct. 1998: 96; "Thoroughly Modern Diva," *Time* 17 Nov. 1997; Allan Ulrich, "Streetcar Uninspired," *The Advocate* [LA], Oct. 27 1998: 77; J. A. van Sant, "States of Desire," *Worldwide North American*, Sept. 1998; and Stephanie von Buchau, "Kindness and Desire," *Pacific Sun* Sept. 23–29, 1998.

SELECT BIBLIOGRAPHY

Adler, Thomas P., *Mirror on the Stage: The Pulitzer Plays as an Approach to American Drama.* West Lafayette, IN: Purdue University Press, 1987.

"A Streetcar Named Desire": The Moth and the Lantern. Boston: Twayne, 1990.

Barranger, Milly S., "New Orleans as Theatrical Image in Plays by Tennessee Williams." *Southern Quarterly* 23 (Winter 1985): 38–54.

"Three Women Called Blanche." *Tennessee Williams Literary Journal* 1 (Spring 1987): 15–30.

Bedient, Calvin, "There Are Lives That Desire Does Not Sustain: *A Streetcar Named Desire.*" In *Confronting Tennessee Williams's A Streetcar Named Desire: Essays in Critical Pluralism.* Ed. Philip C. Kolin. Westport, CT: Greenwood, 1993. 45–58.

Berkman, Leonard, "The Tragic Downfall of Blanche DuBois." *Modern Drama* 10 (Dec. 1967): 249–57.

Bigsby, C.W. E., *A Critical Introduction to Twentieth-Century American Drama.* Vol. II. *Tennessee Williams, Arthur Miller, Edward Albee.* Cambridge: Cambridge University Press, 1992.

Bloom, Harold, ed., *Tennessee Williams's A Streetcar Named Desire.* New York: Chelsea, 1988.

Boxill, Roger, *Tennessee Williams.* New York: Macmillan, 1987.

Bray, Robert, "*A Streetcar Named Desire*: The Political and Historical Subtext." In *Confronting Tennessee Williams's A Streetcar Named Desire: Essays in Critical Pluralism.* Ed. Philip C. Kolin. Westport, CT: Greenwood, 1993. 183–98.

Cahir, Linda Constanzo, "The Artful Rerouting of *A Streetcar Named Desire*." *Literature/Film Quarterly* 22 (1994): 72–77.

Cardullo, Bert, "Birth and Death in *A Streetcar Named Desire*." In *Confronting Tennessee Williams's A Streetcar Named Desire: Essays in Critical Pluralism*. Ed. Philip C. Kolin. Westport, CT: Greenwood, 1993. 167–82.

Ciment, Michael, *Kazan on Kazan*. New York: Viking, 1974.

Corrigan, Mary Ann, "Realism and Theatricalism in *A Streetcar Named Desire*." *Modern Drama* 19 (Dec. 1976): 385–96.

Crandell, George C., *Tennessee Williams: A Descriptive Bibliography*. Pittsburgh: University of Pittsburgh Press, 1995.

"Misrepresentation and Miscegenation: Reading the Racialized Discourse of Tennessee Williams's *A Streetcar Named Desire*." *Modern Drama* 40 (1997): 337–46.

Davis, Walter A,. *Get the Guests: Psychoanalysis, Modern American Drama, and the Audience*. Madison: University of Wisconsin Press, 1994.

Fleche, Anne, *Mimetic Disillusion: Eugene O'Neill, Tennessee Williams, and U.S. Dramatic Realism*. Tuscaloosa: University of Alabama Press, 1997.

Ganz, Arthur, "The Desperate Morality of the Plays of Tennessee Williams." *American Scholar* 31 (Spring 1962): 278–94.

Gronbeck-Tedesco, John, "Ambiguity and Performance in the Plays of Tennessee Williams." *Mississippi Quarterly* 48 (Fall 1995): 735–49.

Harris, Laurilyn J., "Perceptual Conflict and the Perversion of Creativity in *A Streetcar Named Desire*." In *Confronting Tennessee Williams's A Streetcar Named Desire: Essays in Critical Pluralism*. Ed. Philip C. Kolin. Westport, CT: Greenwood, 1993. 83–104.

Hayman, Ronald, *Tennessee Williams: Everyone Else Is an Audience*. New Haven: Yale University Press, 1993.

Holditch, W. Kenneth, "The Broken World: Romanticism, Realism and Naturalism in *A Streetcar Named Desire*." In *Confronting Tennessee Williams's A Streetcar Named Desire: Essays in Critical*

Pluralism. Ed. Philip C. Kolin. Westport, CT: Greenwood, 1993. 147–66.

Hulley, Kathleen, "The Fate of the Symbolic in *A Streetcar Named Desire.*" *Themes in Drama 4, Drama and Symbolism.* Ed. James Redmond. Cambridge: Cambridge University Press, 1982. 88–99.

Isaac, Dan, "No Past to Think In: Who Wins in '*A Streetcar Named Desire*'?" *Louisiana Literature* 14 (Fall 1997): 8–35.

Jackson, Esther Merle, *The Broken World of Tennessee Williams.* Madison: University of Wisconsin Press, 1965.

Kernan, Alvin B., "Truth and Dramatic Mode in the Modern Theatre: Chekhov, Pirandello, and Williams." *Modern Drama* 1 (Sept. 1958): 111–14.

Kleb, William. "Marginalia: *Streetcar*, Williams, and Foucault." In *Confronting Tennessee Williams's A Streetcar Named Desire: Essays in Critical Pluralism.* Ed. Philip C. Kolin. Westport, CT: Greenwood, 1993. 27–44.

Kolin, Philip C., "'Red Hot!' in *A Streetcar Named Desire.*" *Notes on Contemporary Literature* 19 (Sept. 1989): 6–8.

"*A Streetcar Named Desire:* A Playwrights' Forum." *Michigan Quarterly Review* 29 (Spring 1990): 173–203.

"'Affectionate and mighty regards from Vivien and me': Sir Laurence Olivier's Letter to Tennessee Williams on the London Premiere of *A Streetcar Named Desire.*" *Missouri Review* 13.3 (1991): 143–57.

"Our Lady of the Quarter: Blanche DuBois and the Feast of Mater Dolorosa." *ANQ: A Quarterly Journal of Short Articles, Notes and Reviews* 4 (Apr. 1991): 81–87.

"The First Critical Assessments of *A Streetcar Named Desire:* The *Streetcar* Tryouts and the Reviewers." *Journal of Dramatic Theory and Criticism* 6 (Fall 1991): 45–67.

"Eunice Hubbell and the Feminist Thematics of *A Streetcar Named Desire.*" In *Confronting Tennessee Williams's A Streetcar Named Desire: Essays in Critical Pluralism.* Ed. Philip C. Kolin. Westport, CT: Greenwood, 1993. 105–20.

"Reflections on/of *A Streetcar Named Desire*." In *Confronting Tennessee Williams's A Streetcar Named Desire: Essays in Critical Pluralism*. Ed. Philip C. Kolin. Westport, CT: Greenwood, 1993. 1–17.

"Cleopatra of the Nile and Blanche DuBois of the French Quarter: *Antony and Cleopatra* and *A Streetcar Named Desire*." *Shakespeare Bulletin* 11 (Winter 1993): 25–27.

"Bonaparte Kowalski: Or, What Stanley and the French Emperor Have In Common (and What They Don't) in *A Streetcar Named Desire*." *Notes on Contemporary Literature* 24 (Sept. 1994): 6–8.

"'Cruelty and Sweaty Intimacy': The Reception of the Spanish Premiere of *A Streetcar Named Desire*." *Theatre Survey* 35 (Nov. 1995): 45–56.

"'It's only a paper moon': The Paper Ontologies in Tennessee Williams's *A Streetcar Named Desire*." *Modern Drama* 40 (Winter 1997): 454–67.

Tennessee Williams: A Guide to Research and Performance. Westport, CT: Greenwood, 1998.

"Roland Barthes, Tennessee Williams, and *A Streetcar Named Desire/Pleasure*." *Centennial Review* 43 (Spring 1999): 289–304.

Kolin, Philip C. ed., *Confronting Tennessee Williams's A Streetcar Named Desire: Essays in Critical Pluralism*. Westport, CT: Greenwood, 1993.

Koprince, Susan, "Tennessee Williams's Unseen Characters." *Southern Quarterly* 33 (Fall 1994): 87–95.

Lant, Kathleen Margaret, "A Streetcar Named Misogyny." *Themes in Drama 13, Violence in Drama*. Ed. James Redmond. Cambridge: Cambridge University Press, 1991. 225–38.

Leverich, Lyle, *Tom: The Unknown Tennessee Williams*. New York: Crown, 1995.

Londré, Felicia Hardison, "A *Streetcar* Running Fifty Years." In *The Cambridge Companion to Tennessee Williams*. Ed. Matthew C. Roudané. Cambridge: Cambridge University Press, 1997. 45–66.

Murphy, Brenda, *Tennessee Williams and Elia Kazan: A Collaboration in the Theatre*. Cambridge: Cambridge University Press, 1992.

O'Connor, Jacqueline, *Dramatizing Dementia: Madness in the Plays of Tennessee Williams.* Bowling Green, OH: Bowling Green State University Popular Press, 1997.

Pagan, Nicholas, *Rethinking Literary Biography: A Postmodern Approach to Tennessee Williams.* Rutherford, NJ: Fairleigh Dickinson University Press, 1993.

Phillips, Gene D., S.J., *The Films of Tennessee Williams.* Philadelphia: Art Alliance Press, 1980.

"Blanche's Phantom Husband: Homosexuality on Stage and Screen." *Louisiana Literature* 14 (Fall 1997): 36–47.

Quirino, Leonard, "The Cards Indicate A Voyage on *A Streetcar Named Desire.*" In *Tennessee Williams: A Tribute.* Ed. Jac Tharpe. Jackson: University Press of Mississippi, 1977. 77–96.

Riddell, Joseph N., "*A Streetcar Named Desire* – Nietzsche Descending." *Modern Drama* 5 (Feb. 1963): 421–30.

Robinson, Marc, *The Other American Drama.* Cambridge: Cambridge University Press, 1994.

Savran, David, *Communists, Cowboys, and Queers: The Politics of Masculinity in the Work of Arthur Miller and Tennessee Williams.* Minneapolis: University of Minnesota Press, 1992.

Schlueter, June, "Imitating an Icon: John Erman's Remake of Tennessee Williams's *A Streetcar Named Desire.*" *Modern Drama* 28 (1985): 139–47.

"'We've had this date with each other from the beginning': Reading toward Closure in *A Streetcar Named Desire.*" In *Confronting Tennessee Williams's A Streetcar Named Desire: Essays in Critical Pluralism.* Ed. Philip C. Kolin. Westport, CT: Greenwood, 1993. 71–82.

Spector, Susan, "Alternative Visions of Blanche DuBois: Uta Hagen and Jessica Tandy in *A Streetcar Named Desire.*" *Modern Drama* 32 (1989): 545–60.

Spoto, Donald, *The Kindness of Strangers: The Life of Tennessee Williams.* Boston: Little, Brown, 1985.

Tharpe, Jac, ed., *Tennessee Williams: A Tribute.* Jackson: University Press of Mississippi, 1977.

Thompson, Judith J., *Tennessee Williams's Plays: Memory, Myth, and Symbol.* New York: Lang, 1987.

Tischler, Nancy M., *Tennessee Williams: Rebellious Puritan.* New York: Citadel, 1961.

"Sanitizing the *Streetcar.*" *Louisiana Literature* 14 (Fall 1997): 48–56.

Vlasopolos, Anca, "Authorizing History: Victimization in *A Streetcar Named Desire.*" *Theatre Journal* 38 (Oct. 1986): 322–38.

Wolter, Jürgen, "The Cultural Context of *A Streetcar Named Desire* in Germany." In *Confronting Tennessee Williams's A Streetcar Named Desire: Essays in Critical Pluralism.* Ed. Philip C. Kolin. Westport, CT: Greenwood, 1993. 199–222.

Yacowar, Maurice. *Tennessee Williams and Film.* New York: Ungar, 1977.

INDEX